The Invention of Li Yu

D1714669

The Invention of

Li Yu

Patrick Hanan

Harvard University Press

Cambridge, Massachusetts

London, England   1988

Copyright © 1988 by the President and Fellows
of Harvard College
All rights reserved
Printed in the United States of America
10 9 8 7 6 5 4 3 2 1

Library of Congress Cataloging-in-Publication Data

Hanan, Patrick.
The invention of Li Yu.

Bibliography: p.
Includes index.
1. Li, Yü, 1611–1680?—Criticism and interpretation.
I. Title.
PL2698.L52Z65   1988   895.1'8409   87-31144
ISBN 0-674-46425-7 (alk. paper)

Designed by Gwen Frankfeldt

For Anneliese

Preface

Comedy must be acknowledged as the dominant mode in Chinese fiction and drama, from their beginnings right up to the time of such modern masters as Lu Xun and Lao She, however much the notion upsets our preconceptions about tragedy. Nor has humor been an uncommon element in Chinese didactic literature, from the *Zhuang Zi* to the present. It goes without saying that neither comedy nor humor is inconsistent with a serious purpose.

Li Yu, who lived from 1610 or 1611 to 1680, that is to say, through the collapse of the Ming dynasty and the consolidation of the foreign (Manchu) dynasty known as the Qing, was the most wholehearted and versatile exponent of comedy in the history of Chinese literature—the Chinese comic specialist par excellence. He prided himself, above all else, on the comic effects of his work. He did, of course, write some works, a distinct minority in his oeuvre, that cannot be described as comic, and ironically, it is these writings—notably the poems on the cruelty of war and the humiliation of having to shave his head (a loyalty test imposed by the Manchus)—that have been seized on by some scholars as revealing the "true" Li Yu. But, moving as the poems are, they are unremarkable as poetry, and if it were not for the existence of a "false" Li Yu, I doubt that many people would bother to read them. This book is concerned above all with the "false" Li Yu and his generally comic permutations of self, rather than with any search for a "true" Li Yu.

The title refers not to his comedy, but to his invention, by which several things are meant: his invention of himself (the "false" Li Yu); his stress on originality in life and literature; his sheer inventiveness in a multitude of fields; and, finally, the products of that inventiveness, of which the most accessible—all the houses and gardens that he designed and created having vanished long ago—are his fiction, plays, and essays.

Among all premodern Chinese writers of fiction, Li Yu offers us the best opportunity to study his mind and art together: first, because copious writings of his survive in all genres, something that can be said of no other writer; second, because he had a passion for explaining his ideas lucidly and coherently to the reader; and third, because to an extraordinary degree his writing is all of a piece, allowing and even requiring a unified critical approach.

Such, at least, is the approach taken in this book, as well as the book's implied thesis. What I have not attempted to do is to trace Li Yu's ideas to their historical sources. There is little doubt where the main source would lie—in the thinking of He Xinyin, Li Zhi, and especially Yuan Hongdao, those distant, independent followers of the philosopher Wang Yangming. Li Yu's passionate advocacy of the new in life and literature seems to derive from the thought of Li Zhi and Yuan Hongdao, even though neither man arrived at Li Yu's extreme conclusions. Similarly, his belief in the pleasure principle can be related to the thought of He Xinyin and Li Zhi, and his focus on the personal aspect of literature to that of Li Zhi and Yuan Hongdao. But it was no simple transference of ideas that took place. Li Yu seems not to have recognized his indebtedness, if indebtedness it was; and in any case, the ideas on which he drew were common property in the seventeenth century and may have come to him in a variety of ways. More important, the rationale he gives us for his views differs from that of the three men. Tracing his connection to the broad tendencies of which these three were the main representatives would take me away from my aim of showing how Li Yu's ideas and art relate to each other. Moreover, his thinking does not derive solely from these tendencies. Although it would be farfetched to claim him as a pioneer in the school of hard-headed "evidential" (*kaozheng*) scholarship that came to the fore in the Qing dynasty, there is a robust, down-to-earth skepticism about him, a tendency to ask for objective evidence, if only in jest, that contrasts with the prevailing mentalism of Wang Yangming Confucianism and belongs to a new age.

There is one other aspect of Li Yu that cannot be ignored. He wrote not merely to please himself, to impress the public with his ideas, and to gain an enduring reputation; he wrote also to make a living.

The fact that he was a professional writer who depended on the sale of his books conditions most of what he wrote—its content, level, and tone—and needs to be examined alongside his ideas and art.

This study was begun with the aid of a Guggenheim Fellowship and completed with a grant from the Committee for Scholarly Communication with the People's Republic of China. Among the many individuals who have helped me, my greatest debt is to Wu Xiaoling, who lent me his editions of Li Yu's works and also provided me with photographs of the illustrations to some of Li Yu's plays. I am much indebted to Itoh Sohei, who allowed me to use his editions of Li Yu's works, and also to Otsuka Hidetaka, who provided me with a copy of part of the indispensable *Liancheng bi* edition in Saeki Municipal Library. I am grateful to the following for their assistance or advice: Cai Tianming, Chen Yupi, Cui Zi'en, Guo Songnian, Guo Yongfang, Li Shen, Liu Shide, Liu Zaifu, Ma Liangchun, and Xu Juemin of Beijing; Wang Qingping, Xiao Xinqiao, and Xu Shuofang of Hangzhou; Wu Xinlei of Nanjing; He Manzi, Huang Qiang, Jiang Xingyu, and Yuan Zhenyu of Shanghai; Chu Pao-liang, George Hayden, Loh Wai-fong, Victor Mair, Wang Ch'iu-kuei, Diana Wang, Ellen Widmer, and Eugene Wu; Mary Ellen Geer of the Harvard University Press; and Anneliese Hanan.

Contents

Broadly speaking, everything I have ever written was intended to make people laugh.

Is it not astonishing that the world had to wait for Liweng [Li Yu] to invent this?

Li Yu

One. Making a Living

At the approach of winter in 1673, Li Yu, the best-selling Chinese author of his time, found himself stranded in Beijing with no money to stay and scarcely enough money to leave. With him were two girls whom he had brought from his home in Nanjing. As a rule, Li Yu liked to take a concubine or two with him on his patronage-seeking journeys, but on this occasion both girls were pregnant—or at least appeared to be. (In fact, Miss Wang, his favorite, was not pregnant but seriously ill, and would die in the New Year.) To make matters worse, his principal contact in Beijing, Gong Dingzi, President of the Board of Rites—distinguished poet, bon vivant, and a frequent bene-factor of debt-ridden writers and artists—had recently fallen ill and resigned his post. Although Gong's instincts were as generous as ever, he proved to be quite poor, and no doubt this circumstance was the main reason for Li Yu's predicament.[1]

The journey to Beijing had been a long time in the planning. As soon as Li Yu's brilliantly original *Casual Expressions of Idle Feeling* (*Xianqing ouji*) had come from the publisher in late 1671, he had sent copies by messenger to his former patrons in the capital—to President Gong, to Chen Aiyong, Vice President of the Board of Civil Office, to Ke Song, a veteran Metropolitan Censor, and others. Their replies brought appreciation in plenty but not the hoped-for invitations, and so Li Yu broached the matter himself in a letter to President Gong. He is excited to learn, he says, that Gong is arranging to buy the Garden of the Urban Recluse, not far from Li's own minuscule Mustard Seed Garden in Nanjing. As an expert on garden design, Li Yu is eager to help plan the renovations; he will at last be able to apply his ideas on a large scale. He enters then upon a litany of complaints: the failure of his "begging-bowl" (patronage-seeking) journeys, with only one or two exceptions; his numerous children; and his consequent poverty. Finally, he announces a plan to travel from Hanyang, which he is now visiting, to Taiyuan and Beijing, where he expects to stay no more than three months. What he is asking is that Gong put in a word for him with other potential patrons.[2]

He wrote also to Vice-President Chen, a man whom he knew better and with whom he could strike a pose of complete candor. Chen had replied with praise of the book's originality, and Li Yu took this chance to express his feelings to his *zhiji*, a term which, before it became debased to "patron," denoted the friend who was capable of appreciating one's capacities and aspirations.

> Ever since I was seven or eight years old, I have dedicated myself—mistakenly—to becoming a writer. Although I wouldn't dare to claim any major contribution, still, what I write, ranging from poetry and drama to fiction, does have one small merit: it never "knits its brow" in imitation of the great beauty or "picks up the spittle" of famous men. Thanks to my writings, the eyes and ears of the contemporary world have been completely freshened. Had there been no Liweng of the Lake [Li Yu] during these last decades, I wonder how much less talking people would have been able to do, and how many more naps they would have taken?

As "one who has done sterling service in the cause of talk and laughter," Li Yu goes on to compare his treatment with that given to people such as gamblers, chessmasters, singers, footballers, and storytellers, whom the gentry welcome and compete for as guests. Even on the superficial level of skill, *Casual Expressions* has more to offer; it is ingenious and, above all, original. Li Yu has never abused the hospitality he received as he toured the houses of the great; he is "friendly and approachable but never boring"; and yet people allow him to "starve to death beneath their windows."

> Alas! Just so long as Liweng does not die! Once he is dead, there will certainly be people who appreciate his genius and sigh over his fate, people who regret they have not lived

in the same age as he. That sort of *zhiji* I can count on in the future. But if I look for one now, he is not at all easy to find.

Yesterday, on reading the letters I was favored with, I noticed that they urged me to "try to take a little more nourishment" and to "take good care of yourself, for the sake of your genius," at which I couldn't help shedding tears of gratitude. That is why I have cast aside all restraint and unburdened myself like this.[3]

One wonders what Chen made of this outrageous letter. For it *is* outrageous. Li Yu was not obscure; he had had his patrons, including some of the highest in the land. Nonetheless, the sarcasm in the last few sentences evidently gave no offense, and Chen continued to treat him as a wayward genius.

Li Yu wrote a third letter, to Ji Yingzhong, a poet and artist who had spent most of his life traveling about the country living off literary commissions but who had some years before become a regular protégé of President Gong. Li Yu, who had known him as a neighbor in Nanjing, evidently hoped that Ji would reinforce the request to Gong. He sent along samples of the special decorative notepaper he had designed, as requested by Ji, and asked him to show it to "the other gentlemen," who presumably included Gong, and to tell them that he (Li Yu) will bring a supply of it when he comes. He also asked Ji to write a preface for his collected works, and promised to send him the sections of the manuscript he had not yet read. The letter has a breezy tone to it, quite unlike that of the letters to Gong and Chen. Ji is a peer, a fellow poet, a fellow suppliant—not an official.[4]

In the end, the journey did not take place in 1672 as planned, because in Hanyang Li Yu's other favorite concubine, Miss Qiao, fell sick and died. He returned home and postponed the equally ill-fated journey to Beijing until the following year.

In Beijing in 1673, Li Yu was shocked not only by the resignation of President Gong but also by the modest style of living to which the high officials were reduced. These men, who had led lives of proconsular magnificence in the distant provinces where they had hosted him, were here forced, under the watchful eyes of the Palace, to subsist on their official salaries alone. Li Yu tells of going to thank a friend (possibly President Gong) for a donation and, in the friend's absence, noticing a pawn ticket on the man's desk for exactly the amount of the gift. The anecdote comes in the course of his reply to an appeal from Ke Song that Li Yu stay on in Beijing through the spring.

> Let me explain [my reasons for leaving] to my *zhiji*. I have not even half a *mu* of land on which to support a family of several dozen. In the writing trade you depend on one person and one person only. Wherever that person goes, his family looks to him for support. Now that I have come north, my family looks to me in the north to feed them. Besides, I am a small-minded person who is ashamed to ask for favors. I have been roaming the whole country for almost twenty years and have never presumed to outstay my welcome by impoverishing any of my hosts. When I arrive at a place, I first calculate whether it will provide enough to cover my expenses while leaving something over for my family. If it does, I cease to worry about them and can stay a long time. If not, if expenditure exceeds income, one is forced to go about asking for loans, inevitably outlasting one's welcome. When this happens, the host, although he may urge his guest to stay longer, will in his heart be inviting him to leave.
>
> I have been in the capital for several months now, and have observed that the great majority of gentlemen are living on credit. The truth is that the hosts are even worse off than their guest. Hearing of my arrival, they all came to my lodgings and offered me dinner. Older friends were so generous as to "give their cloaks" to me, while newer acquaintances provided me with "chicken and millet" dinners. Yesterday I received a gift of twelve taels. When I went to thank the donor, he happened to be out. I noticed a pawn ticket hidden under the inkstone on his desk and, picking it up, found it was for exactly the amount of the gift! I realized then what a great burden friendship with a poor scholar can be.

He then reiterates his decision to leave:

The Court is largely composed of old friends who hosted me when, as governors and governors-general, they held posts in the provinces. Ask them if Master Li is telling the whole truth or not. I have been like this all my life, and I am not willing to change my principles at a moment's notice. That is why my decision to return south is firm.

There are many gentlemen in the capital besides your honorable self who have urged me to stay, and I have not been able to inform them all. May I trouble you to circulate this letter among them as an official notification of farewell?[5]

To soften the tone of the letter, he accompanied it with a short note thanking Ke for his misplaced concern for an "idle rustic" like himself.[6]

From other letters we learn the outcome of this demarche. Chen and Ke urged the Manchu statesman Songgotu, Grand Secretary, Grand Tutor to the Heir Apparent, and the most powerful Court figure of the time, to persuade Li Yu to stay. (Songgotu had some contact with Li Yu, perhaps after this incident; Li Yu visited him, wrote couplets for the pavilions in his garden, and presented him with some of his famous notepaper.) Songgotu conveyed an "order" through Chen and a Cabinet secretary that Li Yu stay in Beijing and receive a subvention.[7]

It was fortunate that he had not left Beijing during the time it took to work out this arrangement. His bags had been packed for three or four days, he tells Ke, but he was unable to leave because of the high cost of transportation ("the price of donkeys has soared"). He reports receiving the Grand Secretary's order, together with a "salary paid in advance . . . in the light of which, I shall finish out the year in the capital, staying the greater part of the time you urged me to stay. I wanted to stay, and now I am going to—it is almost as if Heaven has had a hand in things."[8]

Far from Heaven's having a hand in it, it would seem that Li Yu had plotted this denouement as shrewdly as he plotted his comedies. If so, it was a bold move in the patronage game. He had chosen to test his own worth as a writer, believing that his powerful friends could hardly fail to respond. He had appealed not just to one patron—although in view of the remarks about the poverty of his old friends, Songgotu was presumably in his mind—but, ostensibly at least, to the whole class of officialdom, in the professed belief that society owed a living to a writer of his accomplishments. His tactics may be outrageous, but at least they are more attractive than the flattering of powerful people—an age-old practice in which he engaged far less often than one might have expected.[9]

In any case, that was the end of the matter. Early in the Chinese New Year, he set off for home with his remaining concubine, who gave birth on the way.[10]

This episode has little intrinsic importance—Li Yu's major works were all in print by this time—but it does illustrate certain recurring themes in his life. The letters amply demonstrate his pride both in his originality and in his ability to stimulate talk and provoke laughter—unusual goals for a writer in traditional China. They reveal also his consummate ability at playing a part, an outrageous part if need be, in literature as in life. And most of all, of course, they show his lifelong incapacity for making ends meet, a fact that conditions most of his best writing.

The episode is also a trifle deceptive. It is well to remind ourselves of the economic power of high and even middle-level officials in imperial China, power so great that the most popular writer of his day was driven to seek their help. But although Li Yu knew many top officials, one should not assume that the friendship was an equal one. His position was far above that of the entertainers whom he mentions in the letter to Chen, but still somewhat below that of a friend. On his side, there is a less than subtle distinction between the way he refers to his patrons, all of whom were officials, and the way he writes of his literary and other friends. In letters to his friends, he often expresses his weariness with lavish food and entertainment and sometimes even disparages the taste of his hosts.[11]

It would be easy to give too much importance to the theme of patronage in Li Yu's life. Despite his claim to have traveled the length and breadth of China for almost twenty years, his long patronage journeys began only in 1666, when he traveled to Beijing, Shaanxi, and Gansu. He arrived home early in 1668, only to set off soon for Guangzhou, from which he returned early in 1669. In 1670 he traveled to Fuzhou and in 1672 to Hanyang. Then in 1673 came the journey to Beijing that I have described.

6

Although the first journey was successful, it enabled him merely to clear his debts, not to buy the site he coveted, he tells us. (Where the money came from to buy the Mustard Seed Garden, in the spring or summer of 1668, we do not know.) The Fuzhou journey was also moderately successful, but the others were failures. Even the trading that he carried on in conjunction with his travels was not always profitable.[12]

Li Yu arranged his journeys by securing one invitation and then building upon it by writing to friends and acquaintances along the way. The invitation for the 1666 journey came out of the blue from the governor of Shaanxi. The 1670 journey was initiated probably through the governor of Fujian, who had been Li Yu's host three years before in Gansu. And the 1672 journey may have been arranged through Ji Yuan, prefect of Hanyang, who had been a friend since the Hangzhou years.[13]

It was a common enough practice for high officials, many of whom were literary men themselves, to patronize writers for reasons of pleasure or prestige or both. In Li Yu's case, it was clearly his fame as a playwright, rather than his reputation as a poet, that made him welcome. In 1666 he met Grand Secretary Wei Yijie in President Gong's company, and Wei actually suggested that Li Yu write a new Southern-drama version of the famous play *The West Chamber*. At the other end of the scale, a local official, in 1667, was distinctly flattered to be asked to write a commentary on Li Yu's latest play.[14] In his approach to patrons, Li regularly dwells on the traditional relationship of *zhiji* to the man of talent, as well as on that of statesman to adviser. He also occasionally hints at the vicarious immortality to be gained from friendship with a genius.

There were other reasons for his welcome besides his fame as a playwright. With his novel ideas, his punditry, and his wit, Li Yu must have been good value as a guest. When he writes of his contribution to talk and laughter, I think he meant an oral as well as a written contribution. It was this, rather than the patronage seeking itself, that caused certain of his contemporaries to disparage him as a "jester."[15]

A common misconception holds that his welcome was due to his little troupe of actress-concubines, notably Miss Qiao and Miss Wang. It is an attractive idea, inevitably suggesting Molière and his players, but it lacks substance. Li Yu received Miss Qiao and Miss

Wang as gifts from his hosts in 1666 and 1667, respectively, and each girl died just six years after she joined him, at the identical age of eighteen. Before either could perform, she had to be trained. I suspect that the play they acted for the birthday of their host's wife on New Year's Day, 1668, was among the first performances they gave. Their last must have been in the latter half of 1672, as Miss Qiao's consumption worsened. They were not taken along on Li Yu's Guangzhou journey, which occupied much of 1668 and a little of 1669, and there is only slight evidence that they accompanied him to Fuzhou in 1670. Therefore the period in which they performed in the Mustard Seed Garden, as well as in Li Yu's lodgings in Suzhou, Hanyang, and other places, lasted less than four years.[16] Furthermore, the small, invited audiences before whom they performed seem to have been Li Yu's literary friends rather than his patrons.[17] Let me add that the lurid gossip surrounding the girls has little credibility; it doubtless sprang from Li Yu's reputation as a writer of erotic fiction.[18]

After the 1673 episode Li Yu made no more journeys to Beijing, but in 1677, at another crisis, he wrote an open letter to his former patrons in the capital pleading for help in desperate terms.[19] He had recently moved his family back to the West Lake at Hangzhou, where the local officials had bought some property for him. But leaving Nanjing meant settling all his debts at once, and so he was forced to sell or pawn everything of value, including the printing blocks for his books. The open letter, as published in his collected works, carries a note by his friend Mao Xianshu, a scholar and poet, the tone of which is dryly sardonic. Few writers in history, in Mao's view, had made as much money from selling their writings as had Li Yu. His poverty was a result of the size of his family and also of his failure to take an official post.

Li Yu constantly blames his poverty on the number of his dependents, who totaled as many as fifty in the early 1670s, including his wife, concubines, children, sons-in-law, maids, and servants. His joy at the birth of his first son in 1660 changed to rueful amusement and then amiable dismay when it was followed by the birth of a second son in 1661, and of third and fourth sons in 1662. His acceptance of Miss Qiao as a gift in 1666 and of Miss Wang and another concubine in 1667, and his purchase of an unnamed girl as personal maid on his journey to Guangzhou in 1668, did nothing to help his balance-sheet either.[20]

Modern scholars, like Li Yu's contemporaries, are sometimes tempted to solve his financial problems for him. But surely it is absurd to chide him for not taking an official position—as if official positions were simply there for the taking!—without reflecting on the effect that the chores and dangers of office would have had on his daringly original kind of writing. He was far more independent as the recipient of piecemeal patronage than he would ever have been in state service.

One undeniable factor in his financial woes was his impulsive nature. I believe it was impulsiveness coupled with a residual optimism that led him to undertake one unsuccessful journey after another, despite his dislike of travel. He preferred to set off on a new journey rather than stay at home and worry over his old debts. Moreover, despite the emphasis he places on the virtue of thrift in *Casual Expressions*, the personal anecdotes he tells us show him satisfying his sensuous and aesthetic desires regardless of the state of his finances. He put his sensuous and aesthetic needs above ordinary prudence, and was proud of doing so—it fitted his idea of himself—and hence it is not surprising that he was chronically in debt.

There is even a certain comedy in Li Yu's emphasis on thrift, a comedy that springs in part from his very human tendency to lecture others on the qualities he himself lacked. But the subject of thrift was also a conscious joke that he directed at those who knew him well— it was as if La Fontaine's grasshopper were lecturing La Fontaine's ant on the virtues of frugality.

In any case, like everybody else who received a classical education, Li Yu did take the civil service examinations, and like almost everybody else, he failed. He came from an obscure family in rural Lanqi County in Zhejiang; none of his ancestors, according to the clan history, had ever held an official post. The best the family could boast was an uncle who may have served as a doctor attached to the county government of Rugao in Jiangsu, where Li Yu's father, it seems, ran a herbalist's shop and perhaps also practiced medicine.[21] Li Yu, explaining why he has never possessed any rare or valuable objects, puts it like this: "I was born into a humble family and then fell victim to extreme poverty."[22] As a youth, he had to borrow books in order to study.[23] Yet a friend, writing a preface for one of his plays in 1658, says that Li's family had always been well off and that they possessed the finest garden in the district.[24] No doubt the truth lay somewhere in between; Li Yu, as always, was pleading poverty, while the friend was doing his best to enhance Li Yu's background.

His father had died by 1626 and his elder brother even earlier, and so Li Yu found himself the head of the family while still a youth.[25] He passed the first civil service examination easily in 1635, impressing the examiner, and entered the prefectural school in Jinhua in 1637, but then failed the crucial provincial examination. Even at this time, his poems show a certain ambivalence toward the examinations and the official career to which they were the key, and it was largely from a desire to please his mother that he continued trying to pass. After her death in 1642, he sometimes felt he had let her down and on one occasion records a guilty dream in which she reproves him for neglecting his studies.[26] These were chaotic years, anyway, in which the province was subjected in turn to rebel troops, government troops, Southern Ming troops, and Qing troops, and Li Yu finally let his half-hearted ambitions die an unlamented death.

I do not think it was moral scruple that kept him from reviving those ambitions under the Qing. He had not held office under the Ming, and hence did not owe the dynasty that highest kind of allegiance. He had been fully as shocked by the depredations of the Ming troops as by those of the rebels, and he heartily despised the corruption of the Southern Ming court in Nanjing. After initial reactions of despair over the slaughter and humiliation over the queue law, by which Chinese males had to shave their heads, he came to accept the reality of Qing power. In the 1650s he went out of his way to make laudatory references to the Manchus in his stories, and he sought and received patronage from high officials, many of whom were Chinese Bannermen. When two of his former patrons, Censor Chen Qitai and Governor Fan Chengmo, died in resisting the Fujian rebellion in 1675 and 1676, respectively, he was moved to write unofficial funeral elegies for them.[27] Yet despite this, there is no evidence that he ever tried to qualify as an official under the Qing. When he left Jinhua for Hangzhou, it was to seek his fortune as a writer.

There were private staff positions that Li Yu might have held without passing the higher examination; in fact, he held one between 1644 and 1646, on the staff of Sub-prefect Xu Xicai of Jinhua.[28] This position, which offered him comparative security in a dangerous time, was really patronage disguised as a secretaryship, and no doubt it came his way because of his promise as a writer. (Xu also gave him his first concubine; Li Yu had been married for many years, without a son.) But this was his only experience of such service; presumably, he was too independent of mind to tolerate it for long. Even the kind of patronage that President Gong extended to Ji Yingzhong would, I imagine, have been too restrictive for Li Yu. A number of his literary friends were secretaries or advisers, and in his poems he invariably commiserates with them and counsels stoicism.[29] (Stoicism, like thrift, was a quality that he honored more in the preaching than in the observance.)

Apart from those in official careers or of independent wealth, Li Yu's friends were advisers or secretaries; or, like Ji, they received steady patronage and coupled it with literary commissions; or they were teachers or lower functionaries, whom he pitied because of their poverty.[30] Many were artists—painters or seal-engravers.[31] If one rules out the long-term dependence of the secretary-adviser and the protégé, and the poverty of the functionary and the teacher, the options that remained to Li Yu were very much the ones he tried: working his own land; selling his writing, his designs, his artifacts—his creativity, in short; composing literary pieces on commission; and collecting piecemeal largesse from patrons, carrying his begging-bowl about China, as he put it.

During the 1640s he had his own land in the countryside, the "Mt. Yi" estate, which was really just a hillock 300 feet high that covered no more than 15 acres of land, little of it arable. In a poem entitled "Planning without Success to Build a Mt. Yi Retreat," he declares his wish to put up a "thatched hut" beside his ancestral tombs in Lanqi County and there live out the pastoral dream of the Chinese writer.[32] When, with the aid of relatives and friends, he managed to buy the property, his life was for a time pleasant, even blissful. A poem recounts the dredging of the stream up to his porch, so that "you can dangle your fishing-line in without putting on a raincoat."[33]

Although according to the clan history the dredging led to a dispute that forced him to leave, Li's own writings say nothing of any dispute; instead, they speak of poverty and famine.[34] Whatever the reason, selling the Yi Garden was a bitter experience. Li Yu had already made a name for himself there as a poet, and the garden figures prominently in his poetry. His first collection, *Juvenilia (Tiaolingji)*, consisted of poems from his youth up into the 1640s. (It was destroyed in the fighting, and all that survives are the works Li Yu could remember.)[35] Some of his earliest essays, for example "Burying the Dog" ("Yi quan wen") and "Expelling the Cat" ("Zhu mao wen"), are apparently also concerned with his life at Mt. Yi. And the sale of the property occasioned his "A Deed of Sale for a Hill" ("Mai shan quan"), in which he informs the purchaser that he, Li Yu, retains title to the hill's name because he has celebrated it in his poetry.[36] On the evidence of these works, he had already found a distinctive voice as a humorous essayist.

The two decades from 1650 to 1670 were those of mature creativity. The drama, fiction, and essays that make up Li Yu's finest work were all written during these years, which were spent first in Hangzhou from the early 1650s and then in Nanjing from about 1661.[37] Both sojourns, but especially the latter, were much interrupted by travel. It was while in Hangzhou that he adopted his best-known pseudonym, Liweng (Old Man in the Bamboo Hat, that is, Fisherman) of the Lake (the West Lake).

He went to Hangzhou to seek his fortune as a writer, and he achieved success there with a new kind of comedy in both drama and fiction. He was driven from Hangzhou, he claims, by one of the results of that commercial success, the pirating of his books. He describes what happened in a letter:

> To my surprise, my new work had only just appeared when the greedy merchants of Suzhou began to covet it. Fortunately, I got wind of their plans ahead of time and pleaded as strongly as I could with His Honor Sun, the Suzhou-Songjiang Intendant, that he post a notice ordering them to cease and desist. That put a stop to their scheme, but no sooner had the Suzhou plot been snuffed out than I suddenly got a message from home to the effect that a Hangzhou publisher had finished reprinting the book and was going to put it on sale in a few days' time. I was detained in Suzhou on other business and could not get back to accuse them, and so I told my son-in-law to visit the authorities and seek redress for the crime. Although the pirates have received a little punishment for their greed, and although the blocks are now being sought, I still don't know what

the outcome will be. Alas! How much is such a petty profit worth, that these people rush after it like ducks to water?[38]

The pirated book was probably Li Yu's *Silent Operas, Second Collection* (*Wusheng xi erji*).[39]

Li Yu went heavily into debt to make the move to Nanjing, taking out a ruinous kind of loan that put the borrower's whole property, even his family, at risk. He wrote to a friend:

Until you take out an army loan, you'll never know the true hardship of being in debt. You really ought to get a taste of it. Last year, for the sake of our "migration," I borrowed one or two hundred taels from an army officer. The harassment of being dunned for repayment was a hundred times worse than the torments inflicted by demons. I have recently repaid half of it, and now I can be called half a man, half a ghost. My sole purpose in going on this journey is to pay off this disastrous debt, lest I become an entry in the register of ghosts. Your letter reports him [the creditor] as believing that I am going in order to escape my debts. The fact is that I am going precisely in order to repay them.[40]

Except for a few poems, Li Yu's own writings during the 1650s all belong to the vernacular literature of plays and stories.[41] In the 1660s, however, although he continued to write plays from time to time, he apparently ceased writing fiction and turned instead to classical Chinese genres of a more orthodox kind: an anthology of letters by recent and contemporary writers, an anthology of court cases by contemporary officials, a set of discussions of historical problems, and so forth. The writing of the period culminated in his book of essays, *Casual Expressions of Idle Feeling*.

In Nanjing, by 1662 at least, he had his own bookshop to sell his books and notepaper, an activity in which he had the help of his son-in-law, Shen Xinyou, as well as of his servants. Shen, born in 1638 or 1639, was an orphan who had married Li Yu's eldest daughter in the Hangzhou period and entered the family as a live-in son-in-law.[42] Later he helped Li Yu with the compilation of several works, and later still, together with Li Yu's and his own sons, he appears to have taken over the business.

As we saw in the letter to Ji Yingzhong, Li Yu had created new designs in decorative notepaper. There were two main types, with eighteen different designs in all, by the time he came to write *Casual Expressions*, in which the notepaper section is just an advertisement for his own products: "The paper may be bought at the same place my books are on sale. Everything I have ever written is assembled there. Readers with an addiction to my work will feel they are taking me home with them after they buy it. Spiritual communion over great distances is entirely dependent on such means, and by now I have *zhiji* throughout the country. My friends are by no means confined to the people I have met!" Directions are supplied in a note: "The door in the Cheng'en Temple in Nanjing that bears the sign 'Famous Note-papers of the Mustard Seed Garden' is the place where they may be bought."

The passage closes with a statement that expresses Li Yu's pride in his creativity, his dependence on profits, and his resentment against those who would rob him of both.

> Permission is granted to copy all the new styles in this book except the notepaper designs, which I get my servants to manufacture and sell as an alternative to making a living by my pen. These may not be reprinted, and I have already given public notice, warning people at the outset. If any bold fellows try to seize the market by reprinting the designs as they are, or else adding or subtracting a little here and there, or slightly altering their shape, thus arrogating other people's achievements to themselves, grabbing others' prof-its while suppressing their names, they will be judged as contemptible as the Wolf of Zhongshan. I shall accuse them in the courts wherever they are and plead that justice be done. As for those who reprint my books in the belief that their wealth and power will protect them, I don't know how many there are in the world, but they are living off my labor, and that is a situation I cannot tolerate. I swear that I will fight them to the death, and hereby give notice to the authorities that this book marks a new policy on my part.
>
> In brief, Heaven and Earth endowed every human

being with a mind and it is up to each one of us to develop his own intelligence. I have done nothing to stultify their minds or prevent them from developing their intelligence. What right do they have to take away my livelihood and prevent me from living off my own labor?[43]

The writings Li Yu lived off in the Hangzhou and Nanjing years are best considered by genre, beginning with his plays, which he wrote throughout the period. His playwriting career may have begun while he was still in Jinhua; in fact, it may have been a play that caused him to leave. The play is the *Lianxiang ban, The Companion Who Loved Fragrance,* to which I shall give the title *Women in Love,* in the sense of women in love with women.[44] From the preface, written by a certain Yu Wei, we gather that the play's lesbian (actually bisexual) passion caused such a scandal in the district that Li Yu was forced to flee. Yu Wei defends the play by arguing that its subject matter is commonplace: "A beautiful girl meeting another by chance and falling in love with her fragrance—everyone has seen that sort of thing!" However, the people in the audience, he tells us, assumed it had a particular reference. When Li Yu had to take his family and flee, Yu Wei persuaded his master to give them lodging, and he was able to observe, he says, that Li Yu's wife and concubine loved each other and that both of them loved Li Yu.

Who was the object of the play's reference? One view holds that Li Yu was portraying the situation in his own household.[45] In the spring of 1645, he had acquired a young widow as his first concubine. Several poems refer to his domestic situation: "On Taking a Concubine" is addressed to the concubine and "Poems on a Virtuous Wife" are addressed to his wife.[46] He explains that although people braced themselves for an outburst of jealousy from his wife, none came; in fact, she proved as fond of the new concubine as he was. The account is more than fantasy, for we soon find the two women collaborating in schemes to increase the chances of their bearing a son.[47] In any case, Li Yu's poems point to something more than sisterly affection: "One pearl, how lucky to have two palms held up to receive it," runs one line. (The palms are those of Li Yu and his wife.) But the very fact

that the girl in the play has the same surname (Cao) as Li Yu's concubine presumably indicates that his own experience was remote from
his mind at the time of composition. It is far more likely that some
other person felt that his own family was being satirized in the play.
This would explain the animus that forced Li Yu's departure and perhaps also the famous oath he swore that he had never satirized anyone
in his plays.[48] If this explanation is right, Yu Wei's remark about the
love between Li's wife and concubine must have been intended to
exonerate him from the charge that the play was a personal attack.

His second play, *The Mistake with the Kite (Fengzheng wu)*, has a
preface by another Yu, Yu Lou of the same literary society as Yu Wei,
and it too implies that Li Yu had been driven away from where he
lived. Although the critique attached to the play praises its innovations
of structure and subject matter, it is actually of a more traditional sort
than *Women in Love*. The play elaborates upon the kind of romantic
imbroglio written by Wu Bing and Ruan Dacheng, with its gossamer
web of deceptions and mistakes that end in marriage.[49] In this case
the kite, sent aloft with love poems attached to it and forced down in
this or that garden, is the agency of both romance and misunderstand-
ing. But it would not be a Li Yu play without some outrageous novelty;
here it is the theme of rape, both real and imaginary.

In what was probably his third play, *Ideal Love-matches (Yizhong
yuan)*, Li Yu put four real late-Ming artists on stage—Dong Qichang,
Chen Jiru, Yang Yunyou, and Lin Tiansu, the last two of whom were
women—and paired them off in "ideal" fictional marriages.[50] The play's
piquancy arises from the fact that Dong and Chen, as famous artists
and littérateurs, feel harassed by the volume of requests and commissions they receive, and are searching for artists whom they can employ
to copy their respective styles. By one of Li Yu's happy imaginings,
Yang and Lin are already eking out a meager living by *forging* the two
artists' paintings. After many vicissitudes, each woman marries the
man whose style she has mastered.

The preface, which must have been written about 1655,[51] is
actually by a well-known woman artist, Huang Yuanjie, who had evidently drawn inspiration herself from Yang and Lin when she set out
on her career. One or two of her notes—she also wrote the commentary—refer to her own experience. In Scene 21, Yang is stung by a
canard to the effect that her paintings were not really hers, but were

the work of some man behind the scenes, and she responds by giving a public demonstration. The note runs: "When I was young, I too suffered from this slander, but I just stood my ground. What harm could they do me? Only in this one respect do I come out slightly ahead of Yunyou. People looking for paintings and calligraphy are very well able to understand."[52] It seems clear that it was Huang who had kindled Li Yu's interest in the two women in the first place.

The Illusory Tower (*Shenzhong lou*) is exceptional in Li Yu's drama for two reasons: its subject matter is fantasy, and it depends on literary sources other than Li Yu's own fiction.[53] In both respects, it offends against his advice as given in the drama chapters of *Casual Expressions*, which were, of course, written much later. Li Yu has deftly joined the material of two fantastic Yuan plays, one of which is based on a Tang tale.[54] The preface is by Sun Zhi, who signs himself a fellow-member of the Xiling (Hangzhou) literary society to which Mao Xianshu and others belonged.[55]

The preface to *The Jade Clasp* (*Yu saotou*) tells a little about the play's composition.[56] Its writer, The Farmer of Yellow Crane Mountain (Huangheshan, probably in Dantu), recounts a visit by Li Yu in late 1655. When the discussion turned to the subject of this play, Li Yu grew enthusiastic and at once set to work, finishing the script in a few days. The topic that captured his enthusiasm was the famous liaison between the Ming emperor Wuzong and the Taiyuan singing-girl Liu Qianqian. In Li Yu's version, which makes free with its historical background, the emperor entrusts the government to eunuchs and high officials while he sets off incognito to find a beautiful and gifted consort. Although he and Miss Liu swear vows of love to each other, he does not reveal his true identity, and on the way back to the capital loses the love token (a jade clasp) that she has given him. It is found by a look-alike of hers, and so on and so forth. After a dollop of disguises, deceptions, mistakes, and coincidences, the emperor marries both Miss Liu and her look-alike.

With his next play, *You Can't Do Anything about Fate* (*Naihe tian*), Li Yu began the practice of making plays out of his own vernacular stories;[57] of the last five extant plays, no fewer than four are based on his stories, three from *Silent Operas* and one from *Twelve Structures*. The reason he did not begin the practice before may simply be that his first five plays preceded his first stories. Many writers had turned stories into plays, but as far as I know, Li Yu was the first to adapt his own. This play is actually advertised in the table of contents to *Silent Operas:* "A play on this subject is about to appear."[58]

In the story Li Yu inverts, as he loves to do, the conventions of the romantic comedy, by which the brilliant and handsome youth marries the brilliant and beautiful girl. Here he propounds a fanciful heavenly law by which people inevitably find themselves married to their opposites in terms of brains and beauty. (The law operates as a means of retribution for one's sins in a former life.) Li Yu makes a few changes in the story's outline in deference to the dramatic form. The ugly hero—for the first time in Chinese operatic history, the *chou* (comic) is the hero of the play—is eventually allowed a metamorphosis (while in the bath) into an attractive man, and Li Yu found it necessary to justify the metamorphosis by giving the hero some moral achievements, if only by proxy.

Sole Mates (Bimuyu), my pun on "soulmates," was drawn from a story in *Silent Operas, Second Collection.*[59] Sole or flatfish are symbols of the loving couple in Chinese literature, like phoenixes, mandarin ducks, and butterflies. They do not appear as agents in the *Silent Operas* story, only as an image in one of its poems. In the play, however, the girl and her lover, having thrown themselves into the river, are transformed by the river god first into soles and thence back into human form. But the distinctive feature of the play remains the same as that of the story—its setting in the theater. The theater is the only medium through which the lovers can express themselves to each other, to their audience, and to us. The writer of the preface, dated autumn 1661, was another woman artist and poet, Wang Duanshu, daughter of the writer Wang Siren.

Li Yu's last three plays were written just before, during, and just after his journey to Beijing and the Northwest in 1666–1668. (The gap from 1661 to 1666 was filled with other kinds of writing.) *Woman in Pursuit of Man (Huang qiu feng*, literally, the She-phoenix Chases the Male) was written early in 1666. It was adapted from a story in *Silent Operas, Second Collection* in which several women compete for the same man and, after diabolical stratagems including deception, slander, and abduction, come to terms and agree to share him.[60] It is another inversion of the romantic comedy; instead of male suitors pursuing the female beauty, here female suitors contend, by foul means rather than fair, for the most handsome and brilliant man of his time. The preface, by the poet Du Jun, Li Yu's steadiest adherent, is in Du's usual moral vein, claiming that the play carries a lesson about lust, jealousy, and deception. We can assume that he knew better.

Be Careful about Love (*Shen luanjiao*) was written by 1667 at the latest, for Li Yu had the manuscript with him when he passed through Xianning in Shaanxi and asked a local official who admired his plays to write a commentary for it.[61] Li Yu told him that the play's first nine scenes were routine enough, but that Scene 10 showed the innovations that would mark his projected new anthology.[62] In this scene the heroine, Miss Wang, who has been abandoned by the callous Suzhou gallants on Tiger Mound, spends the whole night discussing the subjects of men, love, and her future with a fellow-courtesan. The scene is mainly of psychological interest, and perhaps that was Li Yu's point. On the other hand, scenes of psychological interest had appeared in his work ever since *Women in Love*.

Alone among Li's last five plays, *Be Careful about Love* is not adapted from one of his stories. It presents, however, a familiar kind of contrast, that between a libertine and a prudent lover, and, among the women, between a tough-minded realist and an incurable romantic. It thus bears a slight resemblance to a *Twelve Structures* story that places a romantic in opposition to a circumspect hero.[63]

His last play, *The Ingenious Finale* (*Qiao tuanyuan*) carries a preface dated the third month of 1668, shortly after his return. A note to Scene 6 says that the day Li Yu finished the draft he gave these songs to Miss Qiao to sing from behind a screen.[64] (The screen was there for decorum's sake.) The play is based on a *Twelve Structures* story and also, to a slight degree, on a *Silent Operas* story.[65] Its theme is the loss, rediscovery, and recognition of parents and child. Loss and reunion are a staple of the Southern drama, the genre in which Li Yu wrote, but the theme had never been employed with such ingenuity as here. More than coincidence is at work, however. An upper-margin note in Scene 32 remarks that the coincidences would be merely "bizarre happenings" had they not been produced by "human nature," that is to say, by psychological as well as providential logic.[66] The play begins with the hero's recurrent dream of his childhood room and ends with his returning to the room and recognizing it as the scene of his dream. The preface praises the play for this, and also because it concerns itself with a relationship other than that of lovers. Endeavoring, like other preface writers, to raise Li Yu on the literary scale, the writer says that he will never again look on Li's writing as vulgar or plebeian.

Li Yu adapted some famous plays and printed specimens of them in *Casual Expressions*.[67] He also continued, at least until Miss Qiao's death, to write new plays, none of which survive.[68] It is not known whether he ever wrote any of the short plays, of ten or twelve scenes, that he once planned.[69]

The plays were published separately and then in anthologies. Apparently five plays were published in the first Hangzhou period, with a preface by Sun Zhi.[70] They were followed by another anthology entitled *Eight Plays, Earlier and Later (Qianhou bazhong)*, perhaps with a preface by the famous critic Qian Qianyi dated summer 1661.[71] By the time Li Yu wrote *Be Careful about Love*, in 1666 or 1667, he was planning a second anthology of innovative plays, to be known as *Eight Plays, Inner and Outer (Neiwai bazhong)*, which he described in *Casual Expressions* as still unpublished; presumably it never appeared.[72] At one point in *Casual Expressions* he speaks of having written "several tens" of plays, but at another he refers to "the ten in circulation," which are, one assumes, the ten that survive.[73] It is not known exactly when *The Ten Plays of Liweng (Liweng chuanqi shizhong)*, the only extant anthology, was first published.[74]

Li Yu's plays may span twenty years, but his stories (and perhaps also his novel) are concentrated in no more than four or five. He wrote three story collections in all, under the pseudonym of The Fiction Writer Who Awakens the World (Jue shi baiguan). His friend, the gifted, eccentric poet Du Jun, wrote commentaries to all three, under the pseudonym Libationer of Slumberland (Shuixiang jijiu), and for the third collection he also wrote the preface. All three works were well printed and provided with fine illustrations, in some cases by leading illustrators.

The first collection, published about 1656, was entitled *Silent Operas (Wusheng xi)*, to draw attention to its stories' affinity to drama.[75] Like plays, and Li Yu's plays in particular, the stories are built upon neat patterns of correspondences; they have little of the supererogatory, authenticating detail common in fiction; and they rely heavily on monologue and dialogue. In the text, the narrator frequently uses the metaphor of the drama in talking of the story he is narrating. But despite these points of similarity one should not assume that Li Yu's is merely a playwright's fiction. There is a complex relationship linking his drama, fiction, and essays by which each genre appears to have influenced the others.

Silent Operas contains twelve stories, most of which share a common feature, in addition to the fact that they are comedies: they are inversions of normal, accepted, or stereotyped situations in life or literature. As an obvious example, one may cite the story of a liaison between male homosexuals that proves to be an ideal "marriage" and leads to an ideal "widowhood."[76] Many of the stories are outrageously, though wittily, ribald.

They must have met with success, for Li Yu quickly followed them with a *Silent Operas, Second Collection*, containing six stories of medium length.[77] (The stories of the first collection are rather short.) Although the *Second Collection* is not extant, all of its stories survive in a later anthology.

There is a curious political sidelight to this second collection: it may have been published with the assistance of the lieutenant-governor of the province, Zhang Jinyan, and its publication may have been a minor factor in Zhang's downfall.[78] Already established in high office under the Ming, Zhang had been partly responsible for surrendering Beijing to the rebel Li Zicheng, after which he had in turn served the Southern Ming and the Qing. He was lieutenant-governor of Zhejiang from 1654 to 1658, when he was promoted to a post in Beijing. No doubt he had been vulnerable all along because of his changes of allegiance. In any case, in the Emperor's review of high officials held at the beginning of 1660, Zhang was criticized for his life-style and demoted; Metropolitan Censor Wei Yijie followed up with an attack on Zhang as a crony of a purged Grand Secretary; and then another censor, Xiao Zhen, joined in with an accusation of career-long opportunism. One of the charges was that while serving in Zhejiang, Zhang had edited and published *The Silent Operas, Second Collection*, referring to himself as "A Hero Who Was Not To Die" ("busi yingxiong") and saying, among other things, that he "tried to hang himself in the Court waiting room but was rescued by the people next door." That is, by laying false claim to a suicide attempt, he had hoped to whitewash his crime of surrendering the city and make his survival look like a miracle.

Although the reference must be to Li Yu's book, it is hard to imagine where the quoted passages might have appeared. In the course of the preface, perhaps? But in what preface—to a volume of fiction, at that—would the writer refer to himself in such terms? Did Zhang attach a personal, exculpatory note to some story? Again, it seems unlikely; there was a story in that collection in which Li Yu expressed his scorn for just such turncoat officials as Zhang.[79] How, then, does one explain Zhang's involvement with the book? I think we must remain skeptical about Xiao Zhen's claim, and allow for the possibility either that his information was false or that his text has been garbled. We can salvage the possibility that Zhang Jinyan played some part in the publication of the Second Collection, perhaps as the writer of its lost preface. That an official of his eminence should, while on active service, associate himself with a work like Silent Operas would be remarkable in itself. Whatever the truth of Xiao Zhen's claim, Li Yu himself was not affected. By 1666 Wei Yijie, Zhang's accuser, now a Grand Secretary himself, had become one of Li Yu's patrons.[80]

Before long, Li Yu asked Du Jun to edit an anthology drawn from the two collections—a further indication of their success. It was to be a cheaper edition, using the old blocks except for the illustrations. The eighteen or so stories of the two collections were now reduced to twelve—seven from Silent Operas and five from the Second Collection—and published under the slightly misleading title of The Combined Silent Operas (Wusheng xi heji).[81] In the two collections, the titles of each pair of stories had matched, and there had been some connecting references between certain adjacent stories. Du Jun broke up the pairs, rearranged the stories, and replaced their old titles, but he left the references untouched, with the result that they no longer connected the appropriate stories.[82] The edition seems to have been a hasty one, put out for urgent commercial purposes.

Du's preface is astonishingly candid.[83] He identifies the author of the collections as "Master Li" and as "Liweng" and also mentions a couple of Li Yu's plays, perhaps to authenticate the edition in the face of the threat of pirating. He also gives a conventional defense of fiction: that it uses a vulgar medium in order to reach a large audience with its moral message—the same notion that lies behind Li Yu's pseudonym, Fiction Writer Who Awakens the World. The explicit references were excised in successive imprints, as was the reference to the *Second Collection*, perhaps because of Zhang Jinyan's disgrace, while the title was changed to the trite *Liancheng bi (Priceless Jade)*. At this stage, the six stories excluded from the *Combined Silent Operas* were added as a supplement.[84]

The third collection, *Famous Words to Awaken the World (Jueshi mingyan)*, with the alternative and better-known title *Twelve Structures (Shi'er lou)*, carries a preface by Du Jun dated autumn 1658.[85] Its twelve stories, each divided into as many as six chapters, make up a more unified and personal collection than *Silent Operas*. They contain some of Li Yu's own previously published poems; they expound some of his favorite views as we find them in *Casual Expressions*; and they conclude with a story that amounts to a personal statement of his ideas about the relationship of the artist-intellectual to his society. If the stories contain less bawdy comedy, they also demonstrate a more conscious artistic control. The preface is not as revealing as that of *Combined Silent Operas*, but Du's commentary refers to Li Yu and to himself by name.

Li Yu's *Carnal Prayer Mat (Rou putuan)*, a short novel of twenty chapters, is ascribed on its first page of text to The Man of the Way Who Turned over a New Leaf after Being Crazed with Passion (Qingchi fanzheng daoren); because of the book's nature, Li Yu was evidently reluctant to attach any of his familiar pseudonyms to it.[86] It is a classic erotic novel, a subgenre with at least a hundred years of prior history. In it, Li Yu sharply distinguishes the libertine from the ascetic approach to sex, and contrasts both approaches with his own enlightened, commonsensical philosophy. Like most of his fiction and drama, it is essentially a comic work with a moral component. Like his other work, too, it is full of daring narrative and discursive ideas and ingeniously patterned structures.

Carnal Prayer Mat probably appeared after *Twelve Structures*, one story of which contains the germ of several of the novel's narrative ideas,[87] but not very long after. The blatant appeal for sales in the novel's commentary reminds one of Du Jun's preface to the *Combined Silent Operas*. But the main reason for assigning it this approximate date is the fact that, beginning in 1660, Li Yu switched to a different kind of writing.

If the change in his writing is apparent to us, at our remove from him, it must have struck his contemporaries with particular force. "Critics," writes the celebrated Nanjing author Zhou Lianggong in his preface to a collection of legal cases Li Yu had just compiled, "say that Liweng's profligate abuse of his talents in his early writings has been replaced by a dignified and righteous manner." He then proceeds to deny the charge of inconsistency with an argument quite as ingenious as it is unconvincing.[88]

Except for the plays, all of Li Yu's writing during the 1660s was in classical, not vernacular, Chinese. For the most part, too, it was not imaginative literature, although a dash of innovation is generally to be found even in Li Yu's hackwork. This was the decade in which he established his own bookshop in Nanjing, and most of his writing was connected directly with publishing and indirectly with patronage seeking. Asking officials for samples of their legal cases for an anthology supplied him with material for publication, but it also served to pay them a deft compliment.[89]

Such compilations of legal cases, letters, and parallel-prose essays were one kind of activity that occupied him. The other was creative— his own essays and reflections. Here too, he involved his friends and acquaintances, though rarely his patrons, by asking them to write comments on the manuscripts he sent them and then incorporating their comments (with their names attached) as upper-margin notes in the published text. This was not a common practice, and certainly not on the scale on which Li Yu employed it. "The critical comments are rather numerous in my inept writings," he remarks to a correspondent from whom he is asking such a favor.[90] Altogether, his works contain notes by more than 150 different critics, some of whom were responsible for scores of comments. The practice was obviously a selling point and had little to do with patronage.[91]

The earliest of his compilations was *A First Collection of Letters* (*Chidu chuzheng*), which carries a preface by the poet Wu Weiye dated autumn 1660.[92] The anthology, which concentrates on the letters of early Qing writers, has not turned its back on fiction and drama. Its Guidelines (*fanli*) refer to the efflorescence of new kinds of literature in the new dynasty: "even drama and fiction have been produced in great quantity," and the collection itself includes letters written to Li

Yu in praise of *Silent Operas* and the early plays.[93] The book's justification is not only that the letters of the period have been neglected, but also that the letter is the one universal genre in which everyone writes. Put together with difficulty over thirty years, this anthology is merely a go-between, he claims, to solicit readers' contributions to second, third, and fourth collections.

This anthology preceded one by Zhou Lianggong by a good two years,[94] but Zhou's enjoyed the greater success, and that may be the reason Li Yu never delivered the promised sequels. In 1668 or 1669, we find him soliciting letters from Du Jun and Wu Weiye for a follow-up anthology that never appeared.[95]

Li's second kind of compilation met with more success. In 1663 he finished assembling a large volume of legal cases, most of them handled by his contemporaries, which he entitled *A New Aid to Administration (Zizhi xinshu)* and published with a preface dated spring 1663 by Wang Shilu, elder brother of the poet and critic Wang Shizhen.[96] What distinguishes this book from the rest of Li Yu's enterprising hackwork are the two essays prefixed to it: "Modest Suggestions on the Proper Use of Punishments" and "Humble Proposals for Due Care in Legal Cases." Li Yu had displayed a characteristic gall in compiling the anthology in the first place—he had never even served as an official—and he compounds it in these essays, which show his quintessential self emerging from behind the blandly efficient compiler.

Both essays hint at his analytical skill as well as his love of the novel idea (or the novel twist to an old idea). He advises strongly against keeping a woman in prison after she has been charged, not for the obvious reason that she may be raped—one can count on some sense of decency among guards and convicts, after all—but because not even her own family, let alone her in-laws, will ever believe otherwise. "I have often known women to survive the shackles and fetters of prison only to die afterwards of shame."[97]

In the second essay he offers a practical idea, a specimen form on which an official can enter all the details of a homicide. An occasional ironic, personal note is also to be heard. At the end of his long discussion of adultery cases, he advises the judge that, however bawdy the testimony may be, he should at all costs keep a straight face—sound advice from the author of *The Carnal Prayer Mat*.

A Second Collection (Zizhi xinshu erji) appeared a few years later,

with the preface by Zhou Lianggong from which I have quoted.[98] Li
Yu also took a batch of cases that his friend and patron Ji Yuan had
intended for the *Second Collection* and published them under the title
Preserving Life (Qiu sheng lu); they were all cases in which Ji had saved
the accused person from a miscarriage of justice.[99]

Li Yu made two more compilations. A *First Collection of Parallel
Prose (Siliu chuzheng)* was published in 1671 by the Nanjing publishing
house Yisheng Tang, which also brought out *Casual Expressions* at about
the same time.[100] Edited by Shen Xinyou from pieces collected by Li
Yu over more than ten years, it includes the work of patrons and
friends, as well as Li Yu's own writing. The other work was an anthology
of *ci* lyrics, *A Choice of Famous Lyrics (Mingci xuansheng)*, compiled in
1678 at the publisher's request from the work of Li Yu's contemporaries.[101]

The first of his creative compositions was *Discussions of the Past
(Lun gu)*, which he completed in 1664.[102] It is a surprise to find Li Yu
writing history at all,[103] until one realizes that the genre he is writing
in need not entail historical evidence; it may amount to the moral—
or, as in his case, psychological—interpretation of famous historical
anecdotes. It was a genre that gave the writer of iconoclastic temper
the opportunity to *fan an*, that is, to overturn an accepted historical
judgment. (The late-Ming writer Li Zhi is the outstanding practitioner.)[104] Li Yu seized the opportunity, and one can see why; it was
closely akin to the technique of inversion that he used in his fiction
and drama.

The book consists of 133 anecdotes, in chronological order, ex-
tending to the beginning of the Yuan dynasty. The anecdotes and the
traditional comments attached to them, which are mostly drawn from
Zhu Xi's history, *Zizhi tongjian gangmu*, are followed by Li Yu's interpretations. Critical comments on the latter are offered by no fewer
than forty-three friends and acquaintances, who include literary figures
such as Wu Weiye and Yu Huai as well as some noted historians.

The main motive behind the book is Li Yu's love of novelty; he
delights in being the lone voice that challenges the traditional interpretation. Sometimes he is deliberately outrageous, as when he avers
that the First Qin Emperor's burning of the books "was not so unrea-
sonable," merely because of some inconsistency he has found in the
early records.[105] Sometimes he is facetious, as when he observes that

Tang literature flourished as Tang military power declined and goes on to draw a conclusion for policymakers.[106] For the most part, however, he is ingenious, especially in deducing motives from meager facts.

Li clearly regarded the anecdotes, old chestnuts most of them, as so many problems in an intellectual game in which one accepts the "facts" as given and then tries to deduce a utilitarian motive for them. At one point, Shen, his son-in-law, quotes Li Yu as likening problem solving to chess: if you look long enough at the board, a solution will present itself.[107] This seems to have been Li's procedure in interpreting history. For example, he takes the well-known story of the "orphan of Zhao," in which a usurper massacred the entire royal family except for a baby boy who was saved by two retainers.[108] One retainer volunteered to deceive the usurper by pretending that his own baby was the prince, thus sacrificing his own and his baby's lives. The other retainer hid the true prince until the usurper's overthrow, and then waited until the prince was enthroned before killing himself. Li Yu will not accept the argument that he did so for honor's sake; he killed himself because suicide was the only way of validating the prince's claim. Without his death, would the prince have been accepted unequivocally as the true heir? Li Yu comments: "Later people fail to grasp this intention of his and constantly insist that he sacrificed himself for honor's sake. This is a distortion; it shows they have not merely misunderstood the minds of the ancients, they have also misinterpreted their very words!"

He is explicit about his interest in motives: "Those who read the books or discuss the actions of the ancients ought to slight the men's careers and trace their thinking instead, because what the books contain is no more than the dregs of the ancients' lives; their thinking could not be put into words and transmitted. All that we can do is to use our imaginations in order to grasp it."[109] By "thinking" he clearly means motives, and motives for Li Yu invariably mean rational, utilitarian calculations. Why did Han Xin, the renowned Han dynasty general, not avenge himself on the local bullies who had humiliated him in his youth? Why did he reward them instead? Was that the act of a sage? Not in Li Yu's view.[110] Han Xin was a hero, not a sage, and heroes are often stimulated to high achievement by the provocations of petty men. The bullies unwittingly spurred Han Xin on to reach his pinnacle, and Han Xin recognized his debt to them. But there was also an additional, more important, motive: in order to savor his success, a hero needs to have people from his obscure past on hand to witness his triumph.

Jesting as its tone often is, Li Yu's book also bears a message for his own times. His praise for a few great dynastic founders, his lack of concern for legitimacy (he even argues that the absence of legitimacy forces the royal house to try harder), and his impatience with high-minded recluses—all these attitudes connote acquiescence in, and even flattery of, Qing power.[111] He ends his book with the archetypal case of Wen Tianxiang, the Song official martyred at the beginning of the Yuan dynasty. Praising Wen's death, he argues that it was tantamount to suicide, since Emperor Shizu (Khubilai) had actually offered him pardon: "What did the grave and dignified new ruler of the glorious Yuan dynasty have to gain from an official of a defeated country that he should go to such lengths to show him mercy? His sole purpose was to inspire the officials of the nation with an example of loyalty and righteousness. Founders of dynasties must have qualities that greatly surpass those of other men! Coming now to the end of my historical studies, I commend Emperor Shizu of the Yuan as a powerful rein-forcement for the other rulers in history."[112] Like the Mongols of the Yuan, the Manchus of the Qing were an alien dynasty, and praise of the former was easily interpreted as praise of the latter.

Li Yu's most famous book of informal discourse was *Casual Expressions of Idle Feeling (Xianqing ouji)*, published in 1671.[113] It is a book of inventive essays, in a lively, personal style, which are arranged under eight topics: the composition of plays; the production of plays; women's (actually concubines') beauty and accomplishments; houses; furniture and *objets d'art*; food and drink; flowers and trees; health and pleasure. There is nothing quite like it in Chinese literature, or in foreign literature either. Its utterly improbable unity is the unity not only of Li Yu's interests and mentality, but also of his persona and style.

Like *Discussions of the Past*, *Casual Expressions* is festooned with his friends' comments, and like *Discussions* too, it is very much of its time. Its Guidelines are in direct response to the Kangxi Emperor's *Sacred Edict*, promulgated in late 1670, particularly the maxim en-joining a simple, frugal style of living.[114] Li Yu asserts that his book, with the exception of the sections on plays and women, does stress frugality, and, furthermore, that his choice of a frivolous title is designed merely to lure the unwary public into reading an edifying book![115] The claim, as often in Li Yu, is so outrageous as to amount to self-mockery.

If in one sense the book is the summation of his experience as a playwright and also of his lifelong passion for houses and gardens, in another it is the product of the four or five years before its completion. His newly acquired concubines, Miss Qiao and Miss Wang, influenced the sections on acting and women, even though neither girl is mentioned in the text. Li Yu's experience with the Mustard Seed Garden supplied many of the book's ideas on houses, furniture, flowers, and trees. And in a more general sense, the topics of this book were those on which he held forth, in his role of witty pundit, in the houses of the rich and powerful. Although he never ceased to complain of imminent starvation, the five years before the book's appearance were the most satisfying period of his life, aesthetically, sensuously, socially, and even financially. The glow of relative contentment that surrounds *Casual Expressions* testifies to that fact.

In 1670 Li Yu reached the age of sixty by Chinese reckoning—he thought he had been born in 1611, although the clan history says 1610—and the question of literary immortality was much on his mind, in addition to his usual commercial concerns.[116] He wrote *Casual Expressions* to serve both purposes, and also began editing those writings in classical Chinese that he wished to preserve, purging them of anything risqué.[117] Their title was to be *Liweng yijia yan*, or simply *Yijia yan*, which means the words or writings of an independent thinker, reflecting his lifelong concern for originality.[118]

Liweng's Independent Words included poems written at or after the end of 1672, and it was published probably in 1673.[119] Apparently it was a success, for by late 1677 Li Yu was at work on a *Second Collection* (*Liweng yijia yan erji*) at his publisher's request. It appeared late in 1678 or early in 1679, together with an "additional collection" (*bieji*) that consisted of *Discussions of the Past* (*Lun gu*) much abridged and revised by their author.[120]

Among several other works written in the 1670s—rhymebooks for *shi* and *ci* poetry, an edition of the *Sanguo yanyi* (*Romance of the*

Three Kingdoms) with copious comments, a volume of stories about famous women edited by Li Yu—the most notable is the revised and expanded collection of his own *ci* lyrics, *Naige ci (Singable Lyrics)*. [121] The introduction he wrote for it on the nature of the *ci* displays to the full his original and analytical genius as well as his irrepressible authorial self.

Two. Creating a Self

To an extraordinary degree, Li Yu is a visible and audible presence in all his writing. His constant self-reference, playful though it usually is, may strike the reader as unnecessary and even obsessive, but it cannot be dismissed; the conspectus of selves or personae that he insists on presenting to us forms an essential element of his art.

Take the case of *Casual Expressions*, his central or representative work in the sense that it has the closest connections with the others. Even its title declares its subject to be Li Yu's personal concerns, and despite the formidable organizing and analytical power it possesses, it is essentially a book about his practical ideas and pleasures—a "Book of the Self," as it might be called, except that the self with which it deals is almost never explored for its own sake, but only as it reveals itself in its tastes, interests, ideas, and opinions.[1] Even the drama chapters, which constitute the most systematic treatise on the subject in premodern times, are mainly about Li Yu's ideas and practices. The words "I" and "Liweng" are ubiquitous, as he proceeds to reveal with great fanfare what he claims to be his own hard-won, practical secrets. Only two Ming dramatists are referred to with approval, while no contemporary dramatist is so much as mentioned, except, of course, Li himself.[2] Subjects on which he has no ideas of his own to contribute he simply skips over; on music, for example, he candidly admits his ignorance—he merely follows the formula, like a vintner making wine— and passes quickly to another topic.[3] By contrast, on the dialogue of the drama, a subject on which he has much to offer, he goes so far as to conduct an imaginary debate with his admirers and detractors over the merits of his own practice.[4] He is even ready to adapt his arguments as he goes along. Here he is, modifying his earlier advice on women's complexions:

Every reader of this book will know by now that Liweng of the Lake is no fool. Not only is he making a valuable contribution to refined taste, he also deserves to be called an understanding friend to women. When I treated the subject of light and dark complexions before, my pronouncements were rather drastic. And yet they were hardly *too* drastic, for only if you realize your disease is a grave one will you be duly grateful to the doctor who has the power of restoring you to life.[5]

In comparison with his own tastes and practical ideas, we hear little of either knowledge or scholarship. The whole learned tradition to which Li Yu is heir is seldom mentioned and never appealed to, except in jest. He himself is at the center of his work, and his own arguments and experience supply whatever authority it needs. The arguments are constantly personalized, and the experience is frequently brought in to nail down a point—or just to embellish it. Thus we hear, in a discussion of turtle meat as a delicacy, of his three narrow escapes from death.[6] And after telling us how he came up with the idea of arranging flowers inside his bed-curtain, he reports the result:

Once, just as I was about to waken from a sweet dream, I smelled the scent of the winter-sweet and my throat and mouth were filled with a clear, delicate fragrance that seemed to emanate from somewhere inside of me. My body felt light and as if about to ascend, and I concluded I was no longer part of this mortal world. Awakening, I told my wife and children about it: "Who are we, to have such joy? Perhaps I have squandered my lifetime's allotment of happiness," to which they replied: "We've always been poor and lowly; that may be the reason." This is true; it is not some tall story.[7]

On the subject of crabs, one of his great passions, he writes:

All my life I have loved crabs. Each year before they appear, I save up in readiness for them. My family tease me for considering crabs as important as life itself, and so I call the money I save up my redemption money. From the day the crabs appear until the end of the season, I never let an evening or, indeed, a couple of hours go by without indulging in them. My friends know about my craving, and do all their inviting during the crab season. That's why I call the ninth and tenth months Crab Autumn. From my concern lest the crabs slip away too quickly, I have the family prepare crocks and brew wine in readiness for pickling and steeping them. The pickle is called Crab Pickle, the wine Crab Brew, and the crocks Crab Crocks. I once had a maid who was very diligent about seeing to the crabs, and I changed her name to Crab Girl, but I have since lost her.[8]

In his other expository works, such as *Discussions of the Past* or the introductory essays to *A New Aid to Administration*, he breaks all the rules of literary decorum in flaunting his own ideas and ingenuity. In the *Discussions*, his interpretations are presented as the *jeux d'esprit* of a brilliant, original mind with a good share of playful perverseness. Surely no other work in this sober genre has ever resembled Li Yu's!

Even in fiction, where one might expect to find less scope for the self, its presence is still strongly felt. In his stories as well as his novel, Li Yu made over the traditional narrator's persona almost into his own image, so that his personal opinions and comments intrude upon, and even dominate, the narrative. In *Silent Operas*, in addition to the prologues, which are developed into amusing essays, there are long epilogues as well as numerous comments and opinions that are remote from the banal moralisms of fiction; they are sharp comments offered by a recognizable literary persona of Li Yu's.

Such trends are only heightened in his later collection, *Twelve Structures*. Li Yu, as narrator, comments explicitly in his own person, offering us his early poems, discussing them, even telling us his wartime experiences, as well as commenting reflexively on the story. And there is an additional complexity: the characters in some stories represent one persona of Li Yu's while the narrator represents another. The novel *Carnal Prayer Mat* also contains a large measure of comment—the whole first chapter and much else—which is sometimes close to Li Yu's advice on sex in the final chapters of *Casual Expressions*. It also has a running commentary, probably written by him, which adds a further level of interpretation. To the extent that a novelist can be an essayist who offers us his personal opinions, Li Yu is such a novelist.

What of the plays? Apart from the prologue and final scenes, the drama holds no place for explicit comment of the kind I have described. On occasion Li Yu manages to smuggle in a comic self-reference, as when, in *Be Careful about Love,* he gives a fanciful explanation of the Li clan's poverty that has nothing to do with the play.[9] But such cases are the exception; instead, in the drama his expository self is refracted into debate and argument.

His plays are full of argument and discussion, often over points on which he liked to hold forth in life. Debate is a favorite device in his essays and fiction prologues, too, but in the plays the argument is distributed among the characters, who have been created, it would seem, largely to represent attitudes or uphold opinions. As Li insists in his drama chapters, the dramatist must draw a sharp distinction between mind and mouth, that is to say, between his mind and his characters' mouths.[10] But the very insistence with which he emphasizes the distinction reflects, I think, the magnitude of the change he himself had to make in moving from one genre to another, from the superbly opinionated persona of the essays and stories to the ostensibly self-effacing dramatist.

Li Yu's was above all the world of the close-at-hand, even the trivial in life. *Casual Expressions* is entirely devoted to subjects ordinarily held to be inconsequential. Like one strain of Chinese poetry, Li's writing is concerned with the domestic self, not with the self as affected by wider issues.

This becomes apparent in his accounts of his travels. There are poems and letters in plenty that dwell on his personal privations, but practically no observation such as the skilled travel writer loves to impart. He records, with relish, the exotic foods and fruits he encounters in other parts of China, but everything else—cities, mountains, rivers—is merely the backdrop for his trials. Even the famous sites rarely evoke historical musings in him, as they do in virtually every other Chinese writer. Intent on personal fund raising and gustatory adventure, Li Yu seems to have traveled about China almost as if it had no history.

The aesthetic principles that influenced him most were those developed by Li Zhi and embraced by Yuan Hongdao late in the sixteenth century.[11] In Yuan's formulation, literature is the expression of one's *xingling* or personal nature; the more authentic the expression of that nature, with the least obstruction from the forces of tradition and convention, the better the literature will be. As an expressivist theory of the personal nature, an entity that is distinctive for each human being, it celebrates the close-at-hand—that is, immediacy of subject matter and feeling. The theory's usefulness for Li Yu lay in its sanction of his individuality, his expression of self, his concern with the close-at-hand, and his rejection of the authority of tradition. But its descriptive validity in Li Yu's case is still very limited. His forte was the expression of ingenious ideas and creative thought, rather than of feeling. And the medium of his ideas is, of course, not the personal nature as such but the created self—persona, point of view, voice— for which the expressivist theory, in its naiveté, provided no place.[12]

In order to describe the self or selves he created, it is necessary to draw an equation between the personae adopted by Li Yu the writer and Li Yu the man. That he was a "character" in life as well as in literature cannot be doubted, if by character we mean not some eccentric unaware of his eccentricity, but one who consciously plays the role and enjoys it—a performer. He loved dramatizing himself, in his life as in his writing. A revealing quotation occurs in his preface to a new edition of a famous collection of repartee. The editors had changed a word in the title from "talk" to "laughter" in order to suit the tastes of the time, a change that provoked the following expostulation from Li Yu:

> Alas! Are talk and laughter really so far apart? I say that once the ability to talk is gone, jokes will cease to exist, and thus talk is the mother of laughter. Unfortunately, while there are many who love laughter, there are few who are good at talk. People say that my talk elicits others' laughter, and that therefore I am toiling for their benefit, doing all the work while they get all the pleasure. But let me ask you this: *When a play is being performed, who is getting more pleasure, the audience or the players?*[13]

There is abundant evidence that Li Yu loved to play roles in life, and that he deliberately chose contrary viewpoints to defend.

Drama itself, of course, afforded an opportunity for role playing. In a famous passage in his drama chapters, Li describes the joys of writing:

If the genre did not exist, men of talent and heroic action would die of frustration. I was born amid disaster, and have lived a life of poverty; from childhood to maturity, from maturity to old age, I have scarcely known a moment of success. When writing plays, however, I not only gain relief from my depression and resentment, I lay claim to the title of happiest man between Heaven and Earth. I feel that all the joys of rank, riches, and glory are no greater than mine. If one cannot fulfill one's desires in real life, one can produce an imaginary realm in which to do exactly as one wishes. If I want to be an official, then in a flash I attain honor and rank. If I want to retire from office, then in the twinkling of an eye I am among the mountains and forests. If I want to be a genius among men, then I become the incarnation of Du Fu or Li Bai.[14]

There is no more forceful statement in Chinese literature of the joys of imaginative projection.

What are the characteristics of Li's favorite personae? He refers to himself by a variety of titles, but usually as Liweng, the Old Fisherman, or Li Zi, the Master Li. He also uses a variety of metaphors, especially that of the doctor (representing the expert with his specialized knowledge) or of artisans such as the tailor or the carpenter (exemplifying his view of the creative process), all of which are employed for comic purpose. Further, he writes, in almost all the work of his that we have, as a wit and pundit, someone with a reputation to live up to for humorous, original, and even perverse opinion.

The essential point in his discourse is some novel (usually contrary) opinion, wittily expressed. His works are full of claims that he is overturning conventional practice or belief, and he refers constantly to his innovative ideas. His son-in-law Shen Xinyou remarks of a confessional poem: "As everybody knows, my father-in-law has all his life said what others can't say or don't dare to say. What people don't realize is that he also says what others are unwilling to say or are too proud to say."[15] Li Yu's views cut across the boundaries of genre; the same opinions are found in essays, plays, and stories alike. To denote their perverseness, he calls himself "the Stubborn Old Man of the Lake."[16]

After his visit to the Governor of Gansu, he wrote apologizing for his uninhibited sophistry and shocking opinions.[17] As I have suggested, his value for such proconsuls lay not merely in his reputation as a popular playwright but also in his standing as an eccentric, the dispenser of witty, original, and even outrageous remarks. Certainly it was this aspect of him that struck other writers most forcibly. When he visited the poet Wu Weiye, Wu wrote a set of poems on Li Yu's role as jester or comedian.[18] And another poet, Gu Jingxing, a fellow guest in Hanyang in 1672, responded to Li Yu's poems with poems of his own stressing Li Yu's oral wit and wisdom.[19]

It was primarily this persona that gave Li Yu his dubious reputation in his own day and even in ours. He lacked the crucial virtue of sincerity; he seemed incapable of *gravitas*. Although sincerity, in literature at least, is a grossly overrated virtue, a notion that depends on simplistic assumptions about literary creation, the evident lack of it in Li Yu offended against certain deeply held values, and to this day there is a tendency to judge his unrelenting comedy by the standards of Du Fu's poetry and to condemn whatever in his work cannot be explained as *cri de coeur* or social satire. In his own time, his friends felt obliged to defend his persona or apologize for it. Wu Weiye's poems are ambivalent at best, while Gu Jingxing's, although ostensibly laudatory, are actually defensive. Other friends writing prefaces to his works—Sun Zhi, Li Changxiang, Bao Xuan—take a similar line, explaining Li's apparently frivolous jesting as concealing a deeper moral meaning.[20] Sometimes they compare him to Dongfang Shuo, the Han dynasty exponent of political wit and satire, a comparison of which Li Yu must have approved.[21] Sometimes, with a certain justice, they compare him to the iconoclast Li Zhi.[22] But in each case it is clear that their purpose is to defend him from being dismissed as a comedian.

Li Yu himself reflected on the charge in some poems of moral stocktaking written on his sixtieth birthday. The poems purport to tell the truth about himself on a day on which he has been deluged with birthday flattery. But although ostensibly remorseful, they actually take a defiant pride in the self he has created, as the following lines show:

A romantic lad with a shock of white hair,
Jesting all day long as he starves and freezes.

My womenfolk cherish my talent, my friends forgive my
  wildness;
Scorning all about me, I crack my jokes.[23]

Of course, other factors also contributed to his reputation—his
indefatigable patronage seeking, for one, although it would seem to
have weighed more heavily with Li Yu himself than with his contemporaries. (He has one or two poems of genuine remorse, reflecting on
the neglect of friendship to which his patronage seeking has led him.)[24]
Or his ribaldry, from which both Qian Qianyi and Bao Xuan, in writing
their prefaces, seek to defend him.[25] Or the daring and scandalous (to
some) use of his concubines as actresses.[26] Another factor must surely
have been his ambiguous status as a professional writer and entertainer
in a society of literary amateurs, one who mixed vulgarity with refinement in both subject matter and language. All of these factors must
have contributed to the patent lack of reciprocity between Li Yu and
many of his literary friends, by which their names appear more frequently in his works than his name appears in theirs.[27]

To return to Li Yu's personae: there are times when he is more
than the witty, outrageous character; he becomes the inventive genius,
the pioneer. Even here, of course, there is a hint of self-mockery, so
exaggerated are the claims he makes for himself. Describing the varied
uses of the heated chair he has invented, he lets his imagination run
wild, ending up with "a filial son who attends you night and morning,
a devoted wife who keeps you warm or cool—this one object serves
all these functions. When Cang Jie invented the first script, Heaven
caused millet to rain down from the skies and ghosts wailed in the
night, all because the mystical substance of creation had been allowed
to escape. Once this design appears, shall I not suffer the same dread
as the man of Qi for infringing the taboo?"[28]

An allied persona is that of the expert, the possessor of specialized
knowledge, of "secret formulas," which he reveals, with the greatest
of misgivings, only because he is too public-spirited to keep them to
himself. Often, as I have mentioned, he uses the metaphor of the
doctor because of the latter's air of professional authority. (In life, in
keeping with the same persona, Li Yu distrusted real doctors and preferred to treat himself.) At all times he insists on getting full credit
from the reader. Here he is on the invention of the picture window:

"Is it not the most delightful thing you've ever seen or heard of? When you're celebrating with wine and song, how will you be able to forget the inventor, Li Liweng?"[29]

The professional, sharing the secret lore of his trade, merges easily with the practical instructor. As a teacher, Li Yu had a positive lust to be understood, which resulted in the clarity that distinguishes his writing from that of most other Chinese critics. It was not that he saw things in a simpler light, merely that he eschewed those aspects of a subject that defied lucid formulation. And he is as much a master of the general as he is of the effable; his criticism excels in the bold analysis of whole genres rather than in insights into particular lines or images.

Another persona is that of the wise man—patient, resigned, nostalgic for country life, and eager to withdraw from the world. He is a man of sage advice and simple enjoyments, who may be either an ascetic or an epicurean, but who is invariably stoical. This is the persona that appears in such famous essays as "How to Be Happy Though Poor and Lowly."[30]

The last example reminds us, however, how tendentious his claims to these personae really are. The personae are no more than a set of congenial roles that he chooses to play because they are useful for literary and social purposes. Much as his amiable epicureanism, in particular, has impressed his modern interpreters, it was a pose that he deliberately assumed—sometimes, it appears, in contradiction to his other qualities. For example, Li Yu the ardent aesthete, who persuades his wives to pawn their jewelry so that he can buy narcissus blooms, hardly accords with the wise and stoical figure he also wants to cut.[31] He is proud of his action, not apologetic, for it fits the character of the eccentric artist who puts beauty first in life. Elsewhere he depicts himself as impatient, easily bored and tense—a notably fussy man of quicksilver temperament who needs the constant stimulus of the new in order to escape boredom. His eldest daughter, he tells us, was often unable to sleep because of her excitement over a line of poetry or a new design in embroidery; she was an intense person "just like her father."[32] As for his fussiness, it must have been a rare servant who could do his or her housework in precisely the way the master wished. In arguing for the necessity of a drawer in one's table, he remarks: "I am a nervous, impatient man by nature. I often call the boy, and when he doesn't come, I do the job myself. No matter how close the study is, it is a bother to walk there. Once you have a drawer, keep in it all the things you are likely to need in a hurry. It is more than convenient; it is as if you had a genie inside, awaiting your command."[33]

From his writings one can, if one wishes, construct quite a different Li Yu—a childlike figure, tense, impatient, volatile, impulsive, indulged by his womenfolk (and to some extent by his friends) and exploiting that indulgence. It is this Li Yu that accounts most easily for his chronic indebtedness. One of his poems of self-analysis begins: "My wildness is a stubborn trait, irreversible; / My family has grown used to it, and is not resentful."[34] And another contains the line: "Now sad, now joyous, a child's temperament."[35]

The link between his personae in life and literature resolves itself into an equation between Li Yu the writer and Li Yu the talker. A friend such as Li Changxiang, in a preface to Li Yu's *Independent Words*, refers to his "pure talk," thus claiming for him a well-known genre of oral wit; he sees the wit and punditry of Li Yu's travels as related to, indeed equivalent to, the wit and punditry of his writing.[36] Li Yu himself frequently connects talk with literature. In his essay on the *ci* lyric, he claims that "good literature in all ages is just speech with the classical particles added."[37] And in his drama chapters, he answers the question of how to tell whether a person is a potential playwright in the following manner:

> There is no problem at all. Just look at his speech and writing and you'll know. If his speech is neither stuffy nor narrow-minded and if in every ten sentences or so there are one or two that show an independent mind; if his writing is unconventional and if in every piece he writes there are one or two passages that are light and free—then this is a man capable of writing plays. If he lacks these qualities, he should apply his energy to some other field and not waste it on drama.[38]

His Guidelines to *Casual Expressions* describe the book's contents, not inaccurately, as "the newest and most unusual talk."[39] And in his *Discussions of the Past,* his empathy with Dongfang Shuo is immediately apparent.[40] In Li Yu's written work, he frequently refers to oral situations and favors us with some *bon mot* or joke he once delivered. More significant is the fact that the spoken voice—or rather, the suggestion of the spoken voice—is present in some form in all of his best prose, in fiction, drama, and essay, as well as in his best poetry.

Unless they have a Boswell to record them, the great talkers and wits of history are only dimly remembered. Li Yu was evidently such a talker and wit, but like a few of his peers—Oscar Wilde and George Bernard Shaw come to mind, both dramatists—he managed to find a literary correlative for his oral wit. This fact not only preserved his wit, it proved to be the main source of his strength as a writer. One reason he wrote the kind of fiction he did was his predilection for speech; he took the figure of the traditional narrator and replaced it with a persona of himself, while retaining the simulation of the spoken voice.[41]

In his essays he shows himself more continuously aware of an audience than any essayist before him. Humor in the Chinese essay had most often derived from some radical disjunction, such as that between genre and subject matter, resulting in the mock biography, mock petition, and so forth, but Li Yu's humor depends largely on his manipulation of persona and voice. He addresses his readership as if it were a live audience, questioning it, chiding it, teasing it, reassuring it. It is difficult to say whether the rhetoric of his late essays was influenced by his fictional practice, but there is no doubt that his mode of writing in both fiction and essay reflects a similar set of personae.

But if Li's writing, in vernacular as well as classical Chinese, is the simulation of good talk, we must remember that it *is* just a simulation and it *is* literary, and that in both languages it owes something to the tradition of the literary essay. It may simulate talk in its authorial persona, in its language, and in its easy acknowledgment of its audience, but no actual talk is ever as beautifully constructed, as elaborated with deft twists and turns of argument, or as richly studded with *bons mots* as Li Yu's prose.

His gift, in both talking and writing, was less narrative than discursive; he was the exponent of witty, cogent, unorthodox opinion rather than a raconteur. Despite the claims made in Li Changxiang's preface, Li Yu does not belong to the tradition of "pure talk"—those lapidary, profound remarks that, encapsulated in anecdote, constituted the classic form of wit. His bent was toward the comic argument or debate or disquisition. Indeed, his fiction is so heavily weighted with discussion in prologues, epilogues, and elsewhere that some stories can almost be regarded as debates, with the characters serving as the vehicles of ideas and attitudes. And his plays were notorious even in his own time for the amount of speech they contained, speech that is dialectical as much as it is narrative.

It is remarkable how often his essays, too, take the form of a debate or an address. "Argument about the Returning *Sha* Spirits," which may well be his earliest surviving essay, is a debate between the youthful Li Yu and a diviner. "Burying the Dog," another early essay, is his retort to a visitor who protests that Li Yu's grief over his dog's death is excessive. "A Deed of Sale for a Hill" contains Li Yu's message to the purchaser of his Mt. Yi property, and "Expelling the Cat" his addresses to a mother cat and kittens.[42] *Casual Expressions* has only two debates, one over the merits of the dialogue in his plays and the other between Li Yu and a Taoist practitioner over the value of meditation,[43] but in a general sense all of its more formal essays can be regarded as one-sided debates, so carefully structured are they to counter opposing views and imagined objections.

Li Yu's style was developed to suit both his persona and his sense of audience, its main requirement being comprehensibility. "Write as if you were talking face to face, and not to literary men," he remarks in his essay on the lyric, "but to your wives and children and servants."[44] In the case of his informal prose, at least, this advice may not be the hyperbole it seems. The five long letters home that he wrote on his Guangzhou journey closely resemble his more relaxed essays in their structure, style, imagery, and calculated sense of audience.[45] In drama, too, he recommends ordinary rather than original language, and stresses the use of commonplaces, a staple of the spoken language, provided slight emendations are made in them. Literary values, of course, are still uppermost in his mind: "A single line of awkward prose will make the audience grow thorns in their ears, while a few words of fresh and sparkling dialogue will make them snap out of their lethargy."[46]

The notion of an audience, whether real or simulated, was a vital one for him. All of his personae are in the service of Li Yu the entertainer, who shows himself ready to compromise in order to amuse and interest his public. In *Casual Expressions* he appeals explicitly to poor as well as to rich, and implicitly to women as well as to men. In terms of education, he appeals to both middlebrow and highbrow, to the former by his choice of subject and his relatively simple language and treatment, to the latter by the freshness of his ideas and wit. No passage gives a clearer indication of this than the long section on jokes in the drama. If the dramatist neglects jokes and comic byplay, "even the man of taste will nod off." Jokes are "ginseng broth to the audience," keeping them awake and alert.[47] There follows a passage on how to use sexual jokes tastefully (for example, by suppressing half of the idiom or by using imagery). A concern to amuse or shock his audience accounts for Li Yu's occasional deliberate lapses of taste; his outrageous flourishes may be construed as his efforts to keep his audience or readership amused at all costs.

This list hardly exhausts the personae in his writings. There are genres such as the elegy in which none of the personae I have mentioned would have been appropriate. In the informal elegy he wrote on the death of Censor Chen Qitai, one of his patrons, Li Yu effaces himself entirely.[48] Threatened with capture by the rebels, Chen first ordered his womenfolk to kill themselves and then took his own life, and Li Yu in his elegy contrives to praise him for a ruthlessness that runs counter to his usual thinking. In the moving "Combined Biography" of his concubines, Misses Qiao and Wang, Li Yu again effaces himself, giving the biography a far greater force than the poems he wrote on the death of each girl, poems that overflow with explicit emotion.[49] Only at the end of the biography does he ask himself the reasons for the girls' affection for him. Not his looks, surely; he was too old. Nor his genius; neither girl was well enough educated to appreciate it. What then? Disingenuous as his question no doubt is, it fits Li Yu's rather mechanical concept of love as a reaction to attributes (looks, talent) rather than as some more intangible thing, as the notion of sentimental love or *qing* would have it. (On the other hand, the fact that he devoted so long and elaborate a biography to two concubines marks Li Yu as a man of sentiment.)[50]

However, in the biography he wrote of Miss Zhu, the concubine of his friend Mao Xianshu, his old persona cannot be suppressed.[51] Miss Zhu had died while still a virgin, just after nursing Mao back from a long illness. Here Li Yu's farcical imagination takes charge. He cannot refrain from comparing her unconsummated experience with his own dead concubines' fulfillment, and he sends them a message of consolation and congratulation by the medium of Miss Zhu. One cannot but wonder what Mao Xianshu, who had asked Li Yu to write the piece out of admiration for the "Combined Biography," really felt about his friend's response.

In certain other genres, too, Li Yu's distinctive personae are important. His rhapsodies, which are both personal and domestic, treat their subjects with comic exaggeration, showing Li Yu in an independent-minded but playful persona. "A Rhapsody on Not Climbing Anywhere" ("Budeng gao fu") is classic Li Yu, flouting the convention and justifying himself with an elaborate explanation.[52] In the patronage letters, instead of praise for the recipient, there is incessant self-reference replete with exaggeration. And some of the prefaces he wrote for his friends and acquaintances have so much to say about Li Yu, and so little about the book he is supposed to be introducing, that the result is almost embarrassing, and in one case he actually apologizes.[53]

His poems and lyrics show a full range of personae, both explicit and implicit. He was a skillful poet, but whenever his poetry lacks an explicit persona it seems a little derivative, like a brilliant exercise in an established mode. He himself preferred drama to poetry because of its explicitness, and one of the most significant strictures in his essay on the lyric is that the poet should make clear whose voice is being heard.[54] Li Yu's explicit personae in his poetry include the pastoral role of the "literate peasant" with his bucolic joys, as well as the penniless provider harried by debts. One poem shows him as the fervent apostle of the new, insisting on his intellectual independence with his customary panache:

> I claim this merit—I haven't copied the ancients.
> I hold that books, once read, are fit for the fire.
> Since people's hearts are as varied as their faces,
> Why in our writing must we all be the same?
> So as *Independent Words* I name my book,
> And hope that none will ever copy me.[55]

Three. The Necessity of Invention

"Fervent apostle of the new"—the expression can be qualified in several ways. One could show that Li Yu was not as original as he claimed to be or even as he supposed; that when he was original, he was original in conventional ways and in conventional areas, taking vast fields of inquiry for granted; and that, in any case, his protestations were designed mainly for comic effect. One might also attempt to place him in his context of intellectual change, pointing to predecessors who also stressed the value of originality, such as Li Zhi or Chen Jiru, as well as to contemporaries like the philosopher Gu Yanwu.[1] But after all these qualifications have been noted, Li Yu remains an exceptional figure in traditional China.

Newness, according to Li Yu, is a universal value in everything but friendship. Moreover, only the absolute kind of newness will qualify, for yesterday's newness is already obsolete. Here is his most extreme statement, from *Casual Expressions:*

> "In people one seeks only the old, in things the new."
> Newness is a term of approbation for everything in the world, but doubly so for literature. This is what the statement "striving to rid one's writing of clichés—oh, how hard it is!" refers to. And in the art of drama, newness is twice as valuable again as in the other literary genres. Not only is the work of past authors now obsolete, there is a gulf even in my own writing between what I wrote yesterday and what I am writing today. Yesterday's work has appeared, while today's has not, and if we regard what has not yet appeared as new, we must accept what has already appeared as old.[2]

The Necessity of Invention

Our minds need constant stimulation from friends if they are not to grow dull. "One can't be like the chimes of a Western clock that sound of their own accord,"[3] he remarks, striking a new image of his own. Dismembering the term for the Southern drama, chuanqi, he asserts that a play, once it has been seen by thousands in performance, is no longer novel (qi) and thus there is no reason to perpetuate (chuan) it.[4] The typical contemporary play is heavily derivative, "an old priest's patched cloak, a doctor's blended medicine,"[5] while old plays have lost much of their entertainment value: "Whenever I am to see an old play, I am both happy and fearful. Happy, because the musical arrangement will be agreeably familiar and will not make thorns grow in my ears. Fearful, because the subject matter may be all too familiar, causing scales to form over my eyes."[6] Newness is whatever the audience or reader perceives as new, and hence the artist is permitted a certain sleight-of-hand. In describing the "lesser finale" at the end of the first half of a play, Li Yu even compares the dramatist to a magician: "If you keep people puzzled, keep people guessing, it makes for good magic and good drama."[7]

Any doctrine of newness had to contend with one of the most cherished values of Chinese culture: Confucius, as we know, "transmitted but did not create."[8] Li Yu sanctions transmission, but he also validates originality and objects strenuously to our mixing one with the other: "In my humble opinion, if you're going to create, you should create from start to finish; if you're going to transmit, you should transmit from start to finish."[9] It is clear, however, where his preference lies. In his Discussions of the Past, he praises both the Tang emperor Taizong and his minister Wei Zheng for their independence from the cultural tradition. The emperor's writing owed nothing to the classics or even to convention, but sprang from his own personal nature (xing-ling), while Wei's "path-breaking" words were original, not derived.[10]

The past seems to exist for Li Yu mainly as a foil to the new; he possessed neither the passion of the historical scholar nor the literary man's nostalgia for the relics of the cultural past. This is what distinguishes him most of all from the legion of sixteenth- and seventeenth-century writers who turned their attention to the domestic arts. His friend Yu Huai, with his interest in the history of women's shoes and stockings and his nostalgic memoirs of the courtesans of old Nanjing, stands in clear contrast to him. In the whole of Casual Expressions,

46

the essay on women's footwear, which was contributed by Yu Huai, is the only piece that takes a historical approach.[11]

Li Yu's references to the past and its monuments are marked by a playful iconoclasm. He is suspicious of the old texts, believing that many of the figures in them may be fictional.[12] He refers again and again with comic approval to the Qin emperor's burning of the books.[13] In general, he believes that modern products are better than the ancient, and that modern morality is at least no worse than the old.

Naturally he advocates revising the old dramatic masterpieces in order to bring them up to date. Revision does the author a favor; would he not do the same thing himself if he were alive?[14] With regard to antiques, about which he professes to know little, he can only be described as ingeniously obtuse. The value of an antique lies in the evidence of its age, in its patina, he claims; if it were polished up to look like new, people would take little interest in it. "Therefore what people value in an object is not its essential character as a constant quality, but its capacity to change and become new,"[15] he concludes, drawing support for his attitudes to the past but ignoring the point that the historical association of an antique might itself be a value.

Change is a universal principle, except in the Confucian ethical relationships. In literature, as in art and social institutions, nothing is fixed. Li Yu defends the exceptional quantity of dialogue in his plays by maintaining "that there are no fixed rules in literature. There are the originators and there are those who preserve without change. There are those who preserve without change and also those who, while largely preserving the idea, make modest changes of form and establish themselves as independent figures, unconcerned about the criticism and mockery they incur."[16] Here he goes far beyond the notion, common enough in his time, that each age had its dominant literary genre and its dominant trends in moral culture (for example, knight-errantry during the Warring States period). He is referring to the innovations of the individual author.

Not all desire for change is good, however. There is an amusing irony in the sight of Li Yu, apostle of the new, excoriating fashionable trends in life and literature. Modern plays "persistently seek the new, changing not only the things that can be changed but also tampering with those that absolutely must be preserved, in order to display their novelty."[17] He is scathing also about current fashion in dress, hairstyling, and makeup, condemning the ornateness and extravagance that result from a restless search for whatever is new and unusual. One "must make things new in the proper way, and make them unusual in the proper way."[18] The desire for newness must be channeled and controlled.

This last is the mission he sets for himself in the Guidelines to *Casual Expressions:* to join the fashionable trend up to a point, in order to lead it in the right direction. The mission has to be taken with a grain of salt, but only a grain, for he strikes the same theme throughout. In the following passage he is replying to someone who has criticized him for recommending the use of hairpieces:

> "If you follow the old ways in the present-day world, who will pay attention to your ideas no matter how good they are? Far better to go along with the current trend and lead it in the direction of naturalness. Women's hair cannot be without ornaments; it has always been so. But rather than decorate their hair with jewels, it would be better if they were to use hairpieces. Granted, a hairpiece is false, but at least it has come from another woman's head, and so using it as a hairpiece can be considered 'restoring it to its rightful place.' "[19]

He does more than preach the doctrine of newness; he continually protests that he has never violated its precepts:

> In half a lifetime's writing, I have not filched a single word from other people. There have been times when I have been ashamed of my shallowness and times when I have invited ridicule for unsound views, but when it comes to following the beaten path, to chewing other men's spittle and claiming it as the fresh blossoms of my own tongue, not only am I confident that I am innocent, but distinguished scholars throughout the land all realize that I would never stoop so low.[20]

His designs, like his books, must bear his individual stamp: "Every beam and every rafter must come from my own style, so that crossing my land or entering my house is like reading Liweng of the Lake's books."[21] Originality entails certain sacrifices, however, such as a full coverage of the subject: "I hope readers will not expect me to be complete and comprehensive in every fact and word of the topics I cover. This is a book to freshen your eyes and ears; it is not a book for checking and verification."[22] He defends his limited coverage by comparing himself to the medical specialist, who concentrates on the field he knows.[23] When there is some subject he cannot avoid and in which he lacks experience, Li Yu substitutes opinions (*pinglun*) for practical ideas, because opinions can always be original, even without a basis of personal knowledge.[24]

Naturally, he exults in the pride of invention. The question "Is it not surprising that the world had to wait for Liweng to invent this?" recurs as a refrain in *Casual Expressions* and, in a variety of forms, in his fiction as well. At the same time, he is jealously protective of the credit due the inventor, as in his tirade against those who would pirate his designs. And he is concerned lest he be seen as an imitator himself. On his visit to Fujian in 1670, he suggested to the lacquer craftsmen a new method which they were eager to adopt:

> "Lacquerware has been made in Fujian for hundreds of years," said one, "and countless visitors have come from all over the world to buy it, but we have never met with an invention as ingenious as the one you have just described to us. May we have your permission to apply it and make it widely known?"
>
> "Wait a bit," I replied, "until my new book is finished and in print. I'm afraid people may see the results of the process before they read the book and, not knowing who was the inventor, assume that I had plagiarized someone's successful idea. That would be a slander I could never clear myself of."[25]

The field of his invention is that of the visible, tangible world, not the world of fantasy. Li Yu firmly rejects the common assertion that the former kind of subject matter has been exhausted in literature and art.[26] He echoes the dramatist and storywriter Ling Mengchu (1580–1644) with his exhortations to write about visible reality, but he obeys them no more faithfully than Ling.[27] Li indulges often in fantasy, in his plays, his stories, and even in *Discussions of the Past*, yet it is a playful indulgence and one that he quickly acknowledges to the reader.

49

Several of his stories actually turn on natural explanations for apparently supernatural events.[28]

New subject matter is produced by changes in the way human nature expresses itself. (It is certainly not produced by changes in the Confucian principles, which are immutable.) "The expression of human nature becomes more and more novel," asserts Li Yu, citing bizarre manifestations of female chastity and jealousy in the modern age, no doubt facetiously.[29] He relishes the pose of the shrewd observer who is able to discern the reality behind the facade of accepted wisdom. Of course, his adherence to what may be called the reality principle is largely a rhetorical stance, a posture for his manipulations of social reality, a rationalization for his paradoxes.

Comedy, which was Li Yu's specialty, is generally held to be an essentially conservative mode that sets out to mock departures from the social norms and conventions. But in fact, there is another, comparatively rare kind of comedy in which the writer takes as his starting point the inversion of just such a norm or convention, all the while claiming that his inversion represents the reality. Shaw and Brecht were exponents of this comedy in Europe, as was Li Yu in China.[30] It remains a question as to how far, unlike Shaw and Brecht, Li Yu used inversion merely as a comic device. Obviously his concerns were not ideological; nonetheless, the degree to which he chose his heroes and heroines from among the poor, the young, and the subordinate must be given its due, as must his championing of their interests.

Li's technique for making things new in literature, therefore, is that of inversion. The majority of the plots in his fiction involve reversals of accepted situations, resulting in stories and plays about homosexual marriages, bisexual lovers, daring and confident maids and peasant women, upright officials who are more harmful to society than their lax or corrupt brethren, and so forth. A special case is the inversion of a literary stereotype. Often the inversion will overturn some ethical judgment; one story argues that there are no absolute criteria, and that the circumstances of an action must always affect our judgment of it.[31] Or the inversion may be of some formal convention; one play uses the clown (chou) role as the male lead, while The Carnal Prayer Mat begins with a key figure whom we do not meet again until the final chapter. The ingenious use of objects—such as the telescope, introduced into China not long before Li Yu's time—constitutes yet another kind of novelty.[32]

Ribaldry, in which topics and ideas normally suppressed in social intercourse are presented for comic purpose, is another Li Yu specialty. *Carnal Prayer Mat* is an attempt to outdo the erotic novel in comic terms, but Li's stories and plays are also full of ribald, shocking references to things rarely treated in literature: diarrhea, menstruation, castration, a "stone maiden" (girl without a vagina), and so forth. Although Li Yu objected to the audience's demands for exciting action, his plays also contain notable *coups de théâtre*. Of course, these are only the most obvious aspects of his novelty, which can be found at all levels of his work.

Ingenuity (*qiao*) is another type of novelty that Li Yu's commentators praise, coupling it with *xin* ("new") and *qi* ("unusual") in discussing his work. A surprising number of his plays and stories depend on the ingenuity of the characters, who may be taken as surrogates for the author. Almost all of these works have some enterprising hero or heroine, and brilliant schemes (*miaofa*) abound in them. Like Boccaccio's stories, Li Yu's are full of the joy of an ingenious plan beautifully executed and cunningly revealed to the reader.

Ingenuity of argument appears constantly in his essays, and also in his fiction (from the mouths of both narrator and characters) and his plays. It is marked by quick twists and deft (usually comic) images, and it is punctuated by jokes. There is a distinctly logical structure to most of his essays, which are the product of an analytical mind with a passion for organization. His essay on the lyric and his chapters on drama show a degree of organic coherence and logical progression that is rare in Chinese literary discussion. Li Yu is at the opposite pole from the writer of casual notes (*biji*), who reveled in the delicious jumble of his jottings. Similarly, structural ingenuity, evinced in intricate parallels and contrasts of characterization, incident, order, and arrangement, is one of the key qualities of his fiction and drama.

Some kinds of originality are more important than others, according to Li Yu; in matters of language and form, originality may not even be desirable at all. He faces the problem in his essay on the lyric: "In my opinion, when the concept is extremely novel, it actually doesn't matter if the language is a little old. A bewitching beauty will appear all the more beautiful in tattered clothing."[33] If the concept is paramount in the lyric, its equivalent is paramount in the other genres. Li Yu broke with precedent by beginning his drama chapters with the play's construction, a subject hitherto rarely even touched upon. With regard to language, however, he is ambiguous. On the one hand, his insistence on comprehensibility—drama is a "universal instrument" and language should be "like an old friend"—indicates a functional concept of language as a means of communication.[34] On the other, his own practice—the extended similes, the parallelism, the adapted or wittily misapplied commonplaces, the array of stylistic devices— suggests the ideal of literariness. Li Yu shared the vernacular writer's stylistic dilemma between literariness and plainness. He feels compelled to argue for stylistic "exquisiteness," but he cannot bring himself to use the word, which is in disfavor, and substitutes another, *jianxin,* which literally means "piquant and novel."[35]

He often reflects on the processes of composition, and sometimes also on its pleasures. Li's celebrated passage on the joys and consolations of the dramatist's imagination, which I have quoted in Chapter 2, [36] should probably be discounted a little, however. From his plays and stories one can deduce that his true joys were conceptual, based on the paradoxes of ideas, rather than empathetic. Since he wrote no plays himself that would quite fit his own description, it seems likely that the passage was something of a set piece.[37]

A truer account of his own experience may be the passage in *Casual Expressions* in which he expounds his notion of the therapeutic value of self-indulgence:

> I have never known any other obsession than writing, an activity by which all my sorrows are allayed, my anger dispelled, and my feelings of discontent and injustice erad- icated. I consider that all illnesses stem from the emotions and therefore, if I have a medicine to control the emotions, there is no way illness can bedevil me! Hence at the onset of an illness, while moaning and groaning in bed, I come up with the idea for the beginning. If I am able to get up, I set down the details, but otherwise I keep the draft in my mind, awaiting the day that I begin to throw off my illness, which is the day the new work gets finished. Who caused me to write all the works I have published throughout my

career? Most of them came to me from the hand of the imp who controls our fortunes.[38]

But writing a play can also be worse than torture, because the prosodic rules for the arias are more restrictive than those of any other genre. How can the dramatist be expected to keep all the restrictions in mind and also to attend to the words and emotions? "The writing instruments are not your own, but seem to have been borrowed from other people. Your eyes, ears, thoughts cannot be effective; everywhere there is someone tugging at your elbow."[39] About such matters as prosody, Li did not try to be original. He learned the rules thoroughly in the hope that, once learned, they would become second nature and no longer impede his writing.[40]

He believed that only a fierce concentration would allow the writer to come up with ingenious or felicitous ideas and language.[41] One writes and invents better under pressure, just as students outdo themselves in examinations. Li Yu had to have his brush and paper within reach, for by the time the boy brought them the thought might have vanished. Characteristically, he then brings the argument down to earth with a comical account of one of his inventions:

> When the literary man is making rapid progress, the cutting edge of his thought will snap off in an instant if it is distracted. However, one can do without sleep and food, but not without relieving oneself. Does not the saying "Better a private crisis than a public one" apply here? I have often come up with a line and been about to write it down when I was prevented by the need to relieve myself. Then, after I had been out to urinate, the line was gone beyond recall. I had this experience time and again, and so I set about this invention with the greatest urgency. One must make a hole by the side of the study and fit into it a bamboo pipe, which will allow one to relieve oneself indoors. The urine is conveyed outside, and there is an absence of smell as complete as if one hadn't urinated at all. One need not set foot outside, no matter what the weather is like.[42]

As was shown earlier in his account of how he composed on his sickbed, Li claimed not to be the sort of intuitive writer for whom the act of writing was itself the first step, a process he called "composing as one goes along."⁴³ Instead, in both practice and theory, he held to a construction model of the artistic process, drawing a classically sharp distinction between the initial conception and the work of art. The images he chose for the writer were those of the Creator, the tailor, and the builder, each of whom, in Li Yu's account, conceives of a plan and then executes it. He insists that the writer work out a detailed design before starting to write: "Only if you keep your hands in your sleeves at the beginning will you be able to write quickly later on."⁴⁴

He should not be taken too literally, of course. Minor discoveries and inventions abounded in the course of his writing, as shown in his claim that song and dialogue interact with each other: "Provided you are filled with the joy of writing, dialogue and song will quite naturally generate each other. I have often thought of a good line of dialogue that has summoned up boundless inspiration for a song. And there have been other times when a fine song I have written has created endless material for dialogue. Thus both forms stimulate each other."⁴⁵

Li Yu's originality springs, in both practice and theory, not from the activity of the personal nature alone, nor from its mere interaction with the outside world, but from his mind's creative manipulation of that world. His proper field is one in which he can make, manipulate, and invent; hence the emphasis on designs and contrivances in his work. He was a maker rather than a connoisseur, and without room for creativity, his imagination becomes whimsical. In *Casual Expressions*, with no new ideas to offer on the subject of flowers, he resorts to a conventional ranking in which he compares flowers to beautiful women.⁴⁶ His appreciation is rarely passive; even his long section on feminine beauty is devoted to novel, practical advice on women's complexions, hair, makeup, clothes, and shoes, as well as their deportment, accomplishments, and education.⁴⁷ If his experience in bringing up his two young concubines lies behind this section, perhaps they too can be considered his creations. He seems to have fashioned them, much as he fashioned his houses, gardens, and compositions.

There is a connection between creativity, which Li Yu believed to be a human power widely held but rarely utilized,⁴⁸ and his concept of the Creator (*zaowu*), to which he refers constantly, more often, surely, than any other Chinese writer. *Zaowu* is an ancient term denoting, not a god, let alone an anthropomorphic figure, but the force or process of creation.[49] In Li Yu's usage, however, the term is analogous to tailors and carpenters, and anthropomorphism can hardly be ruled out. Nor does he use the word *zaowu* exclusively; Pan Gu, the sage kings, and Heaven (*tian*, in its various compounds) are occasional alternatives. The function of the demiurge or *deus artifex* for Li Yu lay in justifying teleological arguments and also in providing a special line of comedy: Life as the Creator's Mistake. Thus Li Yu blames the Creator for giving us mouths and stomachs, the cause of our insatiable desires: "After calculating the matter from every angle, I must place the blame squarely on the Creator. I am well aware that he has ever since regretted his error, but because an institution is hard to change once it has been established, he has had to go on and on compounding his mistake. This just goes to show how careful we must be in initiating new patterns and how dangerous it is to be hasty in setting up new institutions."[50]

The Creator is more than a *deus artifex,* he is also a disposing god. Here we notice a sharp difference between the essays and the fiction and drama. The Creator is referred to as a disposing god in all three genres, but, unlike Yama and other Buddhist and Taoist deities, he never appears as a character in fiction and drama. The other deities were evidently part of a myth that was accepted in those genres but that was inappropriate in the essay. As a disposer, the Creator is stingy with talent, rations happiness, arranges coincidences as well as marital mismatches, and causes brilliant people to die young. In short, he is a figment suited to Li Yu's comic cast of thought rather than a figure to whom religious awe is due. He may be anthropomorphic in conception, but the conception is an intellectual one, a rational support for Li Yu's generally comic interpretation of the world as well as for his own creative approach to life.

The analogy between the Creator's mind and the author's or inventor's is frequently used. The commentaries to *Carnal Prayer Mat* and other works liken Li Yu's mind to the Creator's and praise his writing as like the Creator's work, using Li Yu's favorite attributes, remarkable (*qi*) and ingenious (*qiao*).[51] But it is creativity of a particular kind that the analogy leads to—the creativity of the artist as the maker or artificer who has a plan or concept to carry out. Every part of his work has its rational function, just as every product of the Creator's mind and hand has its function. This was Li Yu's own intellectual assumption, even if his work as a writer occasionally belies it.

Useful as the Creator is as a model, he is not a source of inspiration. Here Li Yu refers more conventionally to "ghosts and spirits," unseen beings who are responsible for the supreme literary effects that lie beyond the author's intention:

> "Where the mind goes, the brush goes too"—this case refers to something within the writer's powers. But as for "where the brush goes, the mind goes too"—that is something beyond one's complete control. Moreover, there are times when the mind is reluctant to go somewhere but the brush insists, as if there were ghostly beings in charge. Can this kind of writing still be called intentional? Literature does indeed commune with the spirits; that is no falsehood. The most remarkable literature of all time was created not by men but by ghosts and spirits. Men were just the mediums that the ghosts and spirits possessed.[52]

Here Li Yu is speaking with reverence of a masterpiece, *The West Chamber*. But he also refers to supernatural inspiration for his own work, for example in inventing a new kind of lock: "In this I relied on divine art pure and simple, not on human ingenuity. It was as if ghostly beings were waiting inside, begging my help in opening up a new prospect."[53] He claims that the playwright who succeeds in putting himself in a character's place will receive a "blossoming brush" from the spirits.[54] The intuitive artists who design rock gardens must be divinely inspired, for they cannot articulate the reasons for the things they do. This is an art of which Li Yu stands in awe; it cannot be accomplished by mere human effort, and should not be left, as it often was, to literary men.[55]

I have suggested that Li Yu's stress on the playwright's putting himself in his character's place may reflect the drastic change he himself had to make as a dramatist from his usual self-personification. Here is one of his exhortations: "Language is an expression of the mind, and if you want to speak in the place of someone else, you must first think in his place. What else does 'putting yourself in a character's place' mean but dream and spirit journeys? For an upright character, of course, one must put oneself in his place and think upright thoughts; but in the case of an evil character, one must abandon morality for expediency and for the time being think evil thoughts."[56] If one employs the dichotomy between *jing* (the outer scene) and *qing* (the inner world of sense, perception, thought, and emotion), Li Yu is, as one might expect, concerned mainly with the latter. There is no such thing as full description, he realizes; it would be impossible to give a complete list of the attributes of anything. One must start with a character's *qing* and ponder his motives and emotions; "if you give your undivided attention to that, a brilliant insight will surface of its own accord."[57]

But the dramatist is doing far more than just divining his characters' thoughts and emotions. In one passage there is a description of the multidimensional consciousness of Li Yu the dramatist at work: "While Liweng's hand holds the brush, his mouth is on stage. His person is fully present in the place of the actors, but his spirit is circling about looking into the plot and trying out sounds and tones. If they are good, he writes them down directly; if not, he lays aside his brush. This is the reason his plays are visually as well as aurally felicitous."[58]

Like all other writers, Li Yu suffered at times from writer's block. Unlike other writers, however, he tells us about it:

> When you begin to write, your brush flies, your style is powerful, you have a wonderful feeling of mastery, you have a surge of confidence, you are an irresistible force, and you have not the remotest concern about being unable to finish.
>
> If at this point you suddenly find your work slowing, if you have to strain to write haltingly, if your wits are beclouded and remain so all day, it is best to stop. But how many writers are there who have a sharp edge at the time they begin? Does this advice of mine not entail stifling the younger generation and preventing plays from getting written? No, say I. There are ways of restoring and reactivating your inspiration.
>
> To avoid frustration, put your brush down when the writing gets difficult. Go and seek pleasant surroundings, to restore your vitality. Wait until you feel a little more relaxed before picking up your brush again. If you feel the urge to write, go ahead. If not, put the brush down again.

No one has ever failed, after several such attempts, to meet up with divine inspiration.[59]

Li Yu did not always follow his own prescriptions, and he is candid enough to say so. He also has some advice on revision: "Writing that comes from one's own hand is always lovely. When a poem is just finished, every word in it seems brilliant. But just let some time pass before picking it up again, and one will find it to be a mixture of both good and bad. Not only can others distinguish the good from the bad, by this time I myself know what to delete." One should edit every day what one has written the day before, and do a major revision every month. Then follows his confession:

> I can offer this advice, but I cannot practice it, a fault for which others share the blame with me. I spend the whole year on "hunger migrations" and rarely seclude myself to write. When I finish something, most often it is roughly written—a rush job. It is not that I don't want to edit or revise the manuscript, just that I haven't the time. When I finish a play, no sooner have I added the last detail than the publisher snatches it from me. The first half is in press before the second is even complete. And that's not all—the nimbler actors have already engraved it in their hearts and on their tongues; it never gets revised, and so suffers forever from an incurable disease. It is not that I don't strive for verbal economy, but the fact is that Heaven thwarts me at every turn. How shall I put it?[60]

Four. The Primacy of Pleasure

Next to novelty in its various forms, the most important value in Li Yu's work is pleasure—aesthetic pleasure and plain instinctual pleasure. In his essay "Enjoying Oneself," he laments the fact that the Creator rarely lets people live out their hundred years, and that even if he does, the time left free of sorrow and hardship is still terribly short:

> As a result, it is only a nominal hundred years, for in truth we have hardly a year or two of real time left in which to enjoy the blessings human beings should enjoy. Moreover, in the course of the hundred years, we hear of death every day. We hear that those younger than we are have died, as well as those older, and when we check with those of our own age, those whom we call brother, we find some of them are dead too. Alas! What is death that although the Creator knows it to be evil he does not suppress it, but lets not a day pass without our being frightened by either the sight or the report of it? From this point of view, he is the most inhumane being who has ever existed. However, there just may be an explanation for his actions which would show his inhumanity to be the ultimate humanity, after all: our knowledge that we cannot escape death, and our daily hearing of others' deaths, may be intended to instill fear in us, in order to make us enjoy ourselves while there is still time. We are to take warning from the dead.[1]

For Li Yu, all pleasure is derived from an innate faculty which includes the primary instinctual pleasures or drives such as hunger and sex. The indulgence of one's nature (xing) should not "offend against human feeling,"[2] that is to say, against a decent regard for the feelings

59

of others; but with this one reservation, the enjoyment of beauty and sex is mandatory. If you can afford a concubine, why not take one? Li Yu answers his question by humorously quoting the Confucian classic, *The Doctrine of the Mean:* "In a position of wealth and honor, the superior man does what is proper to that position."[3] The only possible reason for restraint would be a jealous wife, in which case bringing a young concubine into your house would indeed be offending against human feeling; it might be tantamount to murder.

Good health results from trusting your nature. When ill, you should ignore your doctor and eat whatever it is you crave. One of Li Yu's recollections concerns the epidemic of 1630, which struck down everyone in his family, himself worst of all. It was summer, the time for wild strawberries to be brought to market and hawked along the streets and lanes. Although wild strawberries were a passion of his, Li's wife concealed the news from him, because the doctor, whom she had consulted secretly, held that they would be dangerous to one in his condition.

> But as it happens the house we lived in was quite close to the street, and the cries of the flower and fruit hawkers would drift in to us from time to time. Suddenly I heard some loud, rapid cries going by our door, and I knew it was the man with the strawberries. I promptly interrogated the members of my family, who confessed to me what the doctor had said. "Hack witch-doctor!" I growled. "How does he know? Buy me some strawberries at once!"
>
> No sooner had the strawberry juice touched my teeth than the knot of melancholy that filled my chest came loose and was engorged by my stomach, at which point my organs and limbs were restored to harmony and I no longer knew what illness was. Observing my reaction, my family realized the doctor was wrong and let me go on eating without restriction. By this means, my illness was cured. It can be affirmed in the light of my experience that there is no illness one cannot cure by oneself and no substance that cannot serve as a medicine.[4]

Tonics may include the presence of a loved one, the demise of an enemy (if necessary, the invalid may be deceived on this point), or the gift of a new play or novel. For Li Yu the act of composition itself, his greatest passion, worked as therapy. Even if indulging the invalid does not cure him, it will at least take his mind off his illness. "In general, the most effective way of controlling an illness is to be able to forget it. If it preys on your mind, that means it is controlling you, which is fatal."[5] On the other hand, he rejects the potions and exercises of the Taoist masters. He also rejects meditation techniques, on the basis of the pleasure principle: he is too lazy to submit to their discipline and too fond, anyway, of physical activity.[6]

As a hedonist, he takes the long-term view; he is the careful husbandman of pleasure. Thus sex, although the greatest of pleasures, should be moderated in summer and winter, the times when it is most tempting: "Why? Well, on winter nights you can't get warm without another person in your bed. Your only worry is that she isn't close enough. But clasping a woman in your arms—that's when desire is generated. In winter, spring, and autumn, one is encumbered by thick, bulky clothing, but in summer one dresses for simple convenience, and it is precisely when people have discarded their clothes that sexual feelings are stirred."[7] Autumn, too, proves to have its perils, with the women looking fetching in their new dresses, and spring, of course, is notoriously dangerous. One must simply leave a little leeway in one's sex life, particularly with a new bride, a situation for which Li Yu has some mental strategies to suggest. In due course, self-regulation will come to seem natural, at which stage there is no time when one cannot make love. "Otherwise, spurn this book as fit only for the flames and damn Liweng of the Lake for his meddling."[8]

In our pleasures, we should satisfy our own tastes, however vulgar they may be, and not let cultured society impose its standards upon us. Li Yu himself wrote his plays to the refined Kunqu music and loathed the popular Yiyang and Siping forms of opera. But with his intermittent tolerance of demotic taste, he remarks:

> I once met a rich and eminent person who was accustomed to the Yiyang and Siping tunes and loathed the coldness of Kun music. However, because people considered the latter refined and significant, he forced his singing-boys to learn it. Every time he listened, he would be knitting his

brows, and his guests suffered terribly on his account. These are the wrong ways of enjoying yourself.

I hold that everybody's nature has its likes and dislikes. Even if your tastes are mistaken or unsuitable, it does no harm to cultivate them. For if you cultivate your own mistakes, they are not mistakes any more.[9]

Pleasure and pain are not directly dependent on objective conditions; they derive from perceptions, and perceptions can be influenced by mental strategies. The experienced hedonist approaches a given pleasure by turning his mind to those worse off than he is, thereby increasing his pleasure quotient by anywhere from twenty to fifty percent. The trouble is that "at the height of ecstasy, his cares all forgotten, his enjoyment will naturally diminish";[10] his only recourse is to build it up again from the beginning by the same strategy. Li Yu is even more generous with mental strategies for minimizing pain or sorrow, particularly in his essay "How to be Happy Though Poor and Lowly."[11] In it, he refrains from the bleak, stoical advice we might have expected, and instead tries to show how a feeling of relative contentment can be engendered by the imagination.

On no account must one force oneself to have pleasure. To engage in sex while sad or distraught is a waste of spirit: "Why? Although bodies are joined, hearts are not. Before the semen has flowed, the woman's essence will already have been emitted. Try forcing a sad person to laugh. The pain of his laughter will be even worse than his sadness, and you will realize that pleasures are not to be indulged in times of grief. But although I can give this advice, I can't practice it in my own case. I just conduct myself more moderately than usual."[12]

He thus presents himself as a practical hedonist, and it is true that much of his writing assumes the basic significance of instinctual pleasure. His notion of enlightened self-interest as a value, which is of paramount importance in his drama and fiction, is a consequence of this assumption. Self-interest—that is, the demands of the individual nature—is the intellectual basis for what sometimes seems like a measure of egalitarianism in his thought, for he insists particularly on the capacities and interests of such subordinate classes as women, young lovers, maids, and menservants. In contrast, although he professes himself a Confucian in rejecting Buddhist and Taoist myth, he rarely stresses the self-sacrificing morality associated with the social obligations.

Pleasure begins with the most ordinary sense impressions, with the sensuousness of the commonplace, including the most basic of all activities, the physical functions of the body. It is to be found in sleeping, sitting, walking, standing, drinking, eating, talking, bathing, listening to music, watching people play chess, looking at flowers, birds, and fish, watering bamboos, and even in the unmentionable: "Even such unseemly actions as taking off your clothes and going to the privy to defecate and urinate will, if done properly, bring their own pleasure. If you will join in the spirit of the occasion, even the most potentially depressing things become pleasures."[13] As ever, he enjoys shocking his readers.

Addressing himself to a general audience, he writes only of immediate pleasures. He never mentions reading (except that a new novel or play is a good tonic to bring to an invalid),[14] nor looking at a piece of Song porcelain or a Ming painting. He argues that, whether an art is major or minor, all that matters is that one be "capable of refining it."[15] In this sense, *Casual Expressions* is devoted to showing that even the lowliest arts and activities can be endlessly refined.

The scene of immediate sensuous pleasure is almost always domestic; his prose dwells on mundane delights. I have quoted Li Yu's account of how he scented the bedroom with flowers and on waking up, smelling the flowers, asked his wife: "Who are we to have such pleasure? Perhaps I have squandered my lifetime's allotment of joy."[16] As an illustration of an equally elemental delight, here is his poem "Fresh From the Bath:"

> In old age I love my bath,
> But fearing to catch a chill,
> I keep the door shut tight,
> So all the light is blotted out
> And I cannot see my withered self.
> (No need to heave a sigh.)
> Bathing quickly is none too pleasant;
> Only a slow bath leaves one content.
> Thrice I add the orchid-scented water.

Languid I feel, as if in drunken sleep.
If you ask me what it's like,
It's like making love with a woman.
But love exhausts the body's essence,
While bathing leaves the face aglow.
Now out, I drape myself, and sit;
I feel I am growing wings,
Superb, I want to soar into the skies.
But alas, my strength is a little low.
So I seize the flaccid moment
To find a pillow and travel to Handan.
My intention is to enter on a lifelong fast.
Please don't urge me to take any food. [17]

The mundane experience is treated from the point of view of the senses, in fact just one sense, for even light is blotted out. It is characteristic of him that sensuousness is expressed as a desire to transcend the senses, and characteristic too that sexual imagery is used in describing sensuous pleasure. Here is a prose piece on the same subject in his more matter-of-fact, instructional style:

> When you strip off your clothes and feel free, first temper the water, taking care to keep it on the lukewarm side. From the stomach to the chest, from the chest to the back, let it only be lukewarm to warm, and there will seem to be no water at all, as if you hadn't even entered the bath, in fact. Wait until you are used to the temperature before adding more hot water. Then keep adding it as you bathe, stirring it together all the while so that you don't feel the heat, and you'll find yourself gradually entering a state of bliss. Only then should you try different positions in the bath, turning yourself over, rinsing yourself this way and that, and never stopping until you have given acute pleasure to your whole body. This is the way to enjoy yourself in the tub. [18]

Too sudden an immersion in hot water would not only be painful, it would risk the enervation of one's vital forces.

In his rhapsody on trance ("Cupping One's Chin in One's Hands"), he describes a sensuous experience that seems to transcend sense. The last lines are as follows:

> I am absorbed in the exquisite savoring of this moment.
> I feel the slightest movement would be toil.
> The understanding will consider it gaining something from
>   silence.
> The ignorant will see in it the boredom of vacillation. [19]

Li Yu may be in a trance in which he claims to be free of the senses, but he glories in the actual sensation of the experience. He describes what purports to be a mystical moment but feels not the mystic's joy, only freedom from the bonds of culture and society, a sensuous savoring of the experience of liberation.

He is universally known as a gourmet, but if the term denotes a passion for an elaborate cuisine, it is a misnomer. Despite the fervor with which they are expressed, Li's tastes are simple. He wrote paeans of praise on the crab, for example, but insisted that it be eaten on its own, not made into soup or other dishes: "All the best things in the world are seen to best advantage on their own. The crab has freshness and plumpness, sweetness and succulence. It is a smooth white like jade, a rich yellow like gold. It has already attained a perfection of color, fragrance, and flavor that nothing else can surpass. Blending it with other flavors is as hopeless an enterprise as lighting a torch to increase the sun's heat or scooping water to increase the river's depth." Crabs should also be prepared and eaten as simply, naturally and quickly as possible:

> When crabs are served, they should be steamed in their shells until tender, then preserved in ice dishes placed on low tables so that guests can help themselves. Eat the meat of each shell or claw the moment you crack it open, to ensure that none of its strength and flavor is lost. The meat goes straight from the crab's shell to your mouth and stomach; is this not the most profound secret there is to eating? With other foods, we can have people do the work for us while we sit back at our ease, but in the case of crabs, melon-seeds, and water chestnuts, we have to do the work ourselves. [20]

He wrote a number of rhapsodies—the rhapsody was the prime genre for sensuous description—and most of them are on tastes: on the crab, but also on fruit such as Suzhou strawberries, Fujian lichees, Fuzhou oranges, Yanjing grapes and apples, and Zhending pears. The rhapsody on Fuzhou oranges speaks of "skin like fine gold, flesh like soft jade," and a poem entitled "Eating Fresh Lichees in Fujian" refers to them as "freshly peeled phoenix eggs" and "crystals flashing light."[21]

On flowers, Li Yu is as ardent as he is on tastes. The winter plum-blossom was a secret passion of his, and to gratify it he sometimes dragged his unwilling companions through the snowy landscape, as in his poem "In Search of Plum Blossom:"

> Knotted with cold the country streams,
> Frozen but alive the poet's urge.
> Hunting for lines with the wind in our faces,
> Looking for flowers with the snow underfoot.
> From the barking and crowing, a village is near;
> With plum-blossom fragrance the roads are filled.
> My only fear is that our time is now short,
> A mile or two and the sun will be down.[22]

He looked forward to the first narcissus as eagerly as to the first crabs and strawberries. One spring, on returning to Nanjing, he had no money left with which to buy narcissi, and his womenfolk felt that he could do without them for one season:

> "Do you want to deprive me of my life?" I replied. "I'd rather lose a year out of my life than miss a narcissus season. Why, it was for the sake of the narcissus that I braved all the snow to travel back here! If I'm not going to see any, I might just as well have stayed there the rest of the year and not returned to Nanjing at all."
>
> Unable to restrain me, my family let me pawn some of their hairpins and earrings and buy narcissi with the proceeds. My passion for the narcissus is no mere quirk! Its color, scent, leaf, and stem set it apart from all other flowers, but it appeals to me most of all by its winsomeness. You can find girls anywhere with complexions like a peach-blossom or waists like a willow frond, girls as sleek as the

mudan or *shaoyao* peonies or as slender as the chrysanthe-
mum or the begonia. But I have never seen a girl to match
the mild beauty of the narcissus, or one with such quiet,
unflaunted charm.[23]

He has many evocative descriptions of women, as in a vignette
in *Twelve Structures* of two girls caught in the rain: "They were about
sixteen, with a rare delicate beauty that dazzled the eye. Their soaking
wet silks clung to their bodies and showed off in all clarity the rich
fullness, the yielding bonelessness, of their figures. Even their soft flesh
and jade-fair breasts seemed half exposed."[24] *Casual Expressions* contains several such vignettes which can only represent his young actress-
concubines Qiao and Wang. Here is one on the subtle erotic pleasures
to be gained from keeping company with a concubine in male attire
(note that Miss Wang played the male lead in the plays Li Yu put on):
"Talking with her, playing chess, drinking tea, burning incense—
although this is just a postscript to her acting, in truth it contains a
rare savor of eroticism."[25] Another vignette seems to refer to the lessons
in reading and writing that he gave both girls:

> It scarcely needs to be said that a girl's learning to read and
> write brings untold benefits, but there is also something for
> the observer to enjoy when she is just beginning her studies.
> All she need do is spread her books on the desk and pinch
> the tip of her writing brush as she sits by a green-gauze
> window or a kingfisher-blue screen; already she forms a
> picture. Ban Zhao continuing the *Han History* or Xie Dao-
> yun describing a snowfall were no more beautiful than she.
> What need is there to criticize her poem before you enjoy
> her company? Ah! How many such pictures there are! And
> what a terrible pity it is that the men in these situations
> regard them as commonplace![26]

Li Yu is trying to inculcate a sensibility in his male readers that has
both a sexual and an aesthetic side to it. How can one bear, he asks,
not to let a girl win occasionally at chess? "Her slender fingers pick
up the chessman and then pause, hesitating where to put it. Quietly
observing her is enough to melt a man's soul. I doubt that there is a
creature in the world so heartless as to force her into defeat."[27]

The outstanding quality in a woman's beauty is *taidu* or *meitai*, a dynamic principle that activates her otherwise lifeless perfection. (In English, perhaps only the words "charm" and "grace" will do.) Abandoning the effable for once, Li Yu admits that the quality is beyond his powers of definition. His attempt appears to mimic a well-known passage by Yuan Hongdao on the equally ineffable quality of *qu,* zest. Li Yu's passage runs: "Charm in a woman is like the flame in the fire, the glow in the lamp, the luster of jewels and precious metals—something without form rather than with form. It is precisely because it is a thing and yet not a thing, because it is formless and yet seems to possess form, that I call it a transcendent thing. A 'transcendent thing' means something uncanny, something that cannot be explained in words." Nonetheless, it is a key factor in causing men to fall in love: "When a woman nowadays has not a single good feature and yet can obsess men to the point of risking their lives to be with her, it is by the witchery of *taidu.*"[28]

For the most part, the eroticism of the essays is suggestive only. But in describing the small, soft feet of the girls of Datong, Li Yu explains their mysterious erotic value while at the same time decrying the kind of foot-binding that hobbles women.

> The girls of Lanzhou have feet that are three inches long at most, and yet they can still fly along at such a speed that men often can't catch up with them. But once you remove their dainty stockings and fondle their feet, you find the feet soft and hard in equal proportions. As for girls whose feet are so soft they feel boneless, it is easy to meet the occasional one, but rare to find them in any number. However, most of the famous courtesans of Datong are like that. In bed with them, once you begin to fondle their tiny feet, you cannot bear to stop. You feel that of all of the pleasures of dallying with courtesans, there is none to equal this.[29]

If ribaldry, so prominent in Li Yu's fiction and drama, is the product of wit and sensuality, it may be said to unite the two sides of his mind. I have already described the sensuous faculty with which he renders his reactions to phenomena, and also his intellectual faculty, that is to say, his analytical and ordering abilities, his ideas and his wit. In contrast, the emotions in his work are seldom either deep or convincing. It is ribaldry, not emotion, that bridges the gulf between the two faculties. Of course, the fact that emotion is slighted in his writing, that his characters seem to have no emotional roots, serves only to describe his work, not to disparage it. It results from his nature as a comic writer, and a particular kind of comic writer at that. One could say much the same of Molière or Shaw.

Although Li Yu rarely distinguishes aesthetic from other pleasures, his writings often justify his aesthetic reactions and also explain to the reader how the effects can best be achieved. Much of *Casual Expressions* consists of such arguments and explanations. There are even occasions when the word *xianqing* (idle feelings), which is part of the book's title, comes to mean aesthetic contemplation.

> If you can truly equip yourself with idle feelings and the eyes of wisdom, everything you see will form part of a picture and everything you hear will be the material of poetry. For example, I am sitting beside my window while someone is walking outside. If it's a girl I see, of course the picture will be of a beautiful woman. But even if it's an old woman or a white-haired old man with walking-sticks, they too form equally indispensable subjects for paintings by the masters. If it is children I see playing, they will form a children-at-play picture. And even if it is cattle or sheep being led to pasture, or dogs barking and chickens cackling, they too are regular material for the writer.

The window he is describing is actually a fan-shaped hole in the wall that frames the world outside, converting everything seen through it into art—a framing device. Li Yu claims to have been the first to use this open or "picture" window to capture the view. He planned to use it on a pleasure boat on the West Lake, but could not afford to build the boat; he applied the idea instead to his house in Nanjing, placing the window opposite a rock in his garden. He describes his reaction on first looking through the window: "As I sat there and watched, the window became a picture instead of a window and the rock a rock in a landscape painting instead of the rock behind my room. I couldn't help bursting into laughter, at which my wife and children came in together and began laughing, too, at the same sight. This is how the Empty Picture or Picture Window came into being." With this device all of visual life, no matter how banal, becomes aestheticized. Li Yu likens the window to the box in which one collects the herbs one needs for medicine, including such lowly plants as Ox Urine and Horse Rump. The fan-shaped window is the "medicine basket of the man of taste."[30]

In a brilliant extended metaphor he likens the flowers that bloom in succession throughout the year to "a complete text of nature's work:"

> The flowering plum and the narcissus are experimental exercises. Their spirit may be bold, but their technique is still rough, and so the flowers are neither truly large nor their colors truly deep. But when the peach, the plum, the crabapple, the apricot, and other trees bloom, the literary mind bursts forth in joy; so powerful is the writer's mood that it seems irresistible. But if their flowers have not reached the limit of size and depth of color, it is because the line of thought is too diverse, too unfocused, and the style too wild and unrestrained, so that their irresistible force is the force of license and not of true mastery. The moment the *mudan* and *shaoyao* peonies bloom, both the literary mind and the style attain the "transformed state," wildness is reined in and becomes mastery, and the hoard is emptied of its splendors, so that one can fairly say that the Creator has used up all of his genius and holds nothing whatever in reserve.[31]

He is much concerned with the correct techniques for enhancing aesthetic pleasure. To the appreciation of the orchid's scent, you must bring not only the right feeling but also the right methods, one of which is to depart from the room the orchids are in and then return to it, so that their scent is enhanced.[32] On one occasion Li Yu gives careful directions for a particular visual and auditory effect: two singers must sing a wistful song to the music of flute and viol from behind a bank of flowers and willow trees.[33] To enhance aesthetic effects, he applies his notable ingenuity to the creating of illusions, of which his living mural of trees and flowers with live birds tethered to it is the outstanding example.[34]

Casual Expressions contains much sheer practical advice as well, to which I cannot possibly do justice. Tables should be made with drawers—to keep odds and ends in—but also with detachable guard-boards to prevent scorching.[35] In cupboards, shelf space is the main requirement; the writer, in particular, needs a filing system "like an apothecary's cupboard."[36] In most cases the ideal solution is both practical and aesthetic, *shiyong meiguan* as the expression has it,[37] and when the two needs clash, Li Yu usually suggests a compromise. If winding paths are more beautiful and straight paths more practical, the answer is to open up a side gate—for practical purposes, when you are in a hurry—but retain your winding path.[38]

Some of his aesthetic values have already been mentioned in other contexts. Novelty, for example, in addition to being his principal general value, is also his prime aesthetic value, to the extent, on some occasions, of leading him into excesses. In the mode of grotesque ribaldry, he is capable not only of amusing but also of shocking and even repelling his audience, and I suspect the same must have been true of some of his visual designs, which entirely ignore his alternative ideal of restrained understatement. Take, for example, his novel design for a name tablet in the shape of a banana leaf, which was to have had a green base and black veins (like the leaf) and its title in yellow or gold.[39] A similar objection might be made to the "living mural." In these cases, he seems to have been carried away by his exuberant delight in the new.

Another value is that of design and patterning. By design I mean prior design, what Li Yu in his drama chapters calls *jiegou*, "construction." It springs from his emphasis on order, system, and logic in all created things, and is related to his need of the Creator as metaphor. In this sense design, which is perceptible by the reader as structural ingenuity, is the principal quality of his plays and stories and an important quality in his essays.

Patterning means not only "fine stitching" in its narrow sense, that is to say, seamlessness or close continuity, but also the ingenious system of correspondences, including both parallels and contrasts, that run through his work and hold it together. In describing the quality of *ji*, which evidently means intricate articulation, Li Yu uses two analogies, the system of veins and arteries in the body and a silk cocoon's internal connectedness. Shifting the mataphor, he says that even when the material seems most disparate, it will prove to contain

joints hidden inside it that connect the whole.[40] This system of patterning, reaching down to the level of the image and the word, is
intended not only to produce a close texture but also to repeat and
reinforce (symbolically, perhaps) the work's themes. It is an aspect in
which the Southern drama excelled, but which in Li Yu is taken to
new heights of subtlety.

At first sight it is surprising, therefore, that Li's other principal
aesthetic values are naturalness and simplicity. His notion of the natural is based on the idea that the innate character of things must not
be transgressed or thwarted. (His pleasure principle rests, essentially,
on the same foundation.) The less elaborated an object is, the better.
Vegetables are superior to whole meat, and whole meat is superior to
mincemeat, which represents a further level of elaboration. Perfume
made from rose leaves is better than the artificial kind. His favorite
remedy for bad breath is a natural one—a single lichee which, if taken
at bedtime, will last the whole night. Song is superior to instrumental
music because it is more natural. Women should discard their jewelry
and "reveal all their natural authenticity." Flowers, as natural objects,
are preferable to manufactured ornaments. (In a pinch, imitation flowers will do.) Natural styles are to be preferred in coiffures, but if you
must wear a hairpiece, at least see that it is made from real hair.[41] (In
Li Yu's stories and plays his heroines have simple hairstyles, but his
ugly and spiteful women often have elaborate pompadour coiffures
covered with bibelots.)

It is an artistic crime to go against the nature of the material you
are using. Li Yu deplores the current vogue for patchwork clothes:
"What crime has the cloth committed that it should be subjected to
death by dismemberment?"[42] In making your rock garden, you must
not "go against the nature" of the rocks you use, just as in teaching a
girl you should take care not to "go against" the natural bent of her
talent.[43] The expression *fu . . . xing,* "to go against the nature of," is
the same one Li uses in speaking of immoral sexual behavior. Sexual
expression fulfills one's nature, but adultery "goes against" the nature
of others, and hence is evil.[44]

If artifice is necessary, it should be as natural as possible. It is
permissible to adapt something, provided you do not lose the "authentic
nature" of the thing you are adapting.[45] If a problem arises, for example,

if the holes in a rock are too perfectly round and hence look artificial, the perception is what counts.[46]

A second-order naturalness is attained by placing objects in the "right" places, for in so doing "you attain the 'transformed state' of naturalness, with the Creator in your hand."[47] Houses should not only fit the terrain, they should also, since they are designed for humans to occupy, be built to a human scale, neither too lofty nor too cramped, turning us into neither dwarfs nor giants.[48] By Li Yu's aesthetic of matching, things cannot be placed side by side unless they are either of the same nature or else similar in form.[49] He hated obvious patterning, such as the linear, square, or "plum-blossom" formations (that is, with one large object surrounded by "petals"), but he did approve of more intricate arrangements, as in the shape of the characters for "heart" and "fire."[50] Powder and rouge, being of the same nature, may go together, but powder can only be applied to pale complexions, which it resembles, not to dark complexions.[51] On the analogy of transitional passages (*guowen*) in literature, Li Yu also develops the notion of transitional colors, bridging the gap between one color and another.[52]

In arguing for a design, he often resorts to an associative logic of design and function—the principle of naturalness at a further remove. The designs on women's shoes should have some association with either shoes or feet.[53] Notepaper designs should be associated with letters or at least with writing.[54] Someone once challenged Li Yu as to why only the novel designs he had demonstrated could be used for name tablets: " 'You're wrong,' I replied. 'In what I do, I seek more than novelty. The essential thing is that designs should reflect some implicit association. People need to choose something to write on before they can use a brush. The ancients, for example, grew banana palms to use as paper and carved inscriptions on bamboo.' "[55] This uncharacteristic use of historical association justifies the banana leaf and bamboo trunk motifs of his name tablets. Against the fashionably elaborate women's hairstyles known as the Tree Peony, Lotus Flower, Spittoon, and Begging Bowl, he argues that they lack just this associative logic. The ancients referred to women's hair poetically as "black clouds" and "coiled dragons" because clouds and dragons belong in the sky. Moreover, there is a certain resemblance; hair is black, and it swirls and coils about the head, and thus has multiple associations, of color, likeness, feeling, and reason. Thus hairstyles may resemble black clouds and coiled dragons but not such unassociated things as peonies and bowls.[56]

The emphasis on simple, frugal living in *Casual Expressions* was partly a reaction to the Kangxi Emperor's *Sacred Edict,* which was issued in 1670 while Li Yu was writing his book, and partly the result of his own desire for the "natural."[57] He himself ate the plainest of plain food; indeed, he was the sensualist of plain fare.[58] Simplicity was an aesthetic value, too, in terms of tasteful understatement (*yadan*).[59] The fashion among literary men of crowding their walls with scrolls is vulgar.[60] In buildings and furniture, the frugal is to be preferred to the lavish, the understated to the flashy. He has seen valuable pieces of furniture in rich men's houses, and been dazzled by them, but for a moment only, because although the materials were superb, their design was atrocious. Quite the opposite may hold true in peasant houses; he has seen and admired the peasants' "pure use of natural means" and recommends adopting and improving their designs.[61] His strongest condemnation is to say that some practice is "a waste of natural resources," while "to make something of no value into something valuable—that shows an immortal's magic."[62] After *Casual Expressions* comes out, he claims, nothing will ever be thrown away again.[63]

Such principles scarcely apply to literature. Despite his insistence on economy and simplicity of language, Li admits that he does not always attain the former, and he shows all of the vernacular writer's ambivalence about the latter. His plays, for all their multidimensional ingenuity, are indeed of simple design; that is to say, they contain few plot leads and relatively few characters and events, because he held that the proliferation of such elements makes the "path of thought" fork and divide.[64] Nonetheless, he felt that simplicity in the sense of artlessness (*laoshi*) induces sleep, while exquisiteness is the "siren of literature."[65] Artlessness may be admirable in a person, but in literature it is anathema.

Writing of drama and the domestic arts, Li Yu upholds neither high nor low taste, as conventionally defined, but affirms his own, which seems to contain elements of both high and low. Addressing a wide audience of varying levels of taste, he had to explain and argue his opinions, not merely enunciate them, a fact that distinguishes his essays from countless works by other writers on the minor arts. Merely by writing in the vernacular genres of fiction and drama, he was placing himself in a different social context from his peers. (This is less true of drama, for some of his friends, and even patrons such as Gong Dingzi, were occasional dramatists, although the plays they wrote were very different form Li Yu's.)[66] By writing commercially, moreover, he was addressing himself to an audience that sought entertainment before all else. Thus farce and ribaldry play a larger part in his fiction and drama than in the work of any other Chinese writer.

But it would be a mistake to regard his ribaldry and farce merely as sops to the audience. Although Li Yu never claimed that good literature was limited to the comic mode, his own preoccupation with comedy was absolute, no doubt because comedy satisfied his notion of the pleasure principle. Remarks such as "broadly speaking, everything I have ever written was intended to make people laugh" and "if there is a single person in the house who doesn't laugh, I get upset"[67] are more than self-deprecation; they accord with Li's implicit belief in pleasure (which excludes, of course, the dark, ambiguous joys of tragedy) as the main purpose of literature. He was the comic specialist par excellence, and within the domain of his comedy, farce and ribaldry were the areas in which his antic imagination was the freest to disport itself, amusing and shocking his contemporaries at the same time.

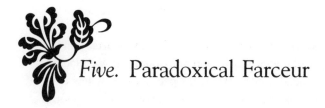

Five. Paradoxical Farceur

Li Yu's stories are named for the two pursuits in which he took the greatest pleasure and pride—writing plays and designing houses and gardens.[1] His first two collections were entitled *Silent Operas (Wusheng xi)*, while the third collection was entitled—or subtitled—*Twelve Structures (Shi'er lou)*, a *lou* being a general term that embraces towers, pavilions, bowers, villas, and the like. *Twelve Structures* is a more closely organized collection than *Silent Operas*, and it is also far more personal, but both works are distinctively Li Yu's; no other writer's fiction stands so clearly apart in conception, theme, plot, and style. Similar qualities mark his only novel, *Carnal Prayer Mat (Rou putuan)*, which I shall describe in the next chapter. So distinctive is his brand of fiction that, although the novel has never actually been proved to be by Li Yu, one has only to read it alongside his stories to feel the truth of the attribution.[2]

The indispensable feature in a Li Yu work is a novel idea that is elaborated with a craftsman's ingenuity and more than a few surprises and shocks. In many stories the ingenuity is that of the characters themselves; because of his delight in invention, he was much drawn to themes of cleverness. As we might expect, the characters he appears to favor are those who follow their own enlightened self-interest in either changing their destinies or making the best of such destinies as they cannot change. Characters often represent ideas or attitudes, but rather than dub them the mere embodiments of ideas it would be truer to say that a particular idea or attitude has been central to their conception. Partly as a result, the stories are full of discursive dialogue and monologue. And all of them, even those that contain their macabre moments, are comedies; Li Yu contrives to make ribald or grotesque comedy out of even the most macabre incident. Sexual comedy, whether romantic, erotic, or ribald, is the most common type.

The volume of narratorial comment is, as we would expect of Li Yu, far greater than in other Chinese fiction. His prologues, although written in the vernacular, often take the form of essays; in fact, they sometimes resemble in structure and mode of argument the kind of essay he wrote later in *Casual Expressions.* Sometimes, too, they contain personal anecdotes, like the essays. The narrator's comment is concerned, in a humorous way, with the various moral and philosophical issues the story raises, and also with its development and progress, stimulating and teasing the reader as he goes along. All of Li Yu's fiction must be perceived through a window of anticipatory and resumptive comment.

The wealth of interpretation is not matched by an equal amount of specific narrative and descriptive detail. The reader is supplied with such information as he needs, but no more; there is none of the authenticating detail common to fiction that gives a strong sense of time, place, and physical presence.

Li Yu's style is also distinctive. Although there are differences between the collections—the *Structures* seems to me, perhaps because it contains more stories about highly educated people, to be somewhat more formal, less exuberant—all of his stories place a premium on verbal fluency and wit. The wit is often that of comic displacement, by which, for example, an image from some incongruous field like that of the bureaucracy or the civil service examinations is applied to a domestic situation—a time-honored gambit at which Li Yu excels. He also misapplies quotations and commonplaces for comic effect, as in his essays. A practiced rhetoric lies behind the style, behind its balance and euphony as well as its use of image, quotation, and commonplace. His expository style tends to build up into complex parallel formations; his narrative prose is witty and economical; and his dialogue has the fluency one expects of a master playwright. There is a remarkable uniformity among the styles, which merge easily into one another; unlike many other writers, Li Yu avoids the use of sharply differing styles to represent the various narrative functions.

Although the basic requirement of a story for him, as for other vernacular authors, is that it relate a morally satisfying narrative, his narrator is sometimes heard to protest *sotto voce* about the moral de-mands of his stories, presenting us with a standard moral interpretation but also mocking it at the same time. The possibility of self-mockery must always be kept in mind in reading Li Yu.

Rather than talk further about the general qualities that mark Li Yu's work, I shall describe some of his finest stories, beginning with his versions (usually inversions) of the romantic comedy, but not nec-essarily proceeding in the order in which the stories were written.

"The Summer Pavilion" ("Xiayilou") in *Structures* shows some of Li Yu's distinctive gifts—novelty of conception, ingenious construc-tion, sly comedy, sensuous description.[3] It is based on a simple, ar-resting idea: the use of a telescope, introduced to China not many decades before, as the means by which a young gallant spies out a beautiful girl to seek as a wife. Without the telescope, he would have had to take a matchmaker's word as to a girl's looks; with it, from the commanding height of a monastery in Li Yu's native Jinhua, he can see inside the compounds of the local families and make his own choice. The telescope, before the hero put it to such creative use, had been regarded in China as an exotic curio. "The Summer Pavilion" is thus a story of cleverness, of the hero's winning of an ideal beauty; it modifies the romantic comedy by placing the emphasis, in Li Yu fashion, on the creative imagination and enterprise of the hero.

But there is much more to it than that; not for nothing does Li Yu put "construction" first among the subjects dealt with in his drama treatise.[4] The raw idea of the telescope's use is ingeniously refined into a narrative that offers us one surprising development after another. To impress the girl, Xianxian, with his suit, the hero, Qu, convinces her through a matchmaker that he is a supernatural being who knows all her secrets. (With his hyperbolically powerful telescope, he can not only tell what she is doing in the compound, he can even read the poem she is writing.) Xianxian's father, one of those strict Confucian moralists mocked by Li Yu, insists that she draw lots among her three qualified suitors. When she draws someone other than Qu, on whom she has now set her heart, she is bold and smart enough to invent an excuse on the spur of the moment; she claims that her dead mother has told her in a dream that Qu is her predestined husband. Her father is naturally suspicious—why did his late wife not choose to appear in *his* dream?—and insists on waiting to see if the wife will return. Xianxian neatly explains her mother's omission as due to her reluctance to disturb him as he lay beside his concubine. As proof of her veracity, Xianxian offers the exact words of a prayer that her father had written out and burned. Needless to say, it is Qu's powerful telescope that has enabled him to read the prayer and tell Xianxian of its contents. Convinced by this proof, her father consents to the marriage.

But the mystery is not yet over. Believing that her bridegroom is an immortal, and hence accustomed only to ethereal pleasures, Xianxian is careful to restrain her passions on the wedding night. She soon finds that he is happily and reassuringly human. But even now, with the mystery explained, both he and she are inclined to venerate the telescope. Qu had appealed to it for help before this last crisis, and Xianxian still feels that "a certain Heavenly intent" has been manifested in her marriage.[5] Later they turn the summer pavilion, in which Xianxian had been resting the day Qu first spied on her, into a family shrine and install the telescope there, for use as an oracle. But although it never fails to give helpful advice, Li Yu insists on a naturalistic explanation: "It is clear that wherever the spirit is concentrated, images of wood and clay can work miracles. It has always been true that worship of the Taoist and Buddhist deities amounts to worshiping one's own mind. It is not as if there really are such things as immortals and bodhisattvas."[6]

The story is not, of course, presented in the order in which I have summarized it. Qu does not even appear in the first of its three chapters. Instead, the story focuses on Xianxian in her compound, slumbering in the pavilion while the little girls of whom she has charge sneak away and frolic among the lotus-flowers in the pond. This is a tableau which, sensuously described, is referred to again and again in the course of the story. The first chapter ends as the gallant gives Xianxian, through the matchmaker, a message indicating that he knows all her secrets—that he has "the eyes of a god," in the matchmaker's words.[7]

Closing with this dubious claim, the narrator addresses his readers: "Gentle readers, having read this far, please put aside all other thoughts and consider the question of how Qu was able to learn everything that went on inside the Zhan household. Was he man or ghost? Was it dream or reality? Let each one of you try to guess, and then, when you find you cannot come up with the explanation, turn to the next chapter for the answer."[8] The answer is as follows: "I daresay my gentle readers have been unable to guess how Qu came to know these things, so let me explain. This incident was the work neither of man nor ghost, and the explanation given you was neither a complete fabrication nor the complete truth. It was all due to a certain device that served Qu as an eye, allowing a flesh-and-blood human being to impersonate a disembodied immortal without any fear that people would doubt his word."[9] The narrator goes on to tell us that Qu had found a telescope in a curio shop and seen its potential.

In Chapter 2 the reader sees everything through Qu's eyes, or rather, through his telescope. On seeing Xianxian writing a love poem and then suddenly crumpling it up, he is startled; he wonders irrationally if she can be aware of his spying. But no, she has hidden the poem out of fear of her father whom Qu now sees approaching. At the end of the chapter the narrator continues in his playful vein: the "novelist" wants to slow the pace of narration,[10] so as to leave the story's climax to the final chapter, a chapter which, with its ingenuities and surprises, I have already described.

I have omitted mention of the prologue, a vital part of any Li Yu story. "The Summer Pavilion," unlike most of Li Yu's stories, does not purport to be illustrating a theme. Instead, it sets out to introduce the skinny-dipping episode with which the story proper opens. Six of Li Yu's own poems are offered (out of an original group of ten) on the pastoral theme of girls picking lotus, after which the narrator launches into an elaborate conceit, enumerating those aspects of the lotus that symbolize girls as lovers and wives. He (now he is Li Yu again) then slips into a personal anecdote: "I once made a humorous remark that people told me was worth preserving, and I would like to repeat it to you, gentle readers, to see if you agree. Frivolous and lewd behavior must have something serious about it if it is to be perpetuated."[11] He proceeds to justify the eroticism of the prologue and the main story by reference to the procreative function of sex. After the digression, he continues: "In speaking of the lotus flowers, I happened to stray on to this matter. Please forgive me for being so garrulous."[12]

The brief transition between prologue and story proper gives the obvious justification for the former: as a lead-in (*yintou*) to the lotus-picking tableau with which the latter begins. In addition, the erotic suggestiveness of the prologue foreshadows the suberotic scene of the little girls romping in the water, giggling at the sight of each others' bodies, like "the lords of the seven states comparing their treasures with one another."[13] The symbol (the lotus) and the symbolized (the girls) merge happily together. Eroticism, although never explicit, runs through the story. Xianxian is described as sexually mature and hence careful to banish provocative thoughts. But once her passions have been stirred by Qu's proposal of marriage, they can no longer be held in check and she languishes in illness. Qu, having once relished, at the end of his telescope, the sight of the little girls' bodies and also of their wrathful mistress as she wakens and punishes the ringleaders, is determined to deflower not merely the "queen of the blossoms,"[14] but also the other blossoms as well. After the marriage the girls, whose secrets are known to him, and who call him Master Thievish Eyes, yield up their maidenheads in due course. There is a final, flippant warning about the dangerous consequences of nudity—Li Yu at his most patently insincere.

"The Cloudscraper" ("Fuyunlou") is another romantic comedy from *Structures,* but it is an even stranger specimen than "The Summer Pavilion."[15] In the conventional romantic comedy, engagements are sacrosanct, but here we have a hero encountering and falling in love with his former fiancée. (His parents had broken off the engagement in favor of a more profitable match.) His ugly and odious wife having conveniently died, the hero now seeks the heroine again in marriage and finds himself indignantly rebuffed. There his suit might have ended, had he not been inspired to ask for the hand of the heroine's maid instead. Nenghong, the maid, who is as beautiful as her mistress and infinitely more enterprising, is the story's dominant figure. By bribing a fortune-teller to set specifications that she knows only the hero can meet, she brings off the seemingly impossible marriage to her mistress. In addition, having privately assured her own future in a compact with the hero, she arranges, by "fixing" some dream interpretations, to have her mistress accept her as a co-equal wife.

This story is thus an aberrant romantic comedy in which the hero ends up with two wives—a not uncommon situation in Li Yu's fiction which has little place for concubines—after the most inauspicious of beginnings. But it is also a cleverness story, which consists of the confident machinations of a mere maid, who serves, it will be noted, her own enlightened self-interest.

There is a long tradition of bold and resourceful maids in Chinese fiction and drama, a tradition out of which Nenghong is an extraordinary development. Here she is in Chapter 3, after spying—from the building called the Cloudscraper—the hero kneeling in supplication to an intermediary and then learning that it is *her* hand he is seeking. She addresses the intermediary:

"All my suspicions have been dispelled by what you've just said. He must be a real romantic, no question about that. Well-known scholars have no trouble finding wives. Why, young ladies are ready for the taking, let alone mere maids! And he actually went down on his knees! Go and tell him that if he'd just been trying to get the mistress, he wouldn't even have been able to get *me* into his house, but since he wants to marry me, he needn't give up all hope of getting the mistress as well. We stand side by side, she and I; there's never any difference between us. His family and ours are sworn enemies, and with an outsider as matchmaker, he'd never get anywhere. Fortunately, the whole family recognizes that I'm quite shrewd. They don't come and meekly ask me for my advice, mind you, but they always sound me out, usually without realizing that they're doing so. If I say go ahead, they go ahead. If I say better not, even if it is something they'd already decided on, they end up unable to do it. In the case of this suit of his, the unfortunate thing is that I was so furious before on the mistress's account that I said some very nasty things about him. The whole family took their cue from me and now they all hate him with a vengeance. That is why his matchmaker didn't get so much as a hearing. If he had told me before proposing to her, I'd have been a willing collaborator from inside the household, and I fully expect the marriage would have taken place by this time. But it would be rather embarrassing for me to change my tune now and start supporting the match, and it would be even harder to jettison the mistress and argue the case for myself. Not even an immortal could pull *that* off! I'll just have to play it by ear and try to come up with something. I'll need to give the appearance of planning things for the mistress's sake, but if the public interest can be served, perhaps the private interest can be served also. Two birds with one stone!"

In Chapter 5 Nenghong arranges a meeting with Pei, the hero, allegedly so that she can check his looks and inform her mistress of them, but actually so that she can reassure herself that he will agree to her demands:

"First: From the moment I join your household, I am no longer to be called Nenghong; I must be referred to by everyone as Second Lady. For the first offense, you will slap yourself across the mouth. If the offender is someone on the staff, the blame will rest with the head of the household, and you will be called to account in the same manner.

"Secondly: I have observed that you are a man of licentious conduct and frivolous mind, and I have no doubt that you're an old hand at love affairs. But from the moment I join your household, you must put a stop to all adultery and whoring. If I find a shred of evidence, you'll never hear the end of it, I assure you! Having knelt down for my sake, you are never to kneel down for anyone else. Should you become an official, you will be permitted to kowtow at Court and to pay your respects to your superiors, but for every unauthorized kneeling you will strike yourself on your feet. The mistress is the sole exception to this rule.

"Thirdly: You must reconcile yourself for the rest of your life to marriage with just the two of us. After me, there will be no further acquisitions. Even if you should succeed in the higher examinations and become Minister or Premier, you will not need a third wife. Should you develop any evil hankerings and so much as mention the word 'concubine,' you will have to bang your head on the ground until it bleeds. If by some chance we are unable to bear sons, endangering the ancestral shrine, you will have to wait until the age of forty before receiving a special dispensation, and even then you will be permitted to take only a personal maid, not a concubine."[16]

This meeting, we have been told,

> was strictly in her own interests. The subject of her becoming his second wife had been raised before, but although Pei had given an oral assurance, he had never put it in writing. How could she be sure that, after the event, he might not be carried away by his own success? A brand new head of household is hardly going to get down on his knees and propose marriage to his wife's maid! What if, by some chance, he were to deny the promise that she had received only at second hand and were to go on treating her as a maid? That is why she had arranged this turn of events, knowing full well that her mistress could not leave to attend the viewing herself but would ask her to go in her stead. She devised this plan to get out of the house and obtain a commitment signed in her presence, so as to avoid any future regrets. In all this, she showed just how secretive she could be. Although it was her own private interests that were at stake, she acted as if with openness and impartiality. Mr. and Mrs. Wei had to explain to her how necessary it was for her to go before she would even ask Mother Yu to arrange a meeting with Pei.[17]

At this point the narrator begins his chapter-closing remarks, invoking the title of Li Yu's earlier collection: "This meeting is bound to result in a fine comedy. Not only does she settle her own marriage, she may even, who knows, win first place ahead of Miss Wei. Keep your honorable eyes peeled as you watch this scene of the 'silent opera.' "[18] The term "silent opera" is aptly used of this story, which establishes a striking character largely by means of dialogue.

The maid's nature is shown again on the mistress's wedding day, when she accompanies the bride to Pei's household. Pei has provided two wedding chambers, and intends to spend the hours before midnight with the mistress and then to find some pretext to leave her bed and stay the rest of the night with Nenghong. But the mistress "clung to outmoded wedding decorum and was not prepared to be fashionably informal; she threw herself into the role of the new bride. No matter how Pei besought her and tugged at her, she refused to go in to bed."[19] Pei, finding himself in the presence of a beautiful bride after a marriage to a wife he had detested, can restrain himself no longer. Making an excuse to leave her bedchamber, he "brought forward to the evening hours what he had planned for after midnight."[20]

Nenghong, at least, is unconventional enough to profit from the occasion. Greeting him warmly, she urges him to go back to the mistress, quoting a couplet from the *Poetry Classic* to reinforce her point.

> But then she began to worry that he really would go back, and so she promptly tried to save the situation by quoting from the *Four Books:* "Having persuaded him to come, give him comfort." In his overwrought state, Pei was afraid to delay a moment longer. Without a word he pulled her towards the bed—a case of being "in too great a hurry to spell out the message." Entrusting herself to experienced hands, Nenghong made no resistance as he undid her sash and took off her gown. Beneath the marriage quilt, she tasted bliss for the first time. To her way of thinking, she had lost none of her respect for her mistress; in fact, she continued to think of her mistress as her primary respon-sibility, and saw herself as an advance party preparing the way for a superior. But it is not clear that she sacrificed very much by this respect of hers. All those who ignore real disadvantages in their concern for a hollow reputation should take warning from Miss Wei's example.[21]

Pei pretends to have nightmares, and Nenghong arranges some fake interpretations to the effect that he must take a second wife if the mistress's life is to be spared. (Note how adept Li Yu's heroes and heroines are at exploiting superstitious beliefs for their own ends.) The mistress feels compelled to seek a second wife, and who is as appropriate as Nenghong? After much demurring, Nenghong agrees, subject to her conditions: "On the occasion of her first wedding, Nenghong had not dissembled at all. But tonight she became the new bride all over again, fighting off his advances and refusing to undress. Why? Not until the first watch had passed would she give the real reason: she wanted him, as on the first occasion, to go first to the mistress's chamber to sleep. Only after she had insisted several times did he go. Ostensibly she was expressing her own desires; actually she was repaying a debt. This was typical of the things she did."[22]

The prologue of this six-chapter story—Li Yu's longest—is an essay on the trouble maids can cause by involving their mistresses in romantic intrigue. Embedded within it is a tongue-in-cheek etymology of the word for maid (*meixiang*), as well as a sordid anecdote of the disaster caused by one such maid. The transitional passage promises a story that will tell of a very different kind of maid, one who brings a beautiful girl and a brilliant young man together in marriage. So different is she that readers are bound to take the story as laudatory. We are firmly assured that the writer knows the classics and realizes that a maid who plays the go-between in her mistress's marriage is no better than a traitor who betrays his country. "Therefore this story is admonitory; it is not intended for emulation."[23] The brief epilogue also claims that Nenghong's virtuous married life is what redeems her unscrupulous scheming.

The narration is managed with almost as much ingenuity as in "The Summer Pavilion," and with just as much brio. If Nenghong is astonished that Pei's proposal is meant for her (in Chapter 3), Pei is just as surprised at her purpose and her tone at their meeting (in Chapter 5). The simulated nightmares and fake interpretations of Chapter 6 have to be explained to the reader *ex post facto*. The narrator ends Chapter 3 with a flourish: "Let us wait until the marital fortunes are told to see how Iron-mouth Zhang begins his spiel and what kind of transition he has to make to bring the subject around to Qilang [Pei]. For although that incident follows directly on this, I must separate one from the other; the story will be all the more interesting for it. As in posing a riddle, if you carelessly give away the answer without making people guess, it will be dull indeed."[24]

I shall pass over "The Pavilion of Combined Reflections" ("Heyinglou"),[25] a romantic comedy of geometrical design, pausing only to note its self-conscious reflexiveness and the disingenuousness of its prologue. The story's resemblance to a play is insisted on throughout, by narrator and characters alike. In Chapter 3 one heroine goes to see the other, in order to persuade her to agree to a joint wedding: "This is not just a social visit. I've come with good news. The 'Combined Reflections' poems have been made into a play which is about to reach its joyous finale. The only difference is that there is an additional

86

heroine. You mustn't be too touchy about it."[26] The repeated references merely emphasize the story's staginess. Li Yu may not be writing parody, but he is certainly mocking a convention.

The prologue is a tightly argued essay in a similar vein, which begins by asserting the impossibility of denying young love:

> If you wait until their desire is stirred, family discipline and fear of the law will prove equally futile. Even if the Jade Emperor were to issue an order for their execution and Yama a warrant for their arrest, even if the hills, streams, trees, and grasses were to turn into weapons and the sun, moon, stars, and planets into missiles, the pair would still risk their lives in order to fulfill their hearts' desire. Even if they were to live for thousands of years and then ascend into Heaven, they would be lonely and bereft as immortals for just so long as their passion went unfulfilled. On the other hand, once their hearts' desires are met, they will still be romantic shades even if after death they have to spend aeons without reincarnation. Are there any regulations that will deter people once they have reached such a state of contempt for life? This is why measures to prevent adultery and sup-press desire have to be taken *before* the affair gets started. And the only successful measures to take before it gets started are to segregate the women's quarters, ban all du-bious activities, and never let boys and girls get close to one another.[27]

After quoting a favorite maxim of the puritans, and throwing in a couple of anecdotes, the narrator makes his transition to the main story: "The story I shall relate today is designed to teach the good family man that in order to nip this evil in the bud he must prevent the slightest semblance of it from appearing, not to mention the evil itself. My story is certainly not designed to expound the nature of romantic passion or to explore a way for lovers that the brilliant and beautiful can follow."[28] The playful tone is reinforced by verbal echoes. "Semblance" is actually the same word as the "reflections" of the story's title and main motif, and "way" is the surname of Mr. Lu, who finds a tripartite solution (one husband, two wives) for the lovers. Li Yu's prologue mocks conventional morality while pretending to uphold it, just as the story itself mocks the efforts of the puritanical father to preserve his daughter's chastity.

The finest romantic comedy in *Silent Operas* is "Contemptuous of Riches and Rank, an Actress Preserves Her Honor,"[29] which Li Yu turned into the play *Sole Mates (Bimuyu)*. Like the other *Operas* stories, it is not divided into chapters, and yet, although no longer than the *Structures* stories I have been considering, it seems to contain more incident and cover more fictional ground than they do.

This story has a novel subject—a student who joins an acting troupe in the hope of seducing a young actress to whom he has taken a fancy. Once inside the troupe, he is foiled by the strict prohibition against sexual relations among actors and actresses, and is reduced to declaring his love to her on stage. He and she compensate for their frustration by throwing themselves into the great romantic roles, which they use as vehicles for their own feelings. The extraordinary passion of their performances bring them a popular success.

Arriving ahead of the others at a temple where they are to perform in celebration of the god's birthday, they finally get a chance to make love and exchange their vows. However, it is also during these performances that a local rich man, while enjoying an intimate moment with the girl's mother, a famous actress of unfastidious morals, asks for her daughter as his twelfth concubine. The mother still hopes to induce her daughter to combine the career of actress with the more lucrative one of courtesan, and so she persuades the rich man to wait a year for his answer, until the next year's celebration of the god's birthday.

During the next year's visit, having failed to get her daughter to compromise her morals, the mother agrees to the rich man's suit in exchange for a reward. The girl argues fiercely, but to no avail. In her final performance before the wedding, she chooses a play that represents her own situation, adapts it as she sings, and, at the close of the great aria in the suicide scene, flings herself off the stage into the river below, where her lover soon joins her.

Both are saved by the god to whom the temple is dedicated. Swept downstream and caught in a fisherman's net, they are found locked together "as if they had been cast into the river while in the act of love."[30] They marry and return to the hero's home, where he studies, then passes the examinations and obtains an appointment. His first wishes are to reward the fisherman with a position and to sacrifice to the god, but the fisherman, happy in his obscurity, declines the invitation to serve. By the time hero and heroine reach the temple, the birthday performances are again in full swing, with the heroine's mother now back in the leading role. The couple stay on their boat, from which they can see the stage, and anonymously request that the troupe perform the same play that the girl chose for her last performance. When the actress comes to the critical point, she breaks down, whereupon the young couple reveal their identity and extend their forgiveness. The hero has been much influenced by the fisherman's arguments, and after one term of duty as an official, he and his wife build a cottage near the fisherman's and take up a reclusive life themselves.

The story is about acting, and it has two great dramatic moments, symmetrically placed: the girl's plunge from the stage and her mother's breakdown while acting the same play on the same stage. But drama is more than the story's milieu. References to it as reflexive metaphor are as frequent as in any of Li Yu's stories. When the hero, receiving his first appointment, elects to thank the fisherman rather than return home, he chooses not to "act out a fine 'returning home in triumph' scene." When he and his wife arrive at the temple the second time, she is in favor of making their identities known to her mother, but he insists: "If you suddenly go off and see her, it will make for a very quiet finale." And the fisherman, arguing for the benefits of the recluse's life, compares an official career to the theater: "No play in the world goes on for ever."[31] But in this story, perhaps because it is about actors, the chosen metaphor is often taken from other genres. "The literary technique is quite new," claims the narrator, noting that the prologue is discursive, not narrative. The hero, in planning to seduce the heroine, hoped to progress from *poti* to *chengti*, the first two stages of the eight-part examination essay. The heroine's attempted suicide was new in two senses, one literal and one figurative: "She wrote a new text here too." And the "technique" of having her curse her suitor from the stage is "even more novel."[32]

Central to the story is the repeated use of the illusory medium of drama to express a truth that cannot otherwise be revealed: in the drama class, when the lovers express their feelings in invented stage dialogue; habitually, as they play romantic roles together; when she adapts a famous play, *The Thorn Hairpin*,[33] to denounce her tormentor before plunging into the river; and when her mother breaks down in acting the mourning scene from the same play.

The story's prologue is another tightly argued essay, on the lowly status of actresses, many of whom double as prostitutes. The narrator promises to show us an admirable actress, "like a magic herb growing out of a dungheap."[34] He then makes a claim about the novelty of his prologue; other stories tell a "minor story" before the main one, while he chooses to generate his main story from a prologue essay, which is a technical innovation to match the story's thematic novelty. Actually, neither this theme—a girl from a sordid background who proves herself a model of virtue—nor the essay prologue itself is in the least novel. The novel point is the narrator's explicit interest in technical innovation.

It is the beginning of the main story that departs from the usual practice. It relates that a particular village in Zhejiang was noted for the number of excellent actors and actresses it produced. The actresses did not, however, like those born in "actress-prostitute" families, use acting as a means of getting customers. They had their own strict limits as to what liberties they would allow—not for chastity's sake, we are informed, but simply to sustain their patrons' interest.

But there was one actress—Liu Jiangxian, the heroine's mother— who did not quite fit the pattern.

> Other lead actresses could play only one role, but she had an exceptional versatility, playing a hero or a heroine, a man or a woman, just as the playwright wished. And she also had another kind of talent, too, which was quite uninhibited; when the main play was over, she would quickly put on a painted face and play the *jing* or *chou* (villainous or comic) roles. Her comic byplay was sparklingly original, and every word of it impressed her audience deeply. They lost their hearts to her, and there was no one who did not want to take her to bed. And she was quite exceptionally accommodating by nature, too. It was not absolutely necessary that you be blessed with Pan An's looks or Cao Zhi's talent; in fact, even if you couldn't read and write, and were as ugly as sin, you could go to bed with her just so long as you could put up a large enough sum of money.

From accepting the ugly as well as the handsome, she came to appreciate the stupid as well as the intelligent, and so before she was thirty she had amassed a large fortune and established her husband as a local worthy of some note.[35]

Only at this point does the narrative turn to her daughter, who is far too moral to suit her mother's standards.

What was Li Yu's purpose here? Stories generally begin, after the prologue, with either the hero or the heroine. Clearly the description of the actress and her milieu is central to the story, and she is also its most interesting character. (In the play *Sole Mates* she really comes into her own.) But it is also true that in Li Yu the discursive element rivals the narrative, and here he exploits a justifiable opportunity for a satirical excursion on professional actresses.

I have mentioned his tendency to use parallel constructions in his vernacular prose. Here, as one example, is his description of the heroine's behavior:

Whereas others thought her the apple of their eye, she thought them a thorn in her flesh. Get her to a party to accompany the guests in their drinking, and she would declare she never drank and refuse to let the winecup touch her lips. Say something personal to her, and her expression would change and she would make an excuse to leave. Rich young men threw away large sums of money to get to know her, but she would not give them so much as a frown or a smile in return, let alone any other favors. Jewelry that was created for her she would not wear even once or twice, but would melt down and use as silver. Clothes that were made for her she would put in the props trunk for the supporting actresses and not wear herself. In her heart she was determined "not to take a second husband" and to keep herself chaste for Tan Chuyu, but she could tell no one of her resolve.[36]

I turn now to stories that, although not themselves romantic comedies, not even the novel kind favored by Li Yu, play against the idea of the romantic comedy. Some are inversions, turning cherished tenets of the romantic comedy on their heads; others are extensions of the comedy into new fields, such as that of homosexual love.

The basic concept of these stories is of greater significance than in those I have just discussed. In those stories, some device or special milieu or particular event was the key; here it is the basic idea itself. ("The Cloudscraper," the story about the maid's dominant role in the family, comes closest to this type.) But although the basic idea is more prominent and the incident wilder and even farcical, the action is still worked out with Li Yu's customary attention to detail, and the style remains witty and fluent.

The most notable inversion is the first story in *Operas*, "An Ugly Husband Fears Marriage to a Pretty Wife but Gets a Beautiful One,"[37] which Li Yu later turned into the play *You Can't Do Anything about Fate (Naihe tian)*. The primary assumption of the Chinese romantic comedy, usually referred to by the term *caizi jiaren* (brilliant youth, beautiful girl), is that the brilliant will marry the fair.[38] (In fact, both the hero and the heroine of the romantic comedy have literary ability as well as physical beauty.) Li Yu, upending the assumption, declares this situation to be the exception, not the rule. But merely to assert and demonstrate the fact would not qualify a story as his, and so the inversion is elaborated into a general rule: the more beautiful and talented the girl, the more likely she is to find herself married to an ugly and stupid husband. The reason is karmic; beauty in a woman is a curse, designed to punish her for some sin in a previous life. Precisely because of her beauty, she will have higher expectations than others, and when she sets eyes on her ugly and cloddish husband, she will be the more cruelly disillusioned.

The prologue begins with the notion that most matches are actually mismatches; they produce in women a condition that is known as "the dumb person's frustration" and "the lifelong ailment" because it can neither be expressed nor cured, short of death. The man in a mismatch at least has some recourse: he can take the "back door" of sleeping with concubines or maids. "But the beautiful wife married to an ugly husband or the talented woman married to a vulgar clod have only two doors to death and none to life—this is real suffering."[39]

The narrator then takes up the adage "a pretty face spells a sorry fate,"[40] and reinterprets it to mean that if you are born with a pretty face it is precisely because you are due to suffer a wretched fate. An anecdote about Yama's awarding of punishments in the netherworld shows that to be born beautiful is the worst of all possible sentences, far worse than to be born into the animal kingdom. Animals have no awareness, and do not live long, anyway, before getting another chance at incarnation, but a beautiful woman will entertain high hopes that are bound to be dashed. "When she finds herself married to an ugly dolt, she will naturally feel frustrated and will spend her time agonizing over her lost hopes, and her days will drag by like years. There is no need to persecute her, for she is perfectly able to persecute herself."[41]

Li Yu, who later disavows the Yama story (there is no "evidence" for it),[42] now steps forward in the persona of a doctor: "The writer of this story is the leading specialist in women's problems."[43] Every girl at the age of eleven or twelve must consult her mirror, and, if she finds any signs of beauty, prepare herself mentally for the worst.

The lengthy epilogue—long epilogues are one of the features of the *Operas* stories—continues the advice:

> I hope that beautiful girls will keep this story on their desks and turn to it as soon as they start grieving over their marriages, telling themselves: "Talented I may be, but certainly not more talented than Miss Zou. Beautiful I may be, but no more so than Miss He. Beauty and talent I may possess together, but surely not in greater measure than Miss Wu. Those three were married to the same husband and lived the same life, never managing to escape, either to Heaven above or Earth below. All I have to endure is that critical period each night." And even that may not be too hard to bear. There is always the chance of conceiving a son and not losing your advantages in old age. Moreover, your husband may not be as ugly as "Not-quite" Que. If his looks are only a degree or two better while his stench is of slightly less rich a blend, if he has only a drop or two more ink in him, be sure you accept him as if were Pan An or Song Yu. Whatever you do, don't go expecting too much.
>
> Having given you my secret formula for the elixir of life,

I shall pack up my medicine bag and leave. You may heed me or not—it's no concern of mine. But I do have some advice for those stupid and ugly husbands of yours:

Your wives are married to you, and they have to make the best of it. You are married to them, and you ought to count your blessings. You must realize that men of any talent would not be blessed with beautiful wives. Who am I, each one of you must ask himself, that I am allowed to consort with my wife? Apart from those critical periods in which you have no choice but to profane her a little, you should treat her as if she were a bodhisattva, burning incense and sacrificing to her; on no account must you pollute her nostrils with your stench or offend her ears with vile language. If you treat her with this kind of respect, you will naturally be able to conceive a son as Que Lihou did. But whatever you do, you must not take this story as grounds for believing that Heaven has ordered you to persecute these fine women, and that you need stop at nothing. You must realize that you are not the one who is to torment them, and that this is not the way by which they are to be tormented. If, by some chance, King Yama had not given your wife a life sentence, she might either have put a fatal curse on you so that she could marry some other man, or else done him to death so as to destroy you. Pretty women are perfectly capable of such things! It was only because of the virtue accumulated over many generations by Que's family, as well as his own capacity for cherishing beautiful women, that he received his magnificent reward. Otherwise, it would have taken only a rebuff from Senior Graduate Yuan to destroy him.

This story of mine gives only the general outline of the doctrine of karmic cause and effect. It does not maintain that all husbands and wives are like this. But we must realize that, whereas it is the norm for a beautiful wife to marry an ugly husband, it is a variant case if a brilliant young man should marry a beautiful girl. Those who represent the norm should rest content with each other. Those who do not should exercise the utmost care. This story exemplifies the norm, but there is another story that follows which concerns a variant case and carries a different explanation.[44]

The story describes the adventures in marriage of Que Lihou, a monstrously ugly and foul-smelling man of small education but great wealth. (*Que* means "lacking," and his nickname, *buquan*, means "not quite"—not quite bald, blind, deaf, and so on.) He uses his money to buy three wives in succession, none of whom can bear the sight or the smell of him. (The first wife has been carelessly betrothed by her father, the second is tricked by Que, and the third, a concubine, is forced by a jealous wife into marrying him.) The first wife, Miss Zou, is noted for her intelligence, the second, Miss He, for her beauty, and the third, Miss Wu, for her combination of both intelligence and beauty. Li Yu's inverse principle works even when Que does not want it to. Badly shocked by his first two marriages to remarkable women, he looks for a homely wife, but, through an unexpected development, ends up with the dazzling Miss Wu.

It is a cleverness story, another of Li Yu's stories of resourceful women, except that in this case the ultimate limitation, set by destiny, cannot be changed. The limitation is mentioned humorously in the prologue and epilogue, but grimly by Yuan, the official whose concubine Miss Wu originally was. His callous treatment of her, and the harsh lecture he reads her, stand in neat contrast to the narrator's humorous remarks.

Li Yu's account of Miss Zou's slow discovery of her new husband's smell and looks is amusingly done. She conceives the brilliant idea of claiming a vocation for Buddhism and setting up a shrine (that is, a sanctuary) in Que's own study. Although frustrated, he hesitates to force her, fearing that she might kill herself. Failing in his attempt to starve her out, he resumes sending in food, but vents his frustration by launching into a tirade outside her door:

> "You stupid, wanton slut! You're not reading sutras or praying to Buddha any more than you're trying to perfect yourself for your next life! You're putting on this act solely because I'm not good-looking or sexy enough to satisfy your lust. If you really want to satisfy yourself, there's no problem. I'll sell you into prostitution and you can stand in some doorway, choose the ones that take your fancy, and drag

them inside to bed. You think because you're a lady and good-looking, while I'm just a common person and ugly, that I'm not good enough for you, is that it? I'm not bragging when I say that the only thing to fear is a shortage of money. If a man can afford to risk a large enough sum, he can marry a princess or even Xishi herself. Take a good look at me, I'm determined to marry someone who comes from a better family than yours and who is better-looking than you, too, someone who will have my children and run the house for me. When that happens, don't have any regrets." To all this, Miss Zou said not a word in reply, but just went on intoning Buddha's name.[45]

Miss He, whom Que tricks into marrying him by employing a handsome substitute at the viewing, is indeed more beautiful. She deliberately drinks herself senseless so as to be able to get through the wedding night, during which Que "rowed the boat slowly, so as to catch the drunken fish."[46] She then asks to visit Miss Zou, and Que allows this, hoping to impress his first wife with this new acquisition. But Miss He tries to use the visit to enlist as Miss Zou's disciple and so gain sanctuary herself. Enraged, Que beats her, but under the beating her genuine beauty of face and conduct becomes apparent: "an artistic charm, a poetic grace, qualities revealed unconsciously that she would have found it impossible to affect."[47] This is the observation of Li Yu's ever-active sensuous eye, but it is also Miss Zou's reaction, for it is this sight that impels her to offer Miss He asylum. The suggestion is that what unites the two women is love rather than friendship.

This time Que decides to find a plain wife, but, by a complicated intrigue, gets the beautiful Miss Wu, who decides to make the best of her situation by sharing it with the other two women, thus lightening the load for each. With a little guile, she succeeds in persuading them to join her.

A very different inversion lies behind the *Silent Operas, Second Collection* story entitled "A Widow Hatches a Plot to Receive a Bridegroom, and Beautiful Women Unite to Seize a Brilliant Poet," in which a supremely brilliant and handsome man becomes the object of unscrupulous competition among several women.[48] The hero, unable at first to find a wife worthy of himself, has formed a liaison with three

96

outstanding Nanjing courtesans who are under the impression that, once he has taken a wife, they will be invited to become his concubines. To secure a grateful and complaisant wife, they therefore offer to conduct the search themselves. Although he agrees, the hero is wary of this conflict of interest, and is therefore an easy mark for an infatuated young widow who deliberately raises his suspicions of the courtesans. A wedding date is set and a sedan-chair sent for the hero, but he never appears at the widow's house. He has been kidnapped by the courtesans, and before he realizes the mistake, he is married to their candidate. They forge a letter of rejection to the widow and, for added insult, send a mechanical sexual contrivance along with it. The widow eventually learns the truth; the hero fakes a terminal illness to put pressure on his captors; and all five women come to terms and agree to share him. Modified, the story served as the source of Li Yu's play *Woman in Pursuit of Man.*

Li Yu's most notable extension of an idea resulted in the *Operas* story "A Male Mencius's Mother Educates His Son and Moves House Three Times," which transfers the ideals of courtship, marriage, filial piety, chaste widowhood, and selfless child raising to a homosexual love affair.[49] As the transition passage between prologue and main story puts it: "Now I shall tell of a licentiate and a beautiful boy who were not willing to give up this way of life and who later actually became husband and wife and did many of the things that virtuous husbands and wives do. Their story represents a variant form of the Three Obligations, an intercalary point in the Five Cardinal Relationships; it is a strange event that official history can ignore, but that unofficial history cannot omit. My purpose in telling it is to make you open up your sleepy eyes."[50]

Several tones are to be heard in this story: ribaldry, expressed mainly in poems (the "bride" turning his back on the groom, and so forth); sensuality, as in the description of the boy baring his buttocks in court ("smooth as a peeled egg"); and calm discursiveness, as in the argument that homosexuality is an abnormality in terms of anatomical complementarity, natural feeling, and effect (without issue).[51] A mixture of the three tones dominates prologue and epilogue and conditions the narrative, which is concerned mainly with the comic possibilities of exemplary behavior—replicating the Confucian family ideals—in a homosexual context.

Li Yu's more explicitly sexual fiction is full of shocks. "The House of Gathered Refinements" ("Cuiyalou") in *Structures* tells how the younger partner in a homosexual *ménage à trois* is drugged and castrated on the orders of a jealous premier.[52] A minor story in *Structures*, "The Hall of the Ten Weddings" ("Shijinlou"), tells of a "stone maiden" who eventually develops a vagina.[53] The hero of *The Carnal Prayer Mat*, intent on a career of sexual conquest, first undergoes a penile transplant, and then, feeling revulsion at the root cause of his wrong-doing, castrates himself. "A Male Mencius's Mother" is no exception; its shocking idea is that the boy castrates himself to ensure that his "marriage" to the licentiate will not be threatened by his growing masculinity. The castration scene is described in grisly detail, as when the licentiate discovers the severed phallus ("a fleshly eggplant"),[54] but also with a note of macabre humor.

Xu, the licentiate, in a romantic gesture, sells all his property in order to purchase You from his father, thus setting in motion the series of reciprocal sacrifices required by the notion of *bao*.[55] When You's self-castration leads to a trial (a jealous rival has accused Xu of responsibility for it), Xu offers to take the beating to which the delicate youth has been sentenced, and dies from its effects. You, who now passes himself off as a woman, cares for Xu's son (from an earlier marriage) as if he were the child's mother, moves away to another city to save the boy from the threat of seduction, and lives to see him succeed in his official career.

Li Yu's other homosexual story, "The House of Gathered Refinements" ("Cuiyalou"), is a more sophisticated, if less exuberant, work. Like other *Structures* stories, it begins on a personal note, with a poem Li Yu wrote "twenty years ago," that is, in 1637 or 1638 when, as a young poet of seventeen or so, he visited Tiger Mound in Suzhou to buy flowers.[56] The poem leads him to the subject of exquisite things (flowers) in a vulgar context (the market), and then to the question of which businesses are the most cultured. Shops that sell flowers, incense, and books, he answers, and also antique or curio shops, which may sell all three commodities. Then he introduces an element of fantasy, which is common in his prologues; he imagines that the owners of these shops are predestined for their roles—that they have been bees, musk deer, and bookworms, respectively, in a former existence. But, of course, not all shopkeepers appreciate what they sell.

Some remain like bees, and can only exploit flowers, not enjoy them.

The transitional passage runs as follows: "I will now tell of several people who were able to undergo a complete transformation and to enjoy such things for their own sake. These men should have confined themselves to hanging out a sign advertising their refined business in order to attract customers. But they also had a sign advertising sensual beauty, which they should never have hung out. Because the moment you hang out that sign, you create trouble for yourself. I would urge all comely young shopkeepers to conduct themselves with the greatest circumspection."[57]

The story is set in a shop that has four departments—for selling flowers, incense, books, and antiques—and is owned by three partners, two of whom are the lovers of the third and youngest. The latter is the specialist in flower arrangements, and the first heading of Chapter 1 runs: "The flower-seller will not sell flowers from the rear courtyard."[58] "Flowers in the rear courtyard" *(houting hua)*, an old song title, is also a well-established euphemism for anal intercourse.

The ménage is described in a lively fashion, and not without a little mockery. Behind the account lie the problems faced by the man of education and taste in adjusting to commerce. The two older men are licentiates who have chosen this business as one that will not declass them; high officials visiting their shop "make an exception in their case"[59] and treat them as literary men.

> On balmy, moonlit evenings, they would collect in the House of Gathered Refinements, and there would be music and singing of consummate artistry which ravished the senses of all who heard it. There was not a single rare or remarkable book they did not read, nor a single strange incense they did not use, nor one exotic flower or plant they did not enjoy. They would touch no antique after the Zhou, or hang on their walls any painting later than the Song. When they had finished enjoying a piece, they would sell it, and the longer it had been in their possession, the higher would be the price that they set; they assumed that society would pay for the pleasures of its three artistic consultants.[60]

Much comedy is made of their domestic arrangements. Although the two older men are married, they take turns each night to "look after the shop"—in reality, to "enjoy the pleasures of the rear courtyard" with Quan, their partner: "By day they earned their money; by night they took their pleasure. Where else in the world could you find two immortals such as these? There was not a single young man in the capital who did not admire them, nor one who was not jealous— admiring of the serenity of their lives, jealous of their rare delights."[61]

The demands of a political tyrant, Yan Shifan, shatter this idyllic scene. Through his aides, Yan hears of Quan's beauty, and pays a much-heralded visit to the shop, accompanied by his entourage. Although Quan is nowhere to be seen in the shop, Yan, the picture of a powerful and ruthless man, is not ruffled, at least on the surface. He simply takes all of their choicest pieces on approval and neglects to pay for them. Eventually, after bribing Yan's steward, the older partners learn the reason they have not been paid: Yan is insisting that Quan visit the palace personally in order to collect the payment. Reluctantly, the partners decide to forgo the money.

> "That shop assistant," they told the steward, "is just a boy. He comes from an old family, who have sent him here to learn the business. We have never even allowed him out; we're afraid his parents would be too worried. No matter whether His Honor pays us or not, we are certainly not going to hand over someone else's child in exchange for money. Moreover, we're owed interest on the money as well. We shall not be back again asking to paid. If, by some chance, the money becomes available, please let us know and we'll come for it."
>
> The steward gave a laugh. "Tell me, gentlemen," he said. "Are you going to keep your shop open now that you've decided not to have the money collected?"
>
> "Of course. Why not?"
>
> "What! You own a shop in the capital, so how can you be so ignorant of who holds power here? As the saying goes, the poor and base can't compete with the rich and mighty. If you don't come and collect the money, it will be a clear sign of your hatred and contempt. Is this master someone

you can afford to hate or insult? If he wanted to sleep with your wives, I could understand. You'd naturally risk your lives to stop him. But all we're talking about is a friend of yours. Sending him along for my master's appreciation is like sending him an antique or a painting; even if it comes back a little the worse for wear, it will still retain most of its value. Why give up thousands of taels for a cupful of vinegar? What's more, after you've given up the money, other things will start happening to you. You'll never be able to feel quite secure again. I urge you against a course of action that will bring you nothing but harm."[62]

Quan visits Yan, but resists his advances. Yan then persuades an elderly palace eunuch to invite Quan to join his staff to tend his flowers and antiques, and to castrate him in order to force him to serve. (Yan expects to inherit the boy, and needs a eunuch if Quan is to mingle later with his own womenfolk.) The account of the forced castration and of Quan's eventual revenge is in Li Yu's grimmest manner, and yet it retains some of the grisly humor I have noted—a combination that some readers may find repugnant.

Eunuch Sha invites Quan to come and prune a bonsai bought at his shop. Since Sha is a eunuch, Quan has no qualms.

Eunuch Sha winked at one of his servants, who substituted some drugged wine and filled the young man's cup with it. Not long after drinking it, Ruxiu [Quan] began to grow limp. His head lolled forward and he slumped in the easy chair and slept a sleep as sound as Chen Tuan's. Eunuch Sha roared with laughter and called out, "Come on, lads! Go to it!" Before the drinking began, he had hidden the castrators behind the rock garden; at his summons they now came forward, pulled off the boy's trousers, then held his organs in one hand, and with a light, deft cut, sliced them off and threw them on the ground for the Pekinese dog.[63]

At the end of the chapter, the narrator asks, "Gentle readers, having read this far, are you able to harden your hearts and feel no pain on behalf of the little shopkeeper?"[64]

Quan is eventually forced to join Yan's household, where he successfully schemes to bring about Yan's downfall and then takes an appropriate revenge.

I turn now to inversions other than that of the romance. One example is the *Operas* story "A Client Patronizes a Prostitute, and a Miserable 'Ghost' Tells of Brothel Injustice," which inverts the cherished theme of the good-hearted singing-girl.[65] The theme is present in the minds of the characters all along, conditioning their behavior. A young hairdresser, seeking to emulate the young oil-seller of fiction and drama who with his solicitous kindness won the most beautiful courtesan of the time,[66] is bilked of all his money and labor. Another *Operas* story, "A Son and Grandson Abandon the Corpse While a Servant Hastens to the Funeral," is an extension, rather than an inversion, of a famous theme—that of A Ji, the servant who selflessly helped a widowed daughter-in-law survive the family infighting after the patriarch's death. It was written up as a biography by the Ming author Tian Rucheng, and later converted into a vernacular story.[67] In both versions the servant sacrifices himself beyond the call of duty and then, with his job done, steps modestly back into his original role. Li Yu's servant is just as unassuming, but after the two heirs have destroyed each other fighting over the property, he inherits it all.

"The House of My Birth" ("Shengwolou"), Li Yu's finest extravaganza, is also an inversion—it recounts the adoption, not of a son or daughter, but of a father and mother.[68] This idea is combined with other elements, for example, the abduction of a child who still remembers, in his dreams, the room in which he lived, and the "human markets" in which the rebels sell off in sacks the women, young and old, whom they have captured. The story is full of the most outrageous coincidences, parodying those of the drama, which are here excused as the work of the Creator. After one particularly neat coincidence, the narrator remarks: "As it turns out, the Creator's ingenuity is a hundred times that of man. It is just as if he were deliberately arranging events so that someone could turn them into a play or story. He has united the two couples and then separated them. He has separated them and then united them. Think of the mental effort it must have cost him! These events rate as novel and ingenious to the ultimate degree!"[69]

Another *Structures* story, "Reformation House" ("Guizhenglou"), may also be seen as an extension of a favorite Chinese literary theme, that of the thief or swindler of genius who is inclined to rob the rich and, occasionally, to help the poor.[70] Li Yu's representative follows the general specifications of the theme; he is a marvelous, imaginative swindler, who moves to the capital to prove his mettle in the big time. We can see why the topic interested Li Yu; it was essentially a cleverness theme of the swindler's ever more sublime exploits, most of which are so brilliant they have to be explained *ex post facto.* Li Yu was indebted above all to a particular hero, Lazy Dragon, in the story by Ling Mengchu, and he was evidently so pleased with his creation that he developed it into the figure of the Knave (Sai Kunlun) in *The Carnal Prayer Mat.*

But Li Yu's swindler is distinctive, too, in his own way. He is a bisexual voluptuary who has dallied with all the finest courtesans and catamites. In a brothel he meets a girl whose husband has sold her into prostitution and who now declares her intention to become a Buddhist nun. The swindler, who has been contemplating retirement anyway because he has reached the peak of his profession, decides to become a Taoist himself, after helping the girl to realize her aspiration.

Another notable cleverness story, this time without literary antecedents, is "The Female Chen Ping Saves Her Life with Seven Schemes,"[71] the companion story to "The Male Mencius's Mother" in *Operas.* (Chen Ping was a legendary tactician.) The brilliant schemer is an illiterate peasant woman who resembles the Nenghong of "The Cloudscraper" in ingenuity. Hers is a natural intelligence that is put to the test when rebels descend upon her village and carry off all of its women. In a series of brilliant stratagems, she not only preserves her chastity but also manages to obtain her captor's booty. Exemplifying self-interest in action, she and her husband buy themselves land with the booty without ever telling anyone where the money came from. In her finest stroke, she has succeeded in getting her captor to affirm her chastity, something people would otherwise never have believed in. There are numerous details of simulated menstruation, swollen penises and vaginas, dysentery, and so forth—the various means by which she staves off actual sexual intercourse. The story is part ribald

comedy, part inversion of social perceptions, part a tribute to enlightened self-interest. It is also, of course, another of Li Yu's stories of
enterprising and ingenious women.

There is one other story that specifically refers to the flouting of
a literary stereotype, "The Spirits Astonish by Switching Wife and
Concubine," in *Operas*. [72] It is concerned with wifely jealousy, a staple
subject of comedy in seventeenth-century literature and one on which
Li Yu also has a conventional and rather tedious story. [73] Here, however,
he changes, if he does not quite invert, the terms of the discussion,
distinguishing envy from jealousy, which refers to sexual desire and is
restricted to women. But instead of deploring jealousy, he defends it
as good in the way vinegar is (to be jealous is to "eat vinegar"); it adds
spice to life. A vinegary wife will exercise some restraint over her
husband: "If I can come and go as the mood takes me, she might just
as well be the madam in a brothel welcoming a client." [74]

But a mere defense of wifely jealousy was not enough of an
inversion for Li Yu; he proceeds to distinguish a "new" jealousy from
the "old": "Plays and novels have exhausted the subject of female
jealousy; there is simply no material left. But the women in plays and
novels are all eating the old vinegar. The new vinegar has never before
been tapped, but will be tasted for the first time in this story of mine.
'Old vinegar' refers to the jealousy a senior feels toward her junior;
'new jealousy' refers to the jealousy a junior feels toward her senior." [75]
Li Yu argues that new jealousy is dangerous because the husband's
sympathies are likely to be with the concubine, in which case the wife
may suffer and perhaps even be driven to her death. By contrast, the
old jealousy may be good for the husband, at least in moderation, and
will probably not harm the concubine, whom he will tend to protect.

So, at least, the prologue claims, in the face of a mass of fact
and fiction to the contrary. In his epilogue, having told the story of
a vindictive, ambitious concubine who would have succeeded in de-
stroying the wife if the spirits had not intervened, Li Yu blithely
disavows what he has said in his prologue. If the wife in his story had
been jealous—with the old jealousy of senior for junior—the spirits
would never have been moved to intervene in her behalf.

I will pass lightly over two other inversion stories. In one, the
narrator professes an absolute belief in the immutability of fortunes as
predicted by the "eight characters" of one's time of birth, but then

proceeds to tell a story that directly contradicts his argument.[76] The impression the story gives, despite its prologue, is that fortunes are all a matter of people's perceptions, but that perceptions have a way of becoming reality. The other story, "A Beggar Scorns High Officials and Upholds Justice," touches on the theme of the Zhengde Emperor and his romance with a singing-girl, the material Li Yu made into his pay *The Jade Clasp*.[77] The central figure in this story is a beggar of heroic magnanimity who tries to raise money to help a girl in distress; he is given a large sum by a brothel patron who proves to be the Emperor in disguise.

The most interesting part is the prologue, in which Li Yu defends beggars on the ground that they have often enrolled loyal officials and writers in their ranks, especially in times of turmoil: "I will now ask two beggars to join us, as an introduction to this story, one a writer living in a time of peace, the other a loyal official in a time of civil war. Their stories are calculated to freshen your eyes and ears."[78] The first prologue story is about Tang Yin, the poet and artist, and the second about a loyal official at the end of the Ming dynasty. The latter story is the most explicit reference in Li Yu's writing to the loyalty crisis. Officials of any integrity gave up their lives or at least their jobs when Li Zicheng captured Beijing; many became beggars. Hunger drove some to seek employment with the dissolute pretender to the Ming throne, but when the Great Army (that is, the Qing) came south, these officials fled, while many of the beggars gave up their lives. Li Yu tells of one beggar who threw himself from a bridge in Nanjing, leaving behind a poem that runs:

> Maintained by the Court for three hundred years,
> The officials flee at the first news of trouble.
> The poorhouse now is where morality lies;
> Even a beggar is ashamed to cling to life.[79]

In the early part of his prologue Li has quoted Chen Jiru, the late-Ming author and wit, to the effect that Buddhism is the nation's poorhouse. He follows it with his own *mot*, that "the beggars' hostel is the Court's greatest pacification camp," that is, that it gives desperate wanderers a refuge and thus reduces the chances of rebellion.[80] Such personal opinions by recent or contemporary authors are unusual in fiction, as Li Yu notes: "These two opinions are both of our own making; they are not clichés inherited from earlier fiction."[81]

One of the finest stories in *Operas*, "A Handsome Lad Raises Doubts by Trying to Avoid Suspicion,"[82] can also be discussed, at least partly, under the rubric of inversion. It is the story that follows "An Ugly Husband," whose epilogue refers to this theme as the variant, not the norm; that is, it will show a brilliant young man marrying a beautiful girl. True, but it is an unusual romance, between a student living next door and a beautiful young wife in an as yet unconsummated marriage. These two end up happily married simply because of her father-in-law's unjust suspicions of her.

A more important inversion consists of the notion that an incorruptible official may be more dangerous than a corrupt one, an insight for which Liu E's *Travels of Lao Can* (*Lao Can youji*) of the early twentieth century is usually given credit. The self-righteous moral certitude of Li Yu's incorruptible official is the cause of the trouble here. Obsessed, puritanical, and also, for good measure, intimidated by his own wife, he is as severe on the subject of sexual morality as he is naive about women: "What he always stressed were the rules of morality. What most angered him was anyone who broke the rules. In the adultery cases that came before him, the plaintiffs invariably won and the defendants as invariably lost."[83]

The story is about self-righteous prejudice, and not only on the official's part. It is full of suspicions of incest and adultery, although neither act ever takes place. The events that give rise to suspicion have their simple, natural cause in the fact that rats steal small items for their nests, yet suspicions of incest and adultery lead to judicial torture and to suicide. Li Yu's occasional ventures into the subgenre of court-case fiction turn out always to be crime cases with nonexistent crimes. Another example is the *Operas, Second Collection* story "A Chaste Girl Preserves Her Chastity but Incurs a Strange Slander, While Friends' Jesting Produces a Bizarre Injustice," in which a shrewd official has to use trickery to convince a suspicious husband that his wife is innocent of adultery.[84]

There are three stories, all in *Structures*, in which the inversion is of a quasi-philosophical nature. The most notable is "The Hall of the Homing Crane" ("Heguilou"),[85] in which Li Yu sets in opposition not a puritan and a bohemian as in "The Pavilion of Combined Reflections," but an obsessed romantic and a model of prudence and self-control. It is an antiromantic story that treats the proper place of love in our lives and the attitude we should adopt toward it.

Much more than love is involved, however. A prudent detachment is recommended toward all personal ideals and goals, as well as a resolute anticipation of the worst possible outcome of every action. Perception is all; no condition in itself is absolutely good or bad: "People in the Eighteenth Hell envy those in the Seventeenth, just as living buddhas in the Thirty-second Heaven long for the Thirty-third."[86] Hence we must live by manipulating our perceptions, in particular by the comparative method of "taking a step back" that Li Yu elaborates in *Casual Expressions*.[87] Behind the psychological strategies lies a metaphysical belief, whether serious or not, in a Creator who is jealous of any excess, including an excess of good fortune, especially when people set too great a store by it. The romantic hero is obsessed with love and marriage, which end in tragedy, while his political career, in which he has never invested any hopes, flourishes mightily. Meanwhile the prudent hero, another of Li Yu's masterminds, successfully practices his bleak philosophy. The story's inversion is explicitly referred to by the commentator, who calls it a "variant form" of the eternal romance and compares its "coolness" to the torrid heat of two earlier Li Yu romances, "The Pavilion of Combined Reflections" and "The Cloudscraper."[88]

The opposed attitudes in "The Hall of the Homing Crane" are set out with all of Li Yu's schematic clarity. Two talented friends, Duan and Yu, differ in their attitudes to love and marriage. Their relationship is rather like that in Li Yu's play *Be Careful about Love* between the cautious, controlled Hua and the romantically obsessed Hou. Duan is "of placid temperament, always prudent about his good fortune while constantly concerned lest things turn out badly. And so he lived one day at a time without hoping for anything from the future." His friend Yu is just as willing as Duan to postpone the examinations, but not marriage, which he thinks of as "the ultimate reality" and "the supreme concern."[89]

The story is set at a time of crisis in the Song dynasty, and the Emperor orders all licentiates to take the examinations in order to increase the supply of officials. Duan and Yu succeed brilliantly despite themselves, and are promptly married to two beautiful girls originally destined for the Palace. (The Emperor has reacted to criticism by grudgingly allowing them to marry others.) The reaction of the two men to their marriages is characteristic. Duan is concerned that he has "infringed the Creator's taboo" and so never really abandons himself to pleasure: "Even when he was making love, the thought would suddenly enter his mind and he would feel a trifle uneasy, as if this beautiful woman were not his wife and as if he were doing something immoral and unjust."[90] In Chapter 2 he holds a long discussion with his wife in which he explains the hubristic dangers of any kind of excess, whether it be in literary talent, examination triumph, or the acquisition of a beautiful wife. He describes also his strategies of circumspection, modesty, and contentment, particularly stressing the agony of parting which, if it is treated as a romantic crisis, can tell on husband and wife and either drive them to an early grave or make them old before their time.

When Duan and Yu are sent on a dangerous mission to the Jurchen, Duan behaves offhandedly, even callously, toward his wife. He names his studio the Hall of the Homing Crane to indicate that he is resigned to the idea of not returning alive. Yu, by contrast, says a tender farewell to his wife, complete with vows of love and promises of an early return. But whereas Duan, with his mental self-discipline, is able to preserve his equanimity in a Jurchen prison, Yu tortures himself with images of sexual love: "Just to think of what they had said to each other in bed, of their passion beneath the quilt, made his soul melt and almost expire."[91] In the eight years of their captivity, Yu comes to see the force of Duan's argument, yet is still too softhearted to apply it. Only when he returns, prematurely old, to find that his wife has pined away does he realize that Duan's principles are those of a true romantic. Yu dies with his aspirations unfulfilled, "because he was too wholehearted in his dedication to sex, and the Creator insists on toppling all heroes and preventing people from fulfilling their hearts' desires."[92] Duan, by contrast, returns to a plump and healthy wife who is, however, understandably resentful of him. Ingeniously, he manages to convince her of the efficacy of his philosophy.

"The Studio of the Three Teachers" ("Sanyulou") is equally schematic.[93] Its main distinction is between Yu, the creative artist, forever in debt, who tears down his creations in order to build them more exquisitely, and Tang, the land-hungry, money-grubbing miser.

Like Li Yu himself, the artist is passionately devoted to domestic art; he is fond of asserting that the three things that matter in life are the house a man lives in, the bed he sleeps in, and the coffin he is buried in, and in these objects he must insist on perfection. The artist's studio has three levels, representing the hierarchy of men's contact with the universe: the first is for entertaining friends, for "learning from people"; the second is for study, for "learning from the past"; and the third, equipped only with an incense burner and a Taoist classic, is for "learning from Heaven."[94] When Tang buys and adapts Yu's main property, the aesthetic gap between it and the studio, which Yu has retained, becomes glaringly apparent. "Just as in a fine landscape painting one has only to add or subtract a plant or a tree to sacrifice the whole artistic conception, after the changes they made the house naturally lost its original character. They had hoped to turn base metal into gold, but they succeeded only in doing the opposite."[95]

Li Yu's last story in *Structures*, "Corrigibility House" ("Wenguo-lou"), is the most personal of all.[96] Its prologue, a memoir of his experiences in the countryside during the civil war, seems designed to make us take the main story personally, too, as an envoi to the whole collection. Its hero, Gu, is another man of placid temperament, with the inclinations of a recluse. He is an artist, a descendant of the famous painter Gu Kaizhi, and like Yu of "The Studio of the Three Teachers," whom he resembles, he is also a persona of Li Yu himself. In his thirties, still unsuccessful in the examinations, Gu gives away his art materials and burns his essays and brushes, saving only his books on agriculture. People ask why he is giving up art as well as study:

> "Painting and calligraphy have nothing to do with the examination system. When you give up studying, that is precisely the time when you should concentrate on art. Why give it up?"
>
> "In today's world," he replied, "true art does not bring you recognition. You get that only by appealing to officials for their patronage. You don't even need to have mastered the art of calligraphy and painting to be esteemed by society. And it is no easy thing for a recluse to be a writer, either; he has to sacrifice most of the advantages he enjoys. Not only is he out of pocket for the paper and ink he gives away

to others, he lays himself open to their ridicule. He's far
better off not trying."[97]

He announces that he is going to move to the countryside, but from
the moment he does so, troubles beset him, all of which turn out to
be hoaxes thought up by his friends to force him to return. The friends
build a house for him where town meets country, and next door to it
his cousin Yin builds his own Corrigibility House, where he can receive
Gu's counsel. The epilogue explains that the story is named for Yin's
house rather than Gu's because receptiveness to advice is a rarer quality
than the wisdom needed to provide it. It is hard not to see in this last
and most unusual story of Li Yu's a half-serious plea for patronage.

Six. Comic *Erotiker*

In *The Carnal Prayer Mat (Rou putuan)*, the sexual comedy that lurks behind Li Yu's stories emerges and takes control. The book treats the place of sexual desire in life with novelty, candor, and imagination, but above all with humor. As a sample of this last quality, I will present an early episode in which the hero, a young Casanova eager to embark on a career of sexual conquest, is required to prove that he has the qualifications for the task. His name is not given, only his sobriquet, Weiyang Sheng, the Before Midnight Scholar—evening being the time that he chooses for his philandering. *Weiyang* is an obscure term in Chinese, and I accordingly translate it as Vesperus, [Master] of the Evening.[1] His worldly friend and mentor, a thief of miraculous powers, is nicknamed Sai Kunlun, a Match for Kunlun, because his feats match those of the legendary Knave of Kunlun (Kunlun nu);[2] I shall simply call him the Knave. In reconnoitering for his burglaries, the Knave sees many women in deshabille or less, the most beautiful of whom he has promised to mention to Vesperus. After much discussion of the kind of mistress with whom Vesperus should inaugurate his career, the Knave asks him point-blank:

> "There's just one thing I'd like to ask you, worthy brother. Your sexual desires are so keen that I'm sure you have what it takes to support them. But tell me, what *is* the size of your endowment? And what is your stamina like? I need to know your capacities if I am to act for you with an easy mind."
>
> Vesperus beamed. "That's one thing you needn't worry about, my good fellow. I'm not boasting when I say that my stamina and endowment are both more than adequate.

They will lay a feast from which even a woman with the heartiest appetite will stagger away gorged and drunk. It will be no pauper's dinner party, I assure you, from which the guest rises sober and ravenous, complaining bitterly of her host's lack of savoir-faire."

"That's very reassuring. Still, it might be as well to take the matter a little further. When you're making love, approximately how many thrusts can you give before having to let go?"

"I've never even counted. Anyone who can keep track of the number is bound to be of very limited sexual powers. I don't abide by any general rule when I'm making love to a woman, but I can assure you that she receives innumerable thrusts before I stop."

"Even if you can't remember the number, you must at least remember how long. Approximately how many hours can you last?"

Vesperus's actual limit was only one hour, but since he wanted the Knave to act for him, he was afraid to admit to so little, lest he give his friend a pretext for reneging. He felt he had to add another hour to his performance.

"I can last a good two hours," he replied. "If I were willing to force myself, I daresay I might be able to last out for half an hour or more beyond that."

"That's nothing out of the ordinary," said the Knave. "It doesn't qualify as a superior performance. Such mediocre ability is ample for everyday sex with one's wife, but I'm afraid it would be quite inadequate for conducting a raid on someone else's compound."

"You're worrying unnecessarily, my good fellow," said Vesperus. "The other day I bought myself an excellent aphrodisiac, which I keep in my room. I have no woman at present, so I'm a warrior without a battlefield. If an assignation can be arranged, I'll take the plunge and apply some of it in advance, and I've no doubt I shall prove to have plenty of endurance."

"Aphrodisiacs can only give you endurance," said the Knave, "they cannot increase your size or firmness. If a man with a large endowment uses one, he'll be like a gifted student taking a ginseng tonic at examination time; in the examination hall, his mental powers will naturally be enhanced, and he will be able to express himself well. But if a student with a very small endowment uses one, he'll be no better off than some empty-headed candidate who couldn't produce a line even if he swallowed pounds of the tonic. What is the point of his sitting in an examination cell for three days and nights, if all he wants to do is to hold out regardless of results? Moreover, most aphrodisiacs are a swindle. Who knows whether yours will work or not? But I'm not concerned about whether you've tested it. What I want you to tell me is the size and length of your endowment."

"There is no need to go into that," said Vesperus. "What I will say, though, is that it is not small."

Seeing that he was not about to respond, the Knave shot out his hand and tugged at the crotch of Vesperus's trousers, trying to free the object in quesion. Vesperus kept evading his reach, refusing to let him do so. "If that's the way things are," said the Knave, "I hereby renounce any further interest in seeing it. Your stamina certainly can't be described as superior. If your endowment should be puny, too, and if by some chance you fail to stimulate the woman and she starts screaming that you are trying to rape her, what a disaster it would be! If you get into any trouble, I will be the one who misled you, and that is something I cannot accept."

Confronted with such vehemence from his friend, Vesperus could only smile gamely. "My endowment is by no means unworthy of notice," he said, "but I do find it a little indelicate to have to produce it in front of a friend, and in broad daylight, too. However, since you're so worried about nothing, I have no choice but to make a spectacle of myself."[3]

A set piece now describes Vesperus's penis as the Knave inspects it; it proves to be tiny. (This is one of the few set pieces in the novel—

an indication of the comic importance of the subject.) The narrative continues:

> The Knave examined it, looked Vesperus in the eye, contemplated for a long time, but said nothing. Vesperus assumed he was astonished at its size.
>
> "It is only like this when limp," he said. "When full of vigor, it is really quite spectacular."
>
> "If this is what it's like when limp," said the Knave, "I can quite imagine what it's like when full of vigor. I've seen all I need to, thank you. Please put it away." Then, unable to contain himself any longer, he put his hand over his mouth and burst out laughing.
>
> "How can you be so ignorant of your own limits, worthy brother? Your endowment is less than a third the size of other people's, and yet you propose to go off and seduce their wives! Do you imagine the women's 'shoes' are too big for the lasts they have at home and that they need your little piece jammed in alongside? When I saw you looking about everywhere for women, I assumed you had a mighty instrument on you, something that would strike fear into the hearts of all who set eyes on it. That is why I hesitated to ask you to show it to me. I never dreamed that it would turn out to be a flesh-and-blood hair clasp, good for titillating a woman inside her pubic hair, perhaps, but useless in the really important place!"
>
> "It will serve at a pinch," protested Vesperus. "Perhaps yours is so massive that you tend to look down on everybody else's. I'll have you know that there are people who have expressed their admiration for this unworthy instrument of mine."
>
> "If anybody admired it," said the Knave, "it must have been a virgin with her maidenhead intact or else some boy who had yet to make his debut. Such people would naturally appreciate it. But apart from them, I'm afraid everyone else would find it as hard as I do to flatter your honorable instrument."

"Do you mean to tell me that *everybody's* penis is bigger than mine?"

"I see them all the time—I must have seen a thousand or two, at least—and I don't think I've ever seen one quite as delicate as yours."

"Let's leave other people's out of it. The husbands of those three women—how do their members compare with mine?"

"Not much bigger—only two or three times the size and length."

Vesperus gave a laugh. "Now I know you're not telling me the truth!" he said. "This proves that you don't want the responsibility of helping me and are just looking for an excuse to avoid it. Let me ask you this: perhaps you really did see the two men in that household as you robbed their houses at night, but as for the woman in the silk shop, you said yourself that you visited her only once, in the daytime, and that you spoke only to her and never met the husband. How can you possibly be sure that his thing is two or three times as big as mine?"

"I saw the other two with my own eyes," said the Knave. "This one I heard about. The day I first met her, I went and asked the neighbors about her husband, and they told me his name. Then I asked them: 'She is such a beautiful woman, I wonder how she manages to get along with her stupid clod of a husband?' 'Although the husband may look coarse,' they told me, 'he is fortunate enough to have an impressive endowment and that is why the two of them scrape along without any actual quarrels.' I then asked: 'How large is his endowment?' Their reply was: 'We've never measured it, but in summer, when he strips down, we've noticed it swinging about in his pants the size of a laundry beater, and so we know it's quite something.' I made a mental note at the time, which is what led me to ask to see yours today. Why else, for no reason whatever, would I want to inspect someone's penis?"

At last it dawned on Vesperus that the Knave was telling

him the truth, and he gradually began to feel depressed. After pondering a while, he went on:

"When a woman goes to bed with someone, it's not only out of sexual desire. It may also be because she admires his mind or is attracted by his looks. If neither his mind nor his looks amount to much, a man is forced to rely on his sexual prowess. Now I happen to be quite well endowed with looks and brains, and perhaps a woman will take that into account and be a little less demanding in the other department. I implore you to see this matter through for me. You mustn't ignore my many strong points because of a single shortcoming and withdraw the favor you offered to do for me as a friend."

"Talent and looks," said the Knave, "are sweeteners for the medicine of seduction. Like ginger and dates, their flavor helps get the medicine inside one's body, but once it's in there, it's the medicine alone that has to cure the disease; the ginger and dates are of no further use. If a man goes in for seduction and has neither looks nor talent, he'll not be able to get himself inside the door, but once he is inside, it is his true powers that are in demand. What are you planning to do with her under the quilt, anyway, write *poems* on her pelvis? If someone with a very limited endowment and stamina manages to get in by virtue of his looks and talent and then gives a disappointing display in the first couple of bouts, he will very quickly get the cold shoulder. A fellow takes his life in his hands when he goes in for adultery, and he therefore hopes for a love affair that will last a lifetime. Why waste your ingenuity if all you have in mind is a couple of nights' fun? We thieves think we have to steal a thousand taels' worth of things in a break-in, just to make up for the stigma of being branded as thieves. For just a couple of items, we might as well stay home, rather than incur the stigma and have nothing to show for it. But let's ignore for a moment the man's desire for long-term pleasure. Even a woman who deceives her husband and takes a lover deserves some sympathy. Think how many precautions she has to take, how many alarms she has to suffer! All well and good if she enjoys the real thing a few hundred or even a few dozen times. But if she is to get no pleasure out of the affair at all, she's no better off than a hen that's mounted by a rooster. The hen scarcely knows what's going on inside her before it's all over. The woman's life has been wasted and her reputation lost, all for nothing! Not an easy thought to live with. Forgive me for what I'm going to say, worthy brother, but while endowment and stamina like yours are all right for keeping your wife on the straight and narrow, they are not enough to sustain any wild ideas about debauching other men's wives and daughters. Luckily, I was shrewd enough to measure the customer before cutting the cloth. If I'd simply set to work without asking your measurements, the garments would have been far too big for you. What a waste of material! And apart altogether from the woman's resentment, I'm afraid you too would have blamed me in your heart, for not acting in good faith but deliberately choosing someone too large for you so as to get myself off the hook. I'm a straightforward sort of fellow, and I put things crudely, but I hope you won't hold it against me. From now on, if you need any money or clothing, I'm only too ready to provide it. But as to this other matter, I cannot do your bidding."

From the forcefulness with which the Knave spoke, Vesperus realized that the affair was a lost cause. He knew, too, that the money and clothing would be stolen goods, and he was afraid of the trouble they could land him in.

"I'm in quite a difficult spot," he said, "but I have not spent all my travel money yet, and I still have a few coarse garments left. I would not want to put you to any expense."

After saying a few things to comfort his friend, the Knave made as if to leave. Vesperus, his hopes dashed, could not find it in his heart to ask him to stay, and showed him to the gate.

After this frustration, did Vesperus curb his desires? Did he reform? The reader is not the only one who is perplexed over these issues; the author is not sure of them himself, and will have to continue into the next chapter before resolving them. Up to this point, although Vesperus's mind has been corrupted, his conduct is without blemish. He is still, believe it or not, a man who could lead a virtuous life.[4]

The hero's discomfiture is all the greater for the fact that he has recently been playing the role of worldly mentor in sexual matters himself. His wife, Scent, is the daughter of a formidable puritan known as Mr. Iron Door. (All the men in the novel are known by their sobriquets; it was the custom in the Yuan dynasty, we are told.) In his straitlacedness and his penny-pinching, Mr. Iron Door is one of Li Yu's most heavily satirized Confucian puritans. Unfortunately, his daughter has imbibed some of her father's prudishness, and Vesperus has to expend much effort in educating her out of her inhibitions. He accomplishes his aim by patient lecturing, complete with visual aids (an erotic album) and some famous examples of erotic fiction. Fresh from his triumph, but chafing under his father-in-law's rule, he has set out to conquer womankind. His humiliation on being rebuffed by the Knave can be imagined. Vesperus is a satirized figure throughout the novel, but nowhere more clearly than when he is contrasted with the gallant but immoral Knave.

Note how carefully the dialogue in this passage is constructed, and how Vesperus's conceit, expressed in a fancy image or two, and with much mock modesty, is punctured by his rough-and-ready companion until, utterly deflated, he is reduced to asking the plain, vulgar question: "Do you mean to tell me *everybody's* penis is bigger than mine?" at which stage, all pretensions gone, he is driven inexorably to his humiliation. Meanwhile the Knave's language steadily increases in passion, and his use of similes—direct, earthy, ribald—becomes stronger and stronger, overwhelming Vesperus's orotund rhetoric. The climax of his speech comes in lines like: "What are you planning to do with her under the quilt, anyway, write *poems* on her pelvis?" Note, too, how his use of the word "delicate" to describe Vesperus's penis echoes Vesperus's own use of the word (it would be "indelicate" to show it to a friend). The whole passage is an excellent example of comic dialogue enlivened by earthy images, two of which are taken up by the commentator in his chapter-closing critique: the comparison of an aphrodisiac to an examination tonic and the description of talent and looks as sweeteners for the medicine of seduction.

A worldly husband who patiently gives an erotic education to a prudish wife and then turns into a philanderer who, to his dismay, finds he lacks the principal requirement of the role—these are merely the first of Li Yu's novelties. The major ones—I stress that they are only the major ones—are the following. Vesperus tries the ascetic life, but rejects it when he sees an advertisement offering a remedy for his shortcoming. He undergoes a successful operation by a Taoist adept in which a dog's member is implanted in his own (Chapter 8), bringing him up to the Knave's standards. (The heavy allegory of the use of an animal's member is pointed out, a trifle unnecessarily, in the end-of-chapter critique.) Thus equipped, he embarks on his first adultery, with the woman in the silk shop referred to earlier. This woman, Fragrance, permits a friend to take her place in the first encounter, so that she can be convinced that adultery with Vesperus will be worthwhile (Chapter 10). She soon after insists that Vesperus elope with her (Chapter 11). But once she is pregnant, Vesperus's attentions wander, first to three beautiful cousins and then to their aunt, all of whom he has admired before. The married cousins try to keep his presence secret from their widowed aunt, but the latter descends upon them one day, and looking suspiciously around, finds a naked Vesperus hidden in a large trunk (Chapter 16). The aunt commandeers him for several days, after which she returns him to the cousins' quarters, where a complicated orgiastic game is played involving the use of a deck of erotic playing cards. Vesperus then hears that Fragrance has given birth, and returns to her. Meanwhile Quan, the husband of Vesperus's first mistress, resolves to gain his revenge by seducing Vesperus's wife, who has been left at home. Ingratiating himself with her father, he enters the house as a servant and has little trouble seducing Scent (Chapter 14). Pregnant, she elopes with Quan, but then, after a miscarriage, finds herself sold into prostitution. While Quan undergoes a religious conversion, Scent becomes a famous courtesan in the capital.

Here Vesperus encounters her, in one of Li Yu's strongest scenes (Chapter 19). He had returned home only to be told that Scent was dead. (Mr. Iron Door cannot bear the disgrace of an eloping daughter.) Vesperus goes on to the capital, to see if the famous courtesan (Scent) can restore his jaded sexual powers with her Taoist technique of "seminal transfusion." She sees him first, and locks herself in her room for fear that he will have her arrested. He persists and she, concluding that she will die anyway in prison or from judicial punishment, hangs herself. Vesperus, accused of causing her death, is still not aware of her identity. Only when lying beside the corpse, awaiting the arrival of the constables, does he realize that the dead woman is his wife.

Vesperus now undergoes a revelation of his own in which he grasps the principle of reward and retribution as stressed by the priest Lone Peak in Chapter 2. The man whom he cuckolded, Quan, has deliberately cuckolded him, and the husbands of the three women with whom he slept have, it so happens, slept with his wife too, during her brief career as a courtesan. Vesperus seeks out Lone Peak in order to join the Buddhist order and adopt an ascetic life (Chapter 20). But for all his resolve, he is still troubled by erotic thoughts and dreams. From one dream in which the cousins and their aunt visit him in his monastery and begin another orgy on the "carnal prayer mat," he is awakened at the critical moment by a dog's barking. He resorts to self-castration.

Like some of Li Yu's stories, *The Carnal Prayer Mat* plays against the idea of the conventional romantic comedy.[5] It is Vesperus's ambition, as expressed to Lone Peak in Chapter 2, to become the most brilliant poet and to marry the world's most beautiful girl. Heaven must somewhere, he reasons, have produced a girl of transcendent beauty to match his own brilliance. The priest, however, rightly sees an endless career of adultery stretching before Vesperus, simply because no one woman's beauty is unquestionably supreme. After his marriage, Vesperus does indeed become obsessed with amorous adventure. He is the most brilliant of poets, he reflects, and Iron Door's daughter is not going to be enough for him all his life. After leaving home, he has the idea of hiding behind the statue of a god in a temple so that he can observe the women who come there to pray for fertility. By this time, he feels he *deserves* the most beautiful women.

His female counterpart is his first mistress, Fragrance, one of Li Yu's strong women, who acts resolutely in her own interest. She herself is a beauty who was married first to a handsome, gifted licentiate in a marriage of the brilliant and beautiful, but her husband proved deficient as a lover, and died soon after the marriage from the sexual demands she made on him. When, as a widow, she is able to choose her own husband, it is this last deficiency she is most concerned to remedy. She chooses Quan, ill-favored, rough-and-ready, uneducated, and not even well off, because of his apparent strength and virility. However, when Vesperus proves equal to Quan as a lover, and handsome and gifted besides, she transfers her affections to him. The staple requirements of the romantic hero, brains and good looks, are desirable, it seems, provided his sexual endowment and stamina are sufficient.

In pursuit of these qualities, she is as determined as Vesperus. Here she is, holding forth to her women friends on the place of sex in life:

> "We behaved improperly in our previous existence and now, having been born female, we must spend all our lives in the women's quarters. Unlike men, we can't go out sight-seeing or visiting friends. Sex is the one diversion we have in our lives. Surely we cannot be forbidden to enjoy that! Still, we were created by Heaven and Earth for marriage, and matched with a husband by our parents; naturally it is right and proper for us to enjoy ourselves with him. Sex with any other men than our husbands would be overstepping the bounds. If our husbands heard of it, it would bring us curses and a beating, and if the news became public, it would cause a scandal. But beatings and scandal aside, if a woman does not have sex, fine, but if she is going to have sex, she should at least see that she suits herself. After all, when you're with your own husband after his day's work is done, you undress, you get into bed together, and you take things from the beginning in an ordered, leisurely way until eventually you reach a degree of ecstasy. What enjoyment is to be got from some furtive, hasty encounter with a lover in which your only concern is to finish up as quickly as possible? What's more, there's never anything to eat when you're famished, and always more than enough when you're well fed, and as with food and drink, you get sick from the continual feast and famine. How ridiculous those women are who go astray! Why didn't they use those same eyes of

theirs to pick out a good husband in the first place as they used to pick out a lover later on? If they're impressed by a mere reputation, let them choose someone cultivated. If it's appearance they want, let them choose someone good-looking. And if it's neither a name nor good looks that attracts them, but the reality of sexual performance, they ought to find someone sturdy and vigorous, who will naturally be able to give them that reality. There's simply no need to abandon one's husband and take a lover."[6]

To the modern reader, these remarks may seem reductive although otherwise unexceptionable, but in traditional China they must have been shocking. It is in this mood of calculated hedonism, modified here only because she is speaking to other women, that she switches her affections from her husband to Vesperus. In her clearheaded boldness she exceeds even Vesperus, the committed philanderer, in whom there is an ever-present pride and conceit.

She is also a more devoted hedonist than he. When her husband returns from a business trip and she can no longer see Vesperus every night, she writes him a letter that virtually forces him to elope with her. She sees herself in a heroic light; having lost her chastity, she resolves to follow the logic of her desires, and to fortify her will, she recalls the cases of women who courageously eloped with their lovers and eventually won public approval. She is a rational heroine, one who reduces everything to a simple set of values based on sexual pleasure.

Li Yu has undermined the romance by bringing to the fore an aspect of life—sexual pleasure—that the genre decorously avoids. The element that is sedulously avoided in this novel is *qing*, the sentimental passion of love, which is, of course, the staple of the romance.[7] The absence of *qing* leads to a concentration on physical qualities and to the exclusion of all feelings other than sexual desire. It prompts Vesperus's endless quest for the ultimate beauty, as well as Fragrance's calculated hedonism and Scent's single-minded seduction of a lover who meets none of her moral and aesthetic values. After Quan's return has put a temporary halt to his affair with Fragrance, Vesperus suffers from "lovesickness," but still hankers after the young women he has seen at the temple.[8] And as soon as Fragrance is pregnant, he looks about for a mistress. What is contrasted here with sexual desire is not *qing*, but asceticism.

In fact, not just *qing* but the whole range of feelings is depreciated. When Scent finds that she has been sold into a brothel, she readily accepts her situation. When Quan has an attack of conscience over selling her, it is less an emotional reaction than a rational response to the sudden revelation of the system of divine retribution. When Vesperus returns home and is told his wife is dead, his emotions are slighted. Even in the dramatic scene in which he discovers that the hanged courtesan is his wife, his reaction is mainly one of realizing the inevitability of retribution.

Li Yu's tendency to slight the emotions and his positive attitude toward sexual love are found in his stories as well as in his novel. The motivation of the heroes of "The Summer Pavilion" or of "The Cloud-scraper," for example, seems not so different from that of Vesperus, although neither hero strays into adultery; the force of *qing*, as senti-mental passion, is weak in both of them. Its presence in Li Yu's other work cannot be denied, especially in some of his plays, but, in general, the notion of *qing* is a thin one—a mere response to attributes, nothing more profound. Much of his comedy, in fact, is based either on the absence of *qing*, or on the danger it presents when taken as an all-consuming passion. This reductionist attitude, diminishing love to a transaction of attributes, runs counter to the main trend in Chinese fiction and drama but accords well with the assumptions of the erotic novel.

Three erotic novels are actually mentioned in *The Carnal Prayer Mat*, first in Chapter 4, when Vesperus brings copies of them home to help in the sexual education of his wife, and again in Chapter 14, when she turns to them for consolation in his absence. What surprises her on the second occasion is their apparent hyperbole in the light of her experience: she is struck by the huge numbers of thrusts they record ("numbered in the thousands and ten of thousands") and by the enor-mous size of the penises they describe.[9] The three novels are *The Lord of Perfect Satisfaction (Ruyi Jun zhuan)*; *The Unofficial History of the Embroidered Couch (Xiuta yeshi)*, by the playwright Lü Tiancheng; and *The Story of the Foolish Woman (Chi pozi zhuan)*.[10] *The Lord of Perfect*

Satisfaction was probably written in the middle of the sixteenth century, and the other two works early in the seventeenth.

Li Yu does not employ the lubricious images found in *The Lord of Perfect Satisfaction* and copied into other novels, including *Jin Ping Mei*; his language is relatively plain, and the imagery that he uses for the sexual organs is ribald rather than erotic. Such sensuality as there is in his writing resides more in the carefully selected detail than in the rhetorical figure.

Nonetheless, *The Carnal Prayer Mat* certainly belongs to the tradition of the erotic novel, in which the most common theme is that of the libertine who gives himself up to sexual excess and is eventually punished for it, a formula that fits both *Jin Ping Mei* and *The Embroidered Couch*. In most erotic novels the retribution, though not derisory, seems inadequate, applied without sufficient literary justification to the libertine's excesses, and no doubt it was in reaction to this inadequacy that Li Yu took the bold step of opening his narrative with the priest Lone Peak. It is a clear sign that Vesperus, after learning his lesson on the "carnal prayer mat," will turn at last to a Buddhist asceticism.

Another area in which Li Yu outdoes his predecessors is the penile implant and castration. One of the universal features of the Chinese erotic novel is its stress on the size of penises. The hero of *The Lord of Perfect Satisfaction* is naturally endowed; others, like Ximen Qing in *Jin Ping Mei* and Master Dongmen in *The Embroidered Couch*, use ointments and the like, but nothing approaches Li Yu's outrageous idea of the implant.

Another typical feature of the erotic novel is its emphasis on the woman's orgasm; her "lewd cries" are unfailingly referred to and sometimes recorded and it is clear from *Prayer Mat* that both men and other women found them supremely erotic.[11] One might also note that the Chinese erotic novel concentrates on the sexually mature and seasoned woman, not on the virgin. Vesperus, like other libertines, is not even interested in virgins. His sexual bouts with the aunt, a widow in her thirties, prove far more satisfactory than those with her nieces.

Other features may be briefly mentioned. Most of the novels, for obvious structural and thematic reasons, build up to a dramatic climax, usually an orgy, before the hero repents or dies. In *The Carnal Prayer Mat*, the climax is an orgy in which Vesperus and the four women take part, playing a game in which the younger women seize the opportunity to humiliate their overbearing aunt. As one has come to expect, Li Yu's orgy outdoes all others.

Although *The Carnal Prayer Mat* is directly related to all three erotic novels, its closest connection is to *The Embroidered Couch*. The latter is a short, well-constructed novel about a libertine, his wife, his young friend, and the friend's widowed mother. After the orgy scenes, it ends in the libertine's Buddhist enlightenment. In *Prayer Mat* the closed circle of people, the tricks they play on one another, and the theme of the sexually inadequate man who is restored to vigor by medicinal means—all these elements are reminiscent of *The Embroidered Couch*.

There are also certain aspects in which *Prayer Mat* diverges from the other erotic novels, by far the greatest being its predominantly comic spirit. Other differences are its relatively plain language, its wealth of discourse, and the prominent place it gives to the retribution theme. The erotic novel's usual competition in sexual stamina between man and woman is here only a minor theme, confined to Vesperus's relations with the aunt. And for all Li Yu's novel ideas, the sexual techniques he describes are unsurprising by the standards of the erotic novel. One technique, fellatio, is hardly mentioned.

Li Yu's most striking addition to the erotic novel is the figure of the Knave, who is based on the gallant thief, a voluptuary, found in "Reformation Hall"[12] (a *Structures* story that contains the germ of the idea of *The Carnal Prayer Mat*.) In *Prayer Mat* his function is to serve as Vesperus's eye, his telescope, and also his mentor; because he is a master burglar, his knowledge of what goes on in people's bedrooms rivals that of a god or devil. He is also a foil to Vesperus; he is educated in practical skills rather than book learning, and he is shrewd and cynical rather than sexually obsessed. A gallant friend, he unstintingly puts his experience at Vesperus's disposal, a gesture for which he is sometimes unjustly rewarded with a measure of suspicion. And he also serves another contrasting function: he represents illicit gain as Vesperus represents illicit sex, avarice and lust being the two main sins of desire.

Adultery, the sexual theft of another man's wife, which violates one of the key Confucian relations, is the crucial sin in Chinese erotic fiction. (The European genre, by contrast, is more concerned with the deflowering of virgins, adultery being the property of the bourgeois novel.)[13] The prologue chapter of *Prayer Mat* mentions retribution for exotic love, but it is left to Lone Peak in Chapter 2 to proffer the cliché "If I don't defile others' wives, my wife won't be defiled by others." Vesperus, the young intellectual, is full of contempt at this: "What you're saying is strictly for the unenlightened."[14] In response, Lone Peak elaborates upon the cliché. Even your adulterous thoughts may be avenged by your wife, for how do you know that her thoughts are not on someone else, too, as you sleep together? But that would be just a minor kind of retribution. If you actually commit adultery, will the gods not observe, will the Creator let your wife remain chaste? According to the critique at the end of Chapter 19, this is the book's "basic intent."[15]

The retribution, which may occur during this life or after it, follows conventions of manipulated coincidence as glaring as those of the romance. Li Yu outdoes all others in the elaborate working out of the this-worldly variety of retribution. As I have mentioned, Quan's revenge for Vesperus's cuckoldry is to cuckold Vesperus, and the husbands of the young women whom Vesperus has seduced also take an unwitting revenge on him by sleeping with Scent. Vesperus's orgies with their wives are echoed by theirs with Scent. Vesperus seeks to restore his exhausted vitality with the new courtesan the wives have told him of—they have learned of her from their husbands—and thus, for his renewed adulteries, he needs the help of the one woman who cannot give it: his own wife. Of such exquisite ironies is Li Yu's retribution made.

After the shock of his wife's death, Vesperus is finally convinced of the retributive principle at which he had originally scoffed. He realizes that retribution is paid out with interest, for whereas he has slept with five or six women, dozens of men have slept with his wife, and whereas Quan's wife is now his concubine, his own wife has become a prostitute. Seeing the force of this-worldly retribution, he hastens to seek Lone Peak's intercession against its other-worldly counterpart.

The priest Lone Peak appears in Chapter 2 before the erotic adventures begin, and then again in Chapter 20, this time to intercede for the now repentant Vesperus. But despite the priest's presence, Buddhism is not of paramount importance in the novel, whose key notion of this-worldly and other-worldly retribution is common to several systems of belief. Lone Peak refers to "the Lord of Heaven who creates all things," to the "supernatural powers," and also to the "Principle of Nature," which is distinctly Confucian, at least in origin.[16] Lone Peak fills two essential, general functions in the novel: he represents an ascetic ideal, and he has the power to intercede for sinners.

The retribution theme, with or without a Buddhist framework, has its own strict laws in Chinese literature. Li Yu's innovation lies in the virtuosity with which he handles it, rather than in any inversion or extension. But at the same time he has a series of remarks in epilogues and critiques that underline the inflexibility of the retribution plot. For example, in the critique at the end of Chapter 17, the longest of the chapters, the commentator, who is probably Li Yu himself, complains that the description of the orgy has gone too far, and then answers his own criticism as follows: "Only the extraordinary debauchery of this chapter could invoke the extraordinary retribution of the next. Allowing them to indulge themselves is done precisely in order to make things worse for them. When you read as far as the extraordinary debauchery that Scent excels in, thereby repaying the debts incurred by her husband, you will realize that the previous few chapters were by no means too extreme in their descriptions."[17] The critique to Chapter 18 takes the argument further: Vesperus's "debauchery and wickedness" have reached their peak: "If one had made his wife stop at adultery and not become a prostitute, it would not have been enough to gladden the reader's heart. Even if she had become a prostitute, and entertained other customers but not Xiangyun's and her sisters' husbands, that would not have been enough either."[18] Li Yu is pointing not only to the virtuosity with which he manipulates the retribution theme, but also to the theme's conventionality and restrictiveness. In the opening argument, Vesperus has described the idea of retribution for adultery as a cliché not worthy of belief by educated people. His mention of a cliché is not merely in character; it is also meant to indicate Li Yu's own mocking ambivalence toward the convention.

What the retribution theme does is sanction the use of correspondences, in which Li Yu is a virtuoso, as may be seen from his stories. Some of the correspondences have been pointed out already. Vesperus's orgy with the wives is paralleled by Scent's with their husbands. Vesperus leaves home to join the orgy, as does Scent. (The husbands invite her to visit their lodgings for a few days.) But the

results are different: Scent restores the husbands' health with her techniques, while the wives drain Vesperus's vitality. Similarly, there are
parallels in plenty between Fragrance and Scent. Both become pregnant by their lovers, and both propose elopement, but Scent has a
miscarriage while Fragrance gives birth to twin daughters. Other correspondences can be picked out almost at random. In Chapter 20
Vesperus kowtows 120 times before the priest, and it was for just 120
taels that he had bought Fragrance from her husband. The kowtows
correspond also to those he made in the temple to attract the attention
of the young women and their aunt. After Vesperus leaves, Fragrance
takes up with a lover, receiving him every night for ten or more nights
before eloping; earlier she had received Vesperus for ten or more nights
while her husband was away.

General contrasts are set up, too, in Li Yu's characteristic way.
There is the contrast between the Confucian puritan and the "enlightened man" with regard to the function of sex,[19] and also the rather
different contrast between the puritan and the libertine, as represented
by Mr. Iron Door and Vesperus, respectively. Scent herself, under her
father's influence, begins as a puritan, and then, under her husband's
tutelage, turns into a libertine. A further set of terms is represented
by Fragrance's husband, as I have mentioned. These are only a sample
of the contrasts built into *Prayer Mat*, whose novel ideas are asserted
in correspondences and contrasts as well as in direct discourse.

Discourse takes several forms in *The Carnal Prayer Mat*. One is comment by the narrator-author—there is no pretense that any distance
remains between author and narrator—in prologue, digression, explanation, and chapter epilogue; another is a character's monologue or
mental soliloquy, or a dialogue or debate between two characters; yet
another consists of quoted documents, such as the erotic album or
playing cards or the notes Vesperus takes on the women he has observed. I do not include the critiques, even though I believe that they
were written by Li Yu, because they are on a different plane from the
text itself. In these various forms, discourse dominates the novel at
least as much as, and probably more than, it dominates Li Yu's stories;
as in the stories, it exemplifies the importance of "talk" in Li Yu's
work.

There is a prodigious amount of it. The genre of the erotic novel tends toward discursiveness anyway, but no other novel can approach the sheer volume of discourse in *Prayer Mat*. It even forms the subject of one critique:

> Fiction writers always confine themselves to narrative and do not write discourse *[yilun]*. Or, if they do write discourse, they develop a piece to serve as prologue before the narration of the story, but then, once into the opening, they quickly wind it up, evidently fearing a hopeless disorder. How can they write of leisurely conversation when their brushes are poised to attack? Only the writer of this book is able to keep calm amidst the panic and cool amidst the heat. In the middle of every tense passage of narrative, he will insert a piece of leisurely discourse, posing and answering his questions in an orderly way, so that the reader, far from finding it a nuisance, is loath to see it end. When the author has finished his discussion, and resumes his narration of the previous events, one observes that his writing dovetails perfectly with what has gone before. A true master of the art! Ever since he invented this mode, he has been the only writer capable of practicing it. Those who imitate his technique merely earn the reader's boredom. [20]

This comment appears at the end of Chapter 5, but it fits several other chapters even better, especially those in which disquisitions interrupt accounts of lovemaking.

Although this remark speaks of prologues as commonplace, Li Yu's own prologue to *Prayer Mat*, which forms the whole first chapter, is far from routine; in fact, it is unparalleled in the Chinese novel. As a discursive prologue on the function and management of sex, it is longer than any of the story prologues. The views expressed in it, although more obviously comical and satirical than those in *Casual Expressions*, are recognizably the same. If the other erotic novels have a prologue at all, it is a dire warning against lust and its consequences, but Li Yu's prologue first offers his commonsense views on sexual enjoyment and then explains why he has written a libertine book instead of a didactic one:

Gentle reader, there is something of which you are evidently unaware. Any successful method of changing the popular mores must resemble the way Yu the Great controlled the floods: if one goes along with the popular mores in order to channel them into a profitable direction, one gets a hearing. In these times, people are reluctant to listen to lectures on the canonical texts, but they love to read fiction. Not all fiction, however, for they are sick of exemplary themes and prefer obscenity and fantasy. Truly, today's morals have sunk to new depths, and anyone with a concern for public morality will want to retrieve the situation. But if you write a didactic work exhorting people to virtue, not only will you get no one to buy it; even if you were to print it and bind it and distribute it free with a complimentary card, the way benefactors bestow Buddhist scriptures on the public, people would tear the book apart for use in covering their wine pots or rolling their tobacco, and refuse to bestow a single glance upon its contents. A far better solution is to captivate readers with erotic material and wait until some moment of absorbing interest before suddenly dropping in an admonitory remark or two to make them grow fearful and sigh: "Since sexual pleasure can be so delightful, surely we ought to reserve our pleasure-loving bodies for long-term enjoyment instead of letting them turn into 'ghosts beneath the peony blossoms,' sacrificing the reality of pleasure for its mere name?" One then waits until the point at which retribution is made manifest and gently slips in a hortatory word or two designed to provoke the sudden revelation: "Since adultery is always repaid like this, surely we ought to reserve our wives and concubines for our own enjoyment instead of trying to 'shoot a sparrow with the priceless pearl,' repaying worthless loans with real money?" Having reached this conclusion, readers will no longer go astray, and if they don't go astray, they will naturally cherish their wives, who will in turn respect them. The moral education of the Southern Zhou and Southern Zhao songs is really nothing more than this: the method of "fitting the action to the case and the treatment to the man." It is a practice that is

incumbent not only upon fiction writers; indeed, some of
the sages were the first to employ it, in their classical texts.
If you doubt me, look at how Mencius in Warring States
times addressed King Xuan of Qi on the subject of Royal
Government.[21]

This is Li Yu's tongue-in-cheek transition from the proper enjoyment
of sex to the subject of his novel. After casuistically citing Mencius
as an exemplar of his method, he expresses the hope that the reader
will look upon his novel as a classic or history rather than as fiction:

> If was from this technique that the author of this book drew
> inspiration. If only the entire reading public would buy and
> read it as a classic or history rather than as fiction! Its
> passages of address to the reader are all either admonitory
> or hortatory; you should pay close attention to their un-
> derlying purpose. Its descriptions of copulation, of the plea-
> sures of the bedchamber, do indeed come close to indecency,
> but they are all designed to lure people into reading on
> until they reach the denouement, at which point they will
> understand the meaning of retribution and be on their guard.
> Without these passages, the book would be nothing but an
> olive which, for all its aftertaste, would be useless if it were
> too sour for anyone to eat. My passages of sexual description
> should be looked upon as the date wrapped around the olive
> that induces people to keep on eating until they reach the
> aftertaste. Please pardon the tedium of this opening; the
> story proper will begin in the next chapter.[22]

Notice the emphasis on people's buying his book. The critique to the
chapter reinforces the point:

> This book sounds extremely enticing. I am sure that when
> it is finished, the entire reading public will buy and read
> it. The only people who may not do so are the puritans.
> The genuine puritans will; only a species of false puritan,
> the kind who try to deceive people with their uprightness,
> will not dare. On the other hand, someone has suggested
> that, although the false puritans won't dare buy it them-
> selves, they just might get someone else to buy it for them,

and although they won't dare read it openly, they just might do so on the sly.[23]

The prologue is a commonsense discussion of sex prefaced to a libertine novel which, in accordance with the requirements of the genre, shows a chain of adulteries culminating in a disaster that leads to penitence. There are three principal attitudes toward sex in the book: Li Yu's own view of sex within the family as pleasure and tonic; Vesperus's initial view of sex with beautiful women as the supreme value; and Lone Peak's severe asceticism. The last two are opposites, and we find most of the characters, all but Mr. Iron Door and the Knave, holding to one or the other, or moving from one to the other. But over both of these dramatically posed alternatives there presides Li Yu's own down-to-earth, unromantic, sensible acceptance of sex.

As I have mentioned, discourse dominates the novel. Chapter 1, the prologue, is all discourse; Chapter 2 offers the debate between Vesperus and the priest; Chapter 3 is dominated by the sexual instruction Vesperus gives his new wife; Chapters 4 and 6 contain the Knave's instruction of Vesperus; Chapter 7 is mainly given over to Vesperus's reflections and the Taoist adept's explanation of his techniques; Chapter 9 is devoted to Fragrance's philosophy; and Chapters 10, 12, 14, 17, and 18 are all at least partly occupied with the explanation of sexual procedures and techniques.

Some of the most notable explanations come right in the middle of scenes of copulation. The X-rated movie stops, as it were, while Li Yu, the lecturer, explains the intricacies of some facet—and then starts rolling again. The practice suits his essayistic bent, but it is also, obviously, intended to tease and interest the reader. For example, the digression on pillows in Chapter 10, in the middle of Vesperus's copulation with Fragrance, is a long disquisition, in question-and-answer form, about the correct number of pillows and their placement, which proves to depend on the shape of the lovers' anatomy. It ends with a trademark Li Yu statement: "There are people who are familiar with the general principle, but no one has hitherto hit on this formula."[24] Again, in Chapter 12, in the middle of a bout with Xiangyun, Vesperus discourses on the remarkable properties of his penis. In Chapter 14, as Quan and Scent make love, their congress is interrupted by the narrator's commentary on Quan's foreplay. And in Chapter 17, Vesperus's lovemaking with the aunt is interrupted by a lengthy disquisition from the narrator on the superior, practical (as distinct from aesthetic) charms of plump women and by a digression from the aunt on erotic stimuli (pictures, books, orgasmic cries).

Much other information is given as well. Notable examples are the Knave's comments on women and sex in Chapter 4; his analysis in Chapter 6 of the problems of seducing rich men's and poor men's wives, respectively, and of the relative weight to be assigned to looks-and-talent as against sexual prowess; the Taoist adept's discussion in Chapter 7 of the means of increasing penile size and stamina; Fragrance's discourse in Chapter 9 on how to choose a husband; the disquisition on pillows in Chapter 10; Fragrance's reflections on adultery and elopement in Chapter 11; the explanation of Xiangyun's natural scent in Chapter 12 (in *Casual Expressions*, very beautiful women are described as exuding their own scent);[25] the satirical account of the erotic novel in Chapters 14 and 17 that I have mentioned; the account of the courtesan's "three superlative skills" in Chapter 18;[26] and Vesperus's reflections in Chapter 20 on the methods open to priests for the relief of sexual tension—the novel has many offhand satirical remarks—and on the general curse of sexual desire.

The discourse is set out analytically, whether it comes from the narrator's mouth or from the mouths or minds of the characters. There are countless lists serving Li Yu's expository purposes: two kinds of this, three kinds of that, five kinds of the other. Another feature is the use of discursive imagery, often with a comic tone. There are also narrative images, almost always used for a comic purpose. The fields from which the images are drawn are those of the examination system, education, medicine, and so forth.[27] In Chapter 7, to explain his dislike of sex with virgins, Vesperus uses the terminology of literary structure: "To practice the real thing, one must wait for a woman in her twenties, who will have a knowledge of 'opening, development, variation, and conclusion.' As in writing an essay, each section has its own technique, each 'leg' its own method of parallelism. A child just beginning to write would never be capable of it."[28] In Chapter 8, when Vesperus's young servant, learning that his master is about to embark on a career of adultery, begs for his share of the spoils, Vesperus replies: "A well-fed general does not starve his soldiers." In Chapter 10, when Vesperus is spurred by Scent's neighbor into renewed sexual effort, he is "like a dozing pupil at school who, upon being beaten by the teacher, redoubles his efforts." In Chapter 14, as Scent, her sexual desires now thoroughly cultivated, is suddenly deprived of her husband, she is "like a drunkard who has sworn off wine, a gourmet who has given up meat." In Chapter 15, when Xiangyun boasts to her cousins about her affair with Vesperus, they gaze at her "like candidates who have just failed the examination coming upon a newly successful one." When she agrees to share him with them, they set to work interrogating her "like youths who have yet to take the Boys' Examination buttonholing a friend as he leaves the examination hall and asking him about the questions." In Chapter 16, Vesperus, who has been hiding naked in a trunk used for storing scrolls, is described as a "live and kicking erotic scroll." When the aunt orders the trunk, with Vesperus still inside it, removed to her quarters, the three young women watch it go "like widows in mourning taking leave of the coffin."[29]

The formal innovations of *Prayer Mat* may be regarded as extensions of features found in the stories. The stories had narrowed, and in some cases closed, the gap between narrator and author by giving the former a distinct authorial persona. In the novel, he is regularly referred to as "the author" or "the author of this book," a usage that is also occasionally found in the stories. In Chapters 13 and 18, when characters assume new names, we are told that "the author of the novel" will continue to use their real names, to avoid confusion.[30] The rhetorical devices used by the author-narrator are similar to those in the stories and even, in some cases, to those in Li Yu's essays. In addition, some of the author-narrator's concerns match those of the essays.

The old, implicit duality of narrator and author has been replaced by an explicit duality of author-narrator and critic. I have mentioned the critiques in *Prayer Mat* that follow every chapter but one. They are examples of self-criticism, an interesting development in the history of fiction in which the author, usually under a separate pseudonym, supplies the commentary to his own work. Critiques and notes are found in the editions of Li Yu's stories, too; some of them are by Du Jun, but others must certainly be by Li himself. In *Prayer Mat* I believe that Li Yu wrote all, or almost all, of the commentary himself. The evidence lies in the defensive tone it adopts toward complaints, real and anticipated; in its insider's knowledge of the novel; in its use of some of Li Yu's favorite verbal gambits; and in its astringency, which is remote from the bland appreciation we find in his friends' comments on his other work.

The critiques make points that it would be difficult for Li Yu to make otherwise, pointing to correspondences and contrasts the reader might have missed and hinting at correspondences and contrasts to come. They also sometimes make shrewd comments on narrative method, such as the author's use of discourse and discursive imagery in Chapter 5. The critique attached to Chapter 16 playfully points out that Vesperus had originally expected that an affair with the aunt would lead to one with her nieces. Events turned out differently, for his affair with Xiangyun led him to the other girls and then, inadvertently, to their aunt. "Who would ever have thought," wonders the critique, "that the author's intention would turn out to be the same as the Creator's?" The aunt, who was to have been the entrée to the others, turns out to be the dessert. It is "the height of novelty, the acme of the fantastical."[31] The critique to Chapter 8 makes several points: that all fiction is fable, and in particular, that the implant of the dog's member is to be taken allegorically; that authors of admonitory fiction like *The Carnal Prayer Mat* run the risk of being considered promoters of the very practices they condemn; and, finally, that the reason the Knave at first mistook Fragrance for a virtuous woman—a point only the astute reader will have noticed—is that she was nearsighted and did not see him clearly enough to flirt with him.

The critiques may add an extra level of privileged commentary to the novel, but they cannot be taken at face value any more than the comments of the author-narrator. In fact, there is a mocking interplay between the two voices that continues to the end of the novel. In his final epilogue the author-narrator blames the plethora of sinners on the twin desires for wealth and women, the invention of which he attributes to "the sage who separated Heaven from Earth": "I shall now sum up the case against the sage with a quotation from the *Four Books*: Was it not the sage himself who invented burial images?"[32] He is adapting Mencius's quotation of a remark by Confucius, who had deplored the use of burial images in human form because he thought they encouraged human sacrifice. Thus, "invented burial images" means "initiated the evil," in this case, the evil desire for wealth and sex, which is in direct contradiction to the sense of the prologue chapter, as the author of the critique promptly points out: "At the beginning of the book, he was grateful to the sage; now, at its close, he blames him. The sage cannot feel either pleased or vexed about it. This truly is a book that mocks everything! Let me spring to the sage's defense with another quotation from the *Four Books*: 'Those who understand me will do so through *The Carnal Prayer Mat*; those who condemn me will also do so because of *The Carnal Prayer Mat*.' "[33] Here he is adapting another Mencian quotation of a remark by Confucius, who was responding to anticipated criticism of his compilation of *The Spring and Autumn Annals*.[34] The *Annals*, a history into which a deep moral meaning is to be read, is sometimes enlisted by fiction writers in order to dignify their humble craft. Li Yu thus ends his book with a double quip.

The critiques also point self-consciously to the novelties in *The Carnal Prayer Mat*'s form: the discursive prologue chapter; the introduction of Lone Peak in Chapter 2, after which he disappears until the end of the book; its intricate system of correspondences and contrasts; and the extent of its discursive element.

If the novel's discursiveness suggests Li Yu's essays, there are other features that suggest the influence of his play writing. Take, for example, its disregard of the traditional chapter. In fiction the chapter was a unit that took care not to be complete; it always made at least a pretense of spilling over into the succeeding chapter. A scene in a play was precisely the opposite; it sought to be a rounded episode in the total movement of the work. But most of this novel's chapters are complete and rounded, like the scenes of a play. At the beginning of Chapter 9, the narrative breaks away and turns to Fragrance; at the beginning of Chapter 13 to Quan; and at the beginning of Chapter 14 to Scent. Chapter 10 even ends anticlimactically, with a discussion of nicknames. When the action does spill over from one chapter to the next, as from Chapters 6 to 7, the author makes a novel confession: even he is not sure of the outcome. The breaks are announced in the epilogue comments of the chapter; at the end of Chapter 2 we are told that Lone Peak will not reappear until Chapter 20, and at the end of Chapter 14 that Scent will reappear only in Chapter 18. The epilogue of Chapter 12 announces that Vesperus will be dropped for two chapters: "From Chapter 2 up to this point, enough has been said about Vesperus's infatuation with sex. Let us now pause for a moment and tell of something else in the next chapter. It will be a couple of scenes, at least, before the male lead comes on stage again."[35] In this and other respects Li Yu was affected by, and indeed was consciously affecting, the techniques of the drama.

Seven. Virtuoso of Fine Stitching

Li Yu's drama, for its part, is related to fiction in an obvious sense—half of his plays are drawn from his own stories—and also in a subtler one; it exploits what might be called the "narrative scene" of the Southern drama, in which a character, major or minor, recounts, explains, or reflects upon the action. *Ideal Love-matches* has narrative scenes featuring Miss Yang (Scene 3), Miss Lin (Scene 4), the phony priest (Scenes 6 and 17), and the priest's maid (Scene 21); in *You Can't Do Anything about Fate*, three scenes (16, 20, 23) are devoted, in whole or in part, to narration by servants; and in *Woman in Pursuit of Man*, a go-between narrates in Scene 28 and a steward in Scenes 6 and 30, while in Scene 15 a servant reviews the kidnapping plot and its effects. The commentator remarks of this last scene that the servant's "exposition" is essential to the play and must on no account be omitted.[1] A narrative component, signaled by expressions such as *ting wo dao lai*, "let me tell you about it," occurs frequently in other scenes as well, in both speech and song.

Narratorial comment, the most prominent feature of Li Yu's fiction, is also delegated to the characters in his plays. In *Sole Mates* it is the hero who tells us, as the narrator has done in the corresponding story, that stage performance magnifies both beauty and ugliness in an actress, just as it is the heroine's mother who recounts to her daughter her three-point formula for success as a courtesan. Scene 13, which consists entirely of discussion between the mother and her daughter's rich suitor, throws a satirical light on the acting profession, much as the narrator has done in his prologue. Reflexive comment, that is, comment on the literary work itself, is also sometimes put into the characters' mouths. It is the *chou* clown in Scene 2 of *You Can't Do*

Anything about Fate who comments on the novelty of his (a clown's) serving as the male lead, and Miss Wu, the clown's third wife, who, in Scene 23, urges "all the pretty and talented women in the audience" to bear their plight with fortitude—part of the narrator's epilogue speech as translated earlier in Chapter 5.[2] In these and other plays, comment is dramatized as dialogue, debate, and soliloquy.

Even in the plays based on Li's stories, much of the most significant and entertaining business is new. In *Sole Mates* the tension of the drama quiz and the schoolroom fight, the savage satire of the local officials' attempts to profit from the heroine's suicide, and the entire pastoral idyll of the rustic wedding have all been added, while the fisherman of the story has been developed into a major figure in the play and the key to one of its themes.

Certain kinds of material, the supernatural for example, are regularly added in the play version of a story. Gods and spirits cause people to fall in love, help them triumph in the examinations, and even provide them with a metamorphosis if necessary; but even though the supernatural, in contrast to the frequent naturalism of most of Li Yu's fiction, is an accepted agent of causation in his plays, it is still not to be taken at face value. In *Woman in Pursuit of Man*, the gods award Lü first place in the examinations on account of his sexual probity, and Du Jun in his preface disingenuously claims that this message constitutes the play's main intent.[3] Lü purports to base his conduct on the *Taishang ganying pian*, a text that evaluates moral and immoral acts and allots appropriate rewards and punishments, but his probity is far removed from the puritanism the text demands.[4] It would be truer to say that he exemplifies Li Yu's commonsense notion of the proper role of sex in life; little difference is to be seen between his morality and that propounded in the prologue to *The Carnal Prayer Mat*. Li Yu is making fun of the morality books by substituting his own commonsense, but still radical, sexual morality for their puritanism.

The other main addition in Li Yu's plays consists of military or political material. Nine of his ten plays contain rebellions or wars, while the tenth, *Women in Love*, presents a diplomatic mission to the Ryukyus. The plays' treatment of the rebellions is not perfunctory, but neither is it graphic. Their rebels are stylized base characters who, despite some brutal actions, contribute mainly to the comedy. A military *(wu)* dimension, affording an opportunity for gross humor and vivid spectacle, seems almost to have been required of the drama as Li Yu practiced it.

As we might expect, some, if not all, of his plays depend on the inversion of social stereotypes or common assumptions. In *Women in Love,* a series of stereotypes about women are upended, including the belief in feminine inconstancy. As Miss Cao sings in Scene 27:

> In "romantic passion,"
> It is we women in the end who take all the laurels;
> I mock those faithless males . . .[5]

Another is the stereotype of woman's proper role. Miss Cao's father, the kind of puritanical paterfamilias so common in Li Yu's work, considers poetry an improper activity for his daughter, but he "can't very well stop her from doing what she enjoys" so long as she does not "show off her talent"; "her poems are only for her own amusement and are not to be shown to others." Miss Cao assents, but sings in a prophetic aside: "What if I met a gifted woman friend to write poems with?"[6]

The play's main innovation is the passion between the two women, beside which the love between Miss Cui and her husband is downplayed; even the husband's wedding to Miss Cao is presented to us only through Miss Cui's and her maid's reactions. Not until the end of the play, when he joins both women in a *ménage à trois,* do we meet the theme of wedded bliss, and in the meantime the women's love for each other has been insisted on. In Scene 10 Miss Cui argues for the husband-and-wife relationship as the closest of bonds, and then, dressed in her husband's clothes, she says to Miss Cao:

> "I'm not really a man, but now, dressed in a man's clothes,
> and gazing on your sweet, delicate face, I feel taken by a
> wild fancy.
> *(sings)* Beloved, my heart aches in vain for you!
> Not only am I in a wild mood, I sense that your love has
> been slightly stirred, too."[7]

Li Yu says in his drama treatise that the plot of a play must have its *zhunao,* or governing element, by which he appears to mean some crucial conjuncture that produces more or less naturally the series of events that make up the play.[8] In *Women in Love* the governing element is, first, the gods' decision that Miss Cao is the perfect wife for Fan, who is already happily married to Miss Cui, and, second, their conviction that the only way to effect a marriage is to have Miss Cui fall in love with Miss Cao. But this is just a charming bit of fantasy that enables a lesbian passion to be treated in a romantic comedy. The real governing element in most of Li Yu's plays is the kind of conceptual paradox or inversion that I have described. In this play, the point is even made by the characters themselves. Sakyamuni, in Scene 5, notes that it is unheard of for wives to feel an affinity for each other, and in Scene 10 Miss Cui remarks on the novelty of the "wedding" of two women; "a false hero and a true heroine are acting out a new play."[9] The audacious social idea is what marks Li Yu's plays, rather than the mechanical notion of the governing element as he describes it. His process of composition must have begun with a daring idea, which he then explored in all its delicious improbability, brushing aside the initial conjuncture. In this play, the women fall in love because of karmic destiny. The Buddhist deities, in discussing Fan and Miss Cao in Scene 5, are not deciding the pair's future, for when the Taoist god arrives his plans are already set; the scene exists merely to allow the deities to comment on the action. We learn from it that the women will fall in love and suffer separation and other vicissitudes, but that they will end up as wives to the same man. This knowledge is given to us early, so that the play can concentrate on the minutiae of event and feeling in their novel relationship.

Different social paradoxes sustain *There's Nothing You Can Do about Fate* and *Woman in Pursuit of Man*, both of which are derived from stories by Li Yu that I have discussed in Chapter 5.[10] It is characteristic of the dramatic versions that the main paradox is echoed on various levels. *Woman in Pursuit of Man* inverts conventional courtship: three women compete viciously for the most handsome and brilliant young man of the time, while, on a lower level, three veteran prostitutes seek the *cachet* of a liaison with the hero. (The scene, Scene 3, is entitled Whoring in Reverse.) Other paradox-centered plays are *The Ingenious Finale*, which, instead of the usual courtship theme, is concerned with the momentous choice, through adoption, of one's own parents; *Be Careful about Love*, which attacks the assumptions of the romantic comedy by demonstrating that the cautious, prudish man makes the better lover; *Sole Mates,* in which drama or make-believe proves to be the medium of truth; and *Ideal Love-matches,* in which two famous artists marry the forgers of their paintings. In each case the main inversion is accompanied by a variety of minor inversions. In *The Ingenious Finale,* for example, the hero arranges a marriage between the father and mother he has adopted, only to find that they are his true parents, after all.

Much of Li Yu's fiction and drama is concerned with the proper role of sexual love. He has no consistent stance toward the subject, but toys endlessly with its various polarities—love and lust, puritanism and libertinism, asceticism and sensuality. His fiction, in comparison with his drama, shows the more down-to-earth attitude; little is said in it of *qing,* love as sentimental passion, and much of love as physical attraction. In the plays, in keeping with the genre, there is a stronger emphasis on *qing,* which, however, still lacks the transcendent power it acquires in the work of certain other playwrights.[11]

A didactic distinction between love and lust is given by Miss Cao to her maid in *Women in Love.* The maid, a comic character, is trying to jolt her mistress out of her depression: "Mistress Fan is a woman, and she has everything you have and nothing you haven't." To which Miss Cao replies that the maid does not understand the distinction between the sentiment of love and sexual desire: "Stupid girl, you know only the cause of lovesickness; you don't grasp the difference between love and lust. From the viewpoint of the heart it is love, but from the viewpoint of the bedchamber it is lust. Only if you set your mind on the illicit passion of the bedchamber will you suffer from lovesickness, and even if you die of it, you'll be no romantic lover, just a lustful ghost. In all history, only Du Liniang is entitled to speak of love."[12] Liniang is the heroine of *The Peony Pavilion,* one of the great romantic comedies of Chinese drama, in which she dies for love without ever having seen the ideal lover she has in her mind.[13] Miss Cao fully expects, after she has died of love, that Miss Cui will follow her example, and so she wants to get this life over with in order to be united with her lover in the next. The maid continues to challenge her:

Maid: Du Liniang may never have set eyes on her lover, but at least she had a romantic dream. You've not had any dreams, Mistress. How do you account for that?

Cao: If you want to talk of dreams, I've enjoyed more than Liniang ever had. I've dreamt of her every night since we parted, she in her scholar's cap and gown, exactly as on the day we took out vows.

(sings) In my dreams I walk beside her,
Hand clasping hand,
Her scholar's cap still on her head,
And we two in love like any husband and wife,
Though she is more romantic than any man.
Liniang's sweet dream may be hard to repeat,
But it is not so loving as mine, night after night.
Even by day I see her standing before me, as in an illusion.[14]

Miss Cao is a lovestruck girl whose impractical, idealistic love is contrasted with the down-to-earth passion of Miss Cui, the play's mastermind.

In *Sole Mates* the hero, Tan, is described in the prologue scene as a romantic (*qingzhong*), the same term he uses of himself when he falls desperately in love with the young actress.[15] He has been on a quest for the ideal beauty and, having seen this girl, he wrestles with the temptation to renounce his studies for her sake. It is hard, he says, to decide between the sage and the madman, the latter representing an indulgence in the emotions, but by Scene 9 he has made his choice and thrown away all hopes of a career. The girl is a different case. She may admire him as the "greatest romantic in history,"[16] but her reasoning is practical; marriage to him represents her best chance to live an honorable life. Having made her decision, she is prepared to die for it, but she is never a romantic in the same sense as he.

In *The Jade Clasp* another grand passion is presented, between the emperor and Liu Qianqian. Love is defined by both of them, and there is close agreement between their definitions. In Scene 4, before even meeting the emperor, Miss Liu asserts that lovers must first fall in love and then vow to spend the rest of their lives together. What if the man goes back on his word, she is asked. But Miss Liu believes that love and lust vary inversely and that one can therefore choose the man likely to be true, a similar notion to the courtesan Wang's idea of "hot" and "cool" lovers in *Be Careful about Love*. In Scene 13 the emperor describes true love as different from sexual love; one falls in love through admiration of the other's good looks and talent, but from that point on, love is unalterable.

The difference between love and lust often corresponds to the difference between the hero and heroine on the one hand and the base characters *(chou* and *jing)* on the other, between whom there is a vast disparity in looks and intelligence. The base characters may be benign comic creations who echo on the earthy level the high-flown passions of the major characters; examples are the servant in *Be Careful about Love* and Miss Cui's gross, comic maid in *Women in Love*. Or they may be antagonists of the major characters, aspiring to make love to *them;* for example, in *The Mistake with the Kite,* the hero and heroine are paralleled by her half-sister and the son of his guardian, both of whom are unprepossessing, ill-educated, frivolous, and rapacious. The latter pair help to define the sensibilities of the former, as well as to provide comedy.

The hero of *The Kite,* Han, and his counterpart, Qi, set out their attitudes toward love and sex in Scenes 2 and 3, respectively, but not in a simple contrast between puritanism and license. Han is neither puritan nor libertine, neither immune to beauty nor averse to sex; instead he has an idealistic, even fastidious attitude toward women. He represents one aspect of *qing,* while Qi represents lust. Their attitudes are put to the test by a bevy of prostitutes who call on them with New Year's greetings. Qi is excited, but Han simply turns his back on them, and is later criticized for doing so:

> *Qi:* Why be so puritanical? When those girls were here, why didn't you act like a romantic fellow and have a word with them, and crack a joke or two, instead of standing there motionless, not saying a word and even turning your back on them, as if you were shy? You're just too prudish for words!
>
> *Han:* I'm not really so prudish. It was just the sight of those ugly women that made me react like that despite myself.
>
> *Qi:* What do you mean? They were enchanting! Easy on the eye!

> *Han (amused, sings):*   Amid the stench of their pow-
>   der and rouge,
>   How can one think of love?[17]

His criteria are at least partly aesthetic, for his ideal woman has natural beauty, charm, talent—and is a capable poet besides. At the same time, even if his attitudes are in general held up to us for approval, he is still on occasion subjected to a certain mockery that issues from, of all people, Qi. In Scene 6, when Qi complains of his "brother's" studiousness, he does so by championing the inventive genius of the sage-kings as against the Confucian paragons and philosophers. The sages and inventors created things for people's enjoyment, unlike the moral philosophers with their dull writings, ninety percent of which should be discarded. The claim overstates even Li Yu's most extreme views, but it is hard not to see in it a little oblique mockery of Han, as representing the Confucian tradition of moral learning, along with a hint of self-mockery.[18]

In Scene 9, reading the poem that Shujuan, the heroine, has written on the kite, Han fancies he sees an erotic meaning in it and imagines the poet to be a natural beauty. He longs to make love to her, and readily falls in with his servant's suggestion that he write his own love poem on another kite and bring it down in the girl's garden. Alas, the kite gets into the wrong hands, and it is Aijuan, the ugly half-sister, who obtains it and tries to seduce him in her direct, coarse way. Escaping from her clutches, Han appeals to Heaven for a romantic dream with which to banish the memory of her attempted seduction, but Heaven answers him only with a nightmare reprise of it:

> *Aijuan:* The other evening you panicked for no reason at all, and we weren't able to fulfull our desires. Tonight I've come specially to join you.
> *Nurse:* Master Qi [Han has been using Qi's name], tonight you can just gobble up this cookie right in front of your mouth.
> *(sings)*   How happy you must feel!
>   How happy you must feel!
>   That you are free to make friends with her,
>   Unburdened now by fear.
> *Han (aside):* From what she says, it's elopement she

is proposing, not just an affair like the other day. This will never do!

Nurse: Master Qi, let's be honest with ourself, shall we? You mustn't miss out on a business opportunity that's landed right on your doorstep.

Han: I'm Han, not Qi. Qi's room is over there. Why don't you go and get him?

Nurse: We're like pawnbrokers, who go according to whoever holds the pawn ticket; we're not concerned with people's real identities. That was your writing on the kite, so you're the one we've come for, whether you're Qi or Han.

Han (aside): The other day the nurse came to my rescue, but now even she is abetting the tyrant in her atrocities. What am I going to do?

Aijuan: Last time I was on my own and couldn't hold you, but now I have someone here to help me. If we have to, we'll carry you to the bed.

(They lay hold of him.)

Han (shouting): A woman raping a man—it's never happened before in history! Police! Neighbors! Help! Help!

(Enter watchmen, singing as they make their rounds.)

Watchmen: There's someone shouting inside the house. We'd better go and see what it is. *(They enter the house.)* A fine thing you're up to, at midnight and all!

Han: The woman is raping the man!

Aijuan: The man is raping the woman!

Watchmen: A man can rape a woman, but hardly the other way around. Let's chain him up and take him before His Honor.[19]

If love and lust are emotions, the terms *fengliu* (free-spirited, romantic, and even libertine) and *daoxue* (puritanical, prudish) signify attitudes toward life and particularly toward sex. Puritanical fathers are satirized figures, but Li Yu's heroes are neither *daoxue* nor *fengliu*. In *Be Careful about Love*, the preface quotes Li Yu as saying that the subject of his play "falls between *fengliu* and *daoxue*,"[20] and in fact the hero, Hua, is a mixture of both qualities who proves to be the ideal lover. His attitude is the cautious, modest acceptance of sex that Li Yu favors in his writings. When Hua analyzes himself in Scene 2, the commentator remarks: "How utterly stupid those people are who see Li Bo and Du Fu's poetry as exemplifying the two types (of *fengliu* and *daoxue*)";[21] in the popular opinion, the two famous poets represented contrasting attitudes to morality. Hua describes himself as "outwardly *fengliu* but inwardly a serious person":

> As I see it, men of talent and virtue belong to two distinct kinds: those who believe in *fengliu* and attack *daoxue* with all their might, and those who honor *daoxue* and malign *fengliu*. In my view, there is a place for pleasure within Confucian doctrine, for a divine purpose is manifested in our idle feelings. In the last analysis, only if one combines *daoxue* and *fengliu* can one count oneself a scholar or man of letters.[22]

If Hua should take a concubine, a course his wife has been urging upon him, his action would exemplify a Heavenly purpose. This is essentially the same credo as that of the hero in *Woman in Pursuit of Man*, whose virtue consists in refraining from adultery, not in abstention from sex with singing-girls and the like.

Hua says deprecatingly that he is a "stuffy Confucian," but only in order to excuse himself before the young rakes who are his companions; he does not wish to join a party at which "girls of good family" are present.[23] In Scene 8, when the courtesan Miss Wang eyes him in admiration, he mumbles that he is a moralistic pedant unworthy of her attention. But this is just his caution speaking, for he is afraid to start an affair he cannot continue. He is not prudish, he explains later, but all too susceptible, and is therefore prepared to sleep only with Miss Deng, because she does not appeal to him and there is no danger of his falling in love.

His friend Hou is the irresponsible romantic. Although not one of the base characters, he exemplifies neither Hua's constancy nor his integrity. He haunts the pleasure quarters looking for beautiful women who admire his talent, but after finding one, he soon abandons her for someone else. He would have preferred Miss Wang—she is more beautiful—but his protestations fail to move her, and he settles for Miss Deng instead. However, he has no compunction about offering her to Hua. Later, on marrying the two wards of a powerful eunuch, he jettisons Miss Deng and has to be shamed by Hua into taking her back again.

The reasons for falling in love are the usual ones in Li Yu, as in the romantic comedy: good looks and talent, the latter demonstrated in poetry. The function of the poems exchanged between the lovers is as much to display poetic ability as it is to convey a message. Some heroines even set the topics of the poems their suitors write, as in an examination! But others, such as the heroines of *The Jade Clasp* and *Sole Mates*, are affected by the recklessness of the hero's love, his willingness to risk all. In several plays, a character's gradual realization that he or she is in love is cunningly revealed. If the rationalizations for love are commonplace in Li Yu, its processes are subtle indeed.

It cannot be said, however, that love is ever expressed with any great intensity. In general, Li Yu is not a writer who sets out to move us. Perhaps *Be Careful about Love* and *Women in Love* are partial exceptions, but I find the emotion in the latter weak during the women's first encounter, and not much stronger even when they are forced to part.[24] The most noteworthy exception is Scene 21, in which the sick (and perhaps dying) Miss Cao attacks her puritanical father (after he leaves the room): "Father, you may be a learned man who has passed the metropolitan examination and been appointed to the Hanlin Academy, but you know nothing of what goes on in the world. You are the one who has destroyed my life—you, the very person who asks what ails me!" After more in this vein, she continues:

> As the old saying goes, we receive our bodies from our parents. Now that I have been condemned to die, I must return mine to its original owner.
> (*sings*) Foul though this leather bag may be,
>   Its seal is still intact;
>   And I hand it back to you as good as new.[25]

Such a passage, which presents emotion in concrete form, is rare in Li Yu.

It seems scarcely valid to consider Li Yu's characters separately, because he obviously created them in relation to one another, as foils, echoes, counterparts, and contrasts, and not merely in pairs, but also in larger and more elaborate groupings. For example, Aijuan's relationship to her mother in *The Kite* contrasts not merely with Shujuan's to *her* mother, but also Qi's to Han. Characters belong to a system that helps to define all those within it. In *Sole Mates* the heroine is defined largely by her likeness to, and difference from, her mother (a clear difference, expressed in heated arguments), her classmates, her lover, and her rich suitor. This is true of Li Yu to a greater degree, I think, than of other Chinese playwrights. From one viewpoint, it reflects the more elaborate patterning of the Li Yu play.

Nonetheless, something can be said about his characterization in general. First, as in the fiction, the characters tend to illustrate ideas and attitudes. I have discussed this in terms of Han and Qi in *The Kite* and of Hua in *Be Careful about Love;* in each case, characters are defined by their ideas of, and attitudes toward, sex and love, in addition to other factors. This is not a simple equation of character and attitude, but a complex relationship in which there is much scope for variety. Li Yu's particular strength is for arguing out subtly, in dialogue and monologue, his characters' impulses, reactions, and rationalizations.

Take Hua, for example. His filial piety at first leads him to reject any contact with Miss Wang, whom he admires; he is afraid that his passionate nature may force him to violate the family code. So Wang takes the initiative—she is one of Li Yu's enterprising women—and proposes the only arrangement she thinks he will accept, a platonic friendship for the discussion of poetry, in the manner of men friends. Hua allows himself to be talked into it; when later, at Hou's urging, he begins sleeping with Miss Wang, he still disclaims any serious attachment.

All of this is worked out in excellent detail. With Hou and his rakish friends, Hua plays, half seriously, the role of puritan. Then, after allowing himself to be deceived into the friendship with Miss Wang, he tries to convey a lack of interest in her by acting parsimoniously. (Ironically, it heightens her admiration; she is tired of admirers who bankrupt themselves in order to impress her.) When she reveals her deception and declares her love for him, Hua is characteristically overcome, not by emotion, but by prudence. How can he let his private passions clash with the family code? Why not seek his father's approval, she suggests, taking the initiative once more. He agrees to try, stipulating with absurd caution a ten-year period of probation in which neither will take another lover.

Minor characters are shrewdly observed, often with a single distinguishing trait. The unfortunate Mr. Yang, father of one of the women artists in *Ideal Love-matches*, is an educated man, deeply in debt, for whom respectability is the key value. In Scene 3, we find him telling the art dealer that "a self-respecting person can't sell off his daughter to repay a debt" and then promptly suggesting that the dealer act as matchmaker. In the same scene the debt-collector, who informs us that scholars may not be afraid of lawsuits but are terrified of losing respect, has deliberately insulted him: "Respect! What do you mean respect? A man owes money, but pushes his womenfolk forward."[26] In Scene 7, Yang reacts angrily to his daughter's suspicion of the art dealer, who has passed himself off as a Buddhist priest:

> Child, he is in a genteel occupation, and in dealing with literary gentlemen all the time, he is totally dependent on his manner as a disinterested friend to get business; that is why he dresses like this. Anyway, you can't tell anything from appearances; you have to try a man out to see what he is like at heart. As they say, you find out someone's true nature when you deal with him over money. People these days wouldn't give you ten cash, let alone ten taels, and they'd still keep you on tenterhooks before you ever got your hands on the money. As casual as you please, this man handed over ten taels to help a struggling scholar. Why, he's a living buddha, that's perfectly clear. We ought to worship him, you and I! How can you make these wild accusations against him?[27]

Men may sometimes be torn between their desires and their sense of duty, as Tan is in *Sole Mates* (he overcomes the sense of duty) and Hua in *Be Careful about Love* (he finds a compromise), or they may act from an ingenuous compassion like the hero of *The Ingenious Finale*. But in general, Li Yu's high and base characters pursue their own interests, in the one case morally, harming no one else, and in the other often immorally. As Li Yu explains, self-interest in love, which arises from one's own nature, is a proper, indeed necessary goal in life, provided it does no harm to others.

This view may seem commonplace, but it is liberating in a society whose dominant ethic is one of self-sacrifice to notions of duty. Self-sacrifice is rare in Li Yu, although it is common, together with self-interest, in the romantic comedy in general. His standard motivation is the self-interest that serves one's natural desires.

The most active characters in pursuit of their love interests are his women. They are bold, resolute, calculating, and resourceful to a degree beyond the creations of other Chinese dramatists. Moreover, within the surprisingly wide limits of their power, Li's women are the masters of their fate. There are precursors for them in the Chinese tradition—Red Duster in the Tang tale and Zhao Pan'er in Guan Hanqing's *Jiu fengchen*, for example[28]—but there is nothing to equal their range in Li Yu's plays and stories.

In *Women in Love*, Miss Cui is a mastermind who carries out a daring scheme in the interests of her own love, while her husband remains passive and Miss Cao helpless. Two half-sisters, the grotesque Aijuan and the beautiful Shujuan, are the moving spirits in *The Kite*. In *Ideal Love-matches*, two women artists manage to drug and drown the villainous priest who threatens them. Miss Liu in *The Jade Clasp* simply informs her "mother" how she intends to choose her husband. In *You Can't Do Anything*, all three women, faced with marriage to the play's appalling hero, show astuteness and daring in coping with their situation. By contrast, little sympathy is shown the concubine who hangs herself rather than marry him.

The young actress of *Sole Mates* is another notable example. When she sees that Tan has fallen in love with her, she calculates that he represents her best chance to escape the life of the actress and—if her mother's example is to be followed—of the courtesan. When Tan gets into a fight with her leading man, she springs to the former's aid. Her astuteness is shown in the way she replies to the love letter he sends her in class; she *sings* her reply, calculating that none of her other classmates will know enough opera to realize she is improvising. In her debate with her mother, she ingeniously counters every argument her mother can raise.[29] Then there is her suicide, which, as we have seen, is not an act favored by Li Yu's positive women. This heroine attempts to kill herself, but in as positive a way as possible. The aim of a heroine's suicide, she reasons, is to cause her lover to "summon her soul" and, by giving writers something to write about, to make her immortal. Why become a "mute martyr?"[30]

The three women of *Woman in Pursuit of Man* are all enterprising, especially the two main adversaries. Xu, a courtesan, feeling her profession to be degrading, actually proposes marriage to Lü, her lover. When he declines to accept her as a concubine before taking a wife, she offers to arrange a marriage for him on condition that he make her his concubine afterwards. (She calculates that the bride she finds for him will be beholden to her.) Hearing of this plan, Miss Qiao, who wants Lü to herself, comes up with a diabolical slander to estrange him from Xu: she insinuates that the courtesan is looking for an ugly wife who will offer her no competition. Xu responds, in the central ruse of the play, by kidnapping the bridegroom as he leaves for his wedding to Miss Qiao. Here she is, observing the kidnapping, as Lü, all unawares, gets into the wrong sedan-chair:

> (sighs): What a fickle rogue! What a treacherous rascal! A good thing it's my chair he's getting into. If he had really been taken to the Qiao house, I could never have seen him again as long as I lived. When we meet again, in a little while, I'll give him such a tongue-lashing, that I will, plus a good bite or two. How else can I vent my fury?[31]

Her fury requires even more venting than that. Determined to humiliate Miss Qiao, she writes a letter of annulment and sends it off, in place of Lü, in the empty sedan-chair. Worse, she draws up a poster, purporting to be by Miss Qiao, that offers a reward for anyone who returns the lost bridegroom. Mortified, Miss Qiao rises to the challenge, and eventually she, Miss Xu, and the latter's candidate for a wife, unable to prevail over one another, settle their differences and buy a house in which to share their marriage to Lü. He, meanwhile, except for passing the examinations, has done little more than serve as the prize in their struggle.

Miss Wang, in *Be Careful*, is an enterprising, self-confident woman who is asking for too much in terms of a husband, in the opinion of her friend Miss Deng. Given the opportunity by the local gallants to choose her own consort for the night, she actually, to their astonishment, exercises her right to choose none of them. To Miss Deng, she appears arrogant; to Hou, who would like to have been her lover, she is "independent-minded and superior";[32] and in her own opinion, she is too honest for her own good. But she does not let honesty affect her shrewdness. Realizing that, if she is ever to get close to Hua, it will have to be by subterfuge, she proposes the platonic literary friendship. Later, when she and Hua have been lovers for half a month and he is talking of returning home, she decides that it is time for honesty again: "Master Hua, these foolish eyes of mine observed countless young men before they ever caught sight of you. When I saw that you were full of doubt and hesitation, reluctant to come near me, I pretended to be naive and put my heart's desire aside for the moment, assuming that once we were in love with each other you would never discard me. But you've stayed just as inflexible from first to last. Your saying we will never marry means the end of all my hopes. You surely don't imagine I'll marry anybody else after you've gone!"[33] And she threatens to kill herself then and there.

About lovers she has her own ideas, as we see from her arguments with Miss Deng. She likes men who are lukewarm at the beginning, for it is a sign they will be ardent in the long run. She is attracted by Hua's refusal to impress her with luxury, for it shows he is unconventional. She appreciates the moralist in him, for it is a sign that he will keep his word. Finally, Miss Wang is a bold planner. She subverts the platonic friendship she had originally proposed, and later, in Scene 24, she accuses a rascally suitor of sedition, aware that the charge is false but aware also that, in a time of civil strife, the authorities will take notice of no lesser crime.

Even Li Yu's last play, *Ingenious Finale,* in which the romantic element is very slight, is not without its enterprising heroine. She realizes that, if she is to marry the hero, she will have to act fast. He is going off on a journey financed by her father, and with his looks and talent, he is sure to get marriage offers in plenty. She cannot speak to him, having never been introduced, and so she writes him a love poem, or rather, in place of the conventional poem, she inverts the opening lines of the first song in *The Poetry Classic.* A few scenes later, all alone, and with the rebels getting closer, she rejects suicide, coolly deciding to try her luck with them.[34] A series of shrewd devices enable her to escape with her honor intact, and at the end of the play we find her calmly smoothing out a quarrel between her father and her husband.

The Chinese play has a well-defined place for gross comedy, among the low or base characters of the *chou* and *jing* (villain) roles. It is a stratum that is particularly important for Li Yu, whose drama chapters stress the value of gross comedy in entertaining even the highbrow audience, let alone the lowbrow, and give advice on how ribald humor can be subtly and tastefully communicated. Li Yu's interest in the base stratum was recognized by the commentator on *Ideal Love-matches,* who remarks of a ribald song by Huang the Natural Eunuch: "Literary men in writing their plays have always suited them to the *sheng* and *dan* roles, not to the 'painted faces.' Only Li Yu is able to make all of them realistic. His is a true all-round talent."[35] He even mixes the strata; in *You Can't Do Anything,* by giving a *chou* the leading male role, he is able to bring gross comedy into the mainstream of the play. At the same time, drama, as the prime medium of psychological presentation, works its own changes on this clown hero (and to some extent on other clowns). He becomes a figure of pathos as well as of fun, an Elephant Man, a grotesque who is savagely aware of his grotesquerie and ready to mock all those more favored than he.

Although some readers may be repelled by them, the comic richness of Li Yu's plays is largely to be found in these roles, which are full of racy language, ribaldry, and burlesque. For example, in *Women in Love,* the *jing* Zhou Menggong, whose very name is ridiculous (it refers to Confucius's dream of the Duke of Zhou), stands for examination chicanery. (Most of the obvious satire of the plays is conducted through the *jing* roles.) In an attempt to cheat his way through the examinations, Zhou copies out some model essays, rolls them up tightly, and tucks them into his anus, from which they are dislodged by an untimely fart just as he is filing into the hall, the public nature of his discomfiture adding to his humiliation. In the same play the maids of the two heroines enact an earthy version of the wedding between their respective mistresses, thus fulfilling a common function of the *chou* characters in Li Yu: to play out in gross counterpoint the actions of the high characters.[36]

In *The Kite* the two base characters, Qi, a *jing*, and Aijuan, a *chou,* lust after heroine and hero, respectively, supplying a cynical commentary to the latter couple's idealistic love. Aijuan attempts to seduce Han, and then, in his nightmare, tries to rape him, while with Aijuan's connivance Qi attempts to rape Shujuan. Hearing the would-be rapist's cries for mercy—Shujuan is threatening him with a sword—Aijuan affects to believe that he is quaking with fear before Shujuan's insatiable sexual appetite. Accused later by Shujuan of connivance, she replies with appalling moral obliquity:

> "My dear, there's a saying that goes like this: 'Offering someone a cup of wine is not a malicious act.' You didn't want to play along, so that's that. What's the point of telling your mother? Let me apologize, and ask your forgiveness."
> *(kneels down)*[37]

In *Ideal Love-matches,* the main *chou* is Huang the Natural Eunuch. He is vain and stupid, an old debauchee who is harmless rather than malicious—like other *chou* characters, he is essentially a figure of fun, the object of gentle satire—and once Miss Yang realizes he is harmless, she treats him with good humor and even affection, unlike the vicious *jing,* a phony priest, whom she fears and detests. In this play the *chou* and *jing* are the outstanding characters, and both are associated with ribaldry. When the priest doubts whether the fan painting he has been offered is a genuine Chen Jiru, the courtesan's servant expostulates: "It's a Chen Jiru landscape done by my mistress. What do you mean, not genuine!" The priest goes on: "Tell her that after I've sold this picture, I shall want to buy that picture *[na hua]."* (*Na hua* is a pun on *nahua,* the sex organ.)

> *Servant:* Reverend father, you're joking again! Although "that picture" is available, it is not for you priests to buy. Well, I've delivered the fan, and now I'll be off. *(exit)*
> *Priest (laughs):* This little bit of business has come right to my door. If the Yang girl is too demanding and doesn't come to hand, I'll turn to this one for relief. Good idea![38]

In *Woman in Pursuit of Man,* the three decrepit prostitutes discuss their declining economic fortunes. Business is off at their house, and one of them suggests it is because men have come to prefer adultery; there are more women "with their doors half open" than there are prostitutes; there ought to be a law against it. Another attributes the downturn to the trend toward homosexuality, which has the advantage of costing less; perhaps they should join the trend, dress up as men, and "open up the back way." The third holds that the reason is not so simple; the real problem is their lack of an endorsement from a literary lion: once the writers "give you a good notice, your business picks up." They should try to ingratiate themselves with some celebrated intellectuals: "Clients these days are just too shrewd. If they hear praise of you, they won't believe it, but just dismiss it as a paid endorsement. The people who recommend you must have personally spent a few nights with you first. If you don't believe me, just take a look at Xu Xianshou next door. Since she took up with Lü, her reputation has boomed, and the gateway to her place is jammed with vehicles. You never saw such a busy scene! She's the one we should be modeling ourselves on."[39]

In *Be Careful about Love*, there is much bawdy joking from the prostitutes in Scene 7, the rakes and their women in Scene 9, and Miss Deng's madam in Scene 12. By contrast, the initial lovemaking between Hua and Miss Wang is skipped (Scene 17). This seems to be a general rule in plays; erotic behavior involving the *sheng* and *dan* (female lead) characters is described by allusive or indirect means, if it is described at all. In his treatment of the *chou* and *jing* characters, by contrast, Li Yu indulges his delight in a ribaldry that shocks as it amuses.

Like other dramatists, Li Yu deplores the popular demand for plays with "hot," or action-filled, scenes:

> I maintain that there is no such thing as hot or cold in drama. All one need fear is that the play does not accord with human feeling. If its scenes of joy and sorrow result from human feeling, it will be capable of making an audience laugh or cry, bristle with outrage, or virtually die of fright. Even if there are no drums or clappers sounding, and the stage is quiet, the audience's applause will

be enough to make the heavens tremble and the earth shake.[40]

Yet his own plays are notable for their *coups de théâtre*, the dramatic equivalent of the comic sensationalism of his fiction or the novel ideas of his essays. Consider the following cases: the rape nightmare of *The Kite*, succeeded immediately by the news of the hero's examination triumph; the mirage in *The Illusory Tower*, for which elaborate stage directions (including a smoke screen) are provided ("everything depends on lightning speed, to astonish and impress the audience");[41] the ugly hero's metamorphosis while in his bath in *You Can't Do Anything*; the plunge of hero and heroine from the stage into the river in *Sole Mates*; the abduction of the bridegroom in *Woman in Pursuit of Man*; and the rebels' selling off of their captives (in sacks) in *The Ingenious Finale*. From this sample, one can see that Li Yu's grosser effects also came from his plays' surprising and occasionally shocking spectacle.

In addition to their spectacular effects, the plays are full of novel theater. The opening of *The Ingenious Finale* is one example; we are taken into the hero's recurrent dream, in which he sees the room where he played as a child. His bed is still rumpled, his toys are still in their trunk, and an offstage voice eerily informs him of the significance of each object. The dream is realized in the play's last scene, in which the hero returns to this very room and discovers his identity. In *The Jade Clasp* the heroine is first heard yawning off stage, as the procuress wakes her. Du Jun's note remarks that "there has never been an entrance like this."[42] Then, as the procuress does the girl's hair, describing the process in detail—it was one of Li Yu's aesthetic and sensual interests—we learn their entire situation from the talk they exchange.

One could go on. Scene 6 in *You Can't Do Anything*, in which Que, alternately groveling and blustering, kneels outside the study in which his wife has locked herself, is lively theater, as is the moment in Scene 26 of *The Ingenious Finale* in which Yao fumbles helplessly with the knot of the sack that holds his fiancée, an incident that, according to the commentator, shows that Li Yu has entered his character's mind.[43] Both are cases in which novel and effective action represents emotion.

But the heart of the Li Yu play is in the characters' interactions.

His fiction may be more conceptually daring, but his plays are of greater psychological interest, an interest that is found, above all, in dialogue. He makes a greater use of speech than other dramatists—one commentator maintains, approvingly, that even his songs have speechlike qualities[44]—and it is in talk, punctuated by an extraordinary number of dramatic asides, that we see the multiple-mindedness that he claims for himself as a dramatist. He is constantly aware of the knowledge, situation, temperament, and motives of his characters. A multiple differential is always in play, and perceptions, major and minor, innocent and guilty, conscious and unconscious, lie behind the talk.

In Scene 12 of *Women in Love,* Miss Cui, already deeply in love with Miss Cao, gently leads her husband to the subject on her mind, while taking care to give him only the minimum of information. Finally, she tells him the story of her and Miss Cao's vow to marry, admitting the idea of a marriage ceremony was hers but claiming that she spoke only in jest and that the girl took it seriously. (The audience knows otherwise.) Her husband, although continuing to profess disbelief, secretly likes the idea, but worries that his wife's love may turn to jealousy. As a tactic, he decides to reject the idea until she has committed herself irrevocably.

> *She:* So long as you're fair-minded, what reason would I have to be jealous?
>
> *He:* You're saying you would have no worries in the short term. I'm talking about the long term. But if you absolutely insist on the match, you ought to write me out a guarantee that you'll never be jealous.
>
> *She (aside):* Look at him, consumed with desire on the inside, but full of protestations on the outside! I've a mind to put a scare in him. *(Turns)* You're definitely against it, then?
>
> *He:* Yes, definitely.
>
> *She:* Since you're so insistent, I can't very well press the issue any further. I'll write her a letter calling off the arrangement and telling her to find another match as soon as possible, so as not to waste all of her youth. Hualing, bring me the writing instruments.
>
> *He (agitated):* Let's just reconsider a moment.

She: There's nothing to reconsider.

(*Their maid brings the writing instruments, and the wife writes.*)

He (*tugging at her arm, stopping her*): It was such a generous offer that girl made, it would be a shame to let her down. Let me get someone to arrange the match.[45]

Throughout, the husband plays a slightly different game from his wife, and occasionally, as here, she is aware of it. Affecting to be skeptical, sometimes even concerned about the danger, he is secretly egging her on to her own greatest desire, one that she dare not confess.

Miss Cui's relations with Miss Cao are an equally interesting example of complex role playing. Both women are deeply in love, but Miss Cui, who is fully in charge of the situation, affects a wry, detached tone while leading Miss Cao toward a declaration of love. For her part, Miss Cao readily accepts the role of the direct, passionately serious, naive younger woman. In Scene 10, she wants to swear sisterhood, and Miss Cui suggests that they extend the vow to include the next life:

> *Cao:* So in this life we are to be unrelated sisters, while in the next we'll be true sisters in the same family?
>
> *Cui:* That won't do. We are surely not going to go on being reborn as women every time?
>
> *Cao:* Then what about being sisters in this life and brothers in the next?
>
> *Cui:* That won't do, either. Brothers generally don't get along very well, and anyway, even the closest brothers aren't as close as the most distant of husbands and wives. Let's be husband and wife in the next existence.
>
> *Cao:* (giggles)

She wonders who would be the husband and who the wife:

> (*sings*): This is no theater, here in the gods' presence;
> I calmly weigh the matter in my mind.
> Has marriage ever been discussed
> Before the souls were given human form?

Well, let it be. We don't even know who would be the man and who the woman. I might even be the husband and she the wife.

(sings):   While the question of our sexes is still unclear,
There's no need to grieve over being the wife.
She may not be Liang Hong nor I Meng Guang.
Even if she proves to be the man, so long as she has the same talents and looks as she has now, I would be willing to be her wife.

(sings):   My only wish is that she not alter her dashing looks;
Small matter if I lose the upper hand.

(Turns to Cui):   Mistress, you and I are true romantics!
See how Maitreya in his shrine laughs at our folly!
There's just one thing that troubles me.

Cui: What is that?

Cao *(sings):*   I fear that our slender thread of feeling,
Once given words, will never be forgotten,
But will engender love in the life to come.

Cui *(to the maid):* Hualing, light the candles, we want to make our vows.

Maid: You become a dragon by dressing up as a dragon, as the saying goes. If you want to be husband and wife, you ought to dress the part.

Cui, Cao: How do we do that?

Maid: Over there is the master's study with all of his clothes in it. Dress up in them and take your vows as husband and wife, letting the bodhisattvas be your witnesses. Then in the next life you'll never be able to break the contract.

Cui *(laughing):* The wench is having her little joke, but there *is* something in what she says. Why not go and get the clothes, then?

Second Maid: All we need now is someone to officiate.

Maid: That's no problem. The men in my family have been officiating at weddings for generations and I learned the words as a child. Here are the cap and gown from the study, all ready for you. Why don't you put them on?

(Brings them the clothes.)

Second Maid: My mistress will be the groom.

Maid: No, mine will. *(They banter with each other.)*

Second Maid: Very well, let's get them to try the clothes on. The one they fit best will be the groom.

(Cao tries on the clothes.)

Maid: The cap comes down to her eyebrows and the gown trails on the ground. It doesn't fit!

(Cui tries them on.)

Maid: Look, the cap is not too big nor the gown too long. A perfect fit! Kindly make your bows.

(Wearing a scholar's cap, the maid officiates, while the second maid assists the bride. The girls bow to each other.)

(Nun enters and, coming upon them unexpectedly, roars with laughter and retreats in surprise.)

(Cao and Cui finish making their bows and burst into laughter.)[46]

At the end of the scene, they decide that the only solution is for Miss Cao to marry Miss Cui's husband too. Since her father would never consent to let his daughter be a mere concubine, their plan calls for Miss Cui to be relegated nominally to concubine while Miss Cao takes her place as wife. When, after many vicissitudes, Miss Cao is finally able to marry, she is overwhelmed with nervousness, which she expresses in a discussion with Miss Cui in Scene 31. She is upset at the thought of parting from her lover, even briefly, and is worried about the wedding night.

Cui *(joyfully)*: Thank heavens, all of our worries are now over! My dear, do dress your hair and put on your makeup.

Cao *(sits gloomy and silent, paying no attention to her)*.

Cui: What! To think of the endless efforts I've put in to get this good news, and you not only aren't pleased, you look all sad and bitter. Why?

Cao: It was you I promised to marry, not him. Even if I do marry him, it will only be for your sake. How can you send me ahead on my own, while you keep out of sight?

Cui: What would you suggest, then?

Cao: The only thing is to tell Father everything, that you and I . . .

Cui: How do you mean, you and I?

Cao (is overcome with embarrassment, while Cui laughs).

Cui: How can such an intelligent girl say such a silly thing? That father of yours would not be an easy man to tell everything to. And even if you did, he'd get his back up the minute you mentioned it.[47]

Miss Cao is the nervous bride here, but she is also acting in her usual role vis-à-vis Miss Cui. Throughout, Miss Cui's thoughts have been erotic and practical, Miss Cao's passionate and idealistic, expressed in moral terms. The two maids, in their farcical imitation of their mistresses' wedding, are coarse and ribald, supplying the explicit physical reference that is lacking even in Miss Cui's speech and song.

Li Yu shows his finesse in individual motives whenever an experience is related. A common element in his early plays is some strange event selectively retold under different circumstances. For example, the incident in *Women in Love* in which Miss Cui and Miss Cao fall in love is first enacted on stage, and then told and retold no less than four times, differently on each occasion. Miss Cui tells her husband in Scene 12; he tells his friend in Scene 14; Miss Cui tells Miss Cao's father in Scene 24; and Miss Cao tells her father in Scene 36. For good measure, the incident has been foretold by the gods in Scene 5.

Similarly, in *The Kite,* the story of the kite—really two incidents—is repeated again and again, selectively, with each teller leaving out the pieces of the story he finds embarrassing. In *The Illusory Tower* the initial meeting between Liu and the two dragon girls is told and retold, defensively each time. Shunhua, in telling her parents, makes out as good a case for herself as she can, as does her cousin in telling *her* parents.[48] Shunhua's father is furious, but her mother feels humiliated, believing that the episode reflects on the way she has brought up her daughter. Then the girl's choleric uncle, Red Dragon, enters, and *he* has to know what has happened. Although this time the mother minimizes the incident as much as possible, Red Dragon is all for killing the niece, whose honor he considers irremediably sullied. Her father decides instead to hasten the highly unsuitable marriage that Red Dragon has cavalierly arranged for her. The girl wants to kill herself, but wonders whether her beloved will ever hear of her death, and so she decides to stall in the hope of sending him a letter first.

Psychological subtlety is shown also in the scenes of reflection and tension. Scene 17 of *The Jade Clasp* consists almost entirely of Miss Fan's thoughts as she ponders what to do with the clasp the stranger has dropped. For reasons unclear to her, she cannot bring herself to discard it, and by the end of the scene she realizes she is in love with its owner. In Scene 8 of *The Ingenious Finale*, Yao discovers gradually by introspection that the slight reluctance he feels about departing on his journey is due to his love for the girl next door. Scene 11 of *Woman in Pursuit of Man* is full of strained silences, as Lü, who has heard the slanderous gossip about Miss Xu, treats her coldly but without telling her why. She sits mending his clothes and puzzling over his attitude until she comes upon a love poem from Miss Qiao in one of his pockets. Each has been holding something back; Lü cannot bring himself to mention his betrothal to Miss Qiao, and Miss Xu feels reluctant, because of his attitude, to tell him of the marriage she has just arranged for him.

In *Be Careful about Love*, Scene 13 consists of Miss Wang's anguished thoughts as she waits for Miss Deng to tell her whether Hua will agree to the platonic friendship she has offered him. Her mood runs the gamut of joy, suspicion, resentment, self-reproach, and boredom. In the following scene, she and Hua keep up their elaborate pretense that neither has any romantic interest in the other. It is precisely in such ingeniously "cold" scenes as these that Li Yu is at his best as a dramatist.

Be Careful about Love is one of his coldest plays, if only because of its antiromantic theme. Li Yu told his commentator that Scene 10, which treats Miss Wang's dilemma, differed in style and content from the rather routine earlier scenes.[49] It certainly has less obvious action; it consists of a long discussion between Miss Wang, who has been abandoned by the local gallants on Thousand Man Rock because of her refusal to choose any of them as her consort for the night, and her friend Miss Deng, who has returned to keep her company. Miss Deng reproaches her for her arrogance:

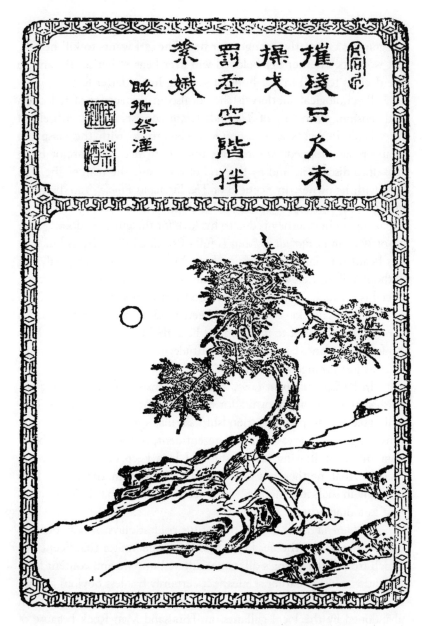

Miss Wang is abandoned for the night on Thousand Man Rock. Woodcut illustration from *Be Careful about Love* (the Yishengtang edition of *Liweng chuanqi shizhong*).

Deng: My dear, the temperament you displayed today was quite extraordinary, even for you. If all of us prostitutes behaved as arrogantly as you did, where would we
be?

Wang: I know, but the very sight of those boors made
me feel as if I'd come face to face with enemies from a
former life. I couldn't help standing up for myself and giving
them a piece or my mind. It must have been fated to happen.

(sings):   I was bound to incur disaster.

           In my heart I tried to conform,

           But couldn't help taking a moral line.

           I met up with rogues,

           And they were all gentility,

           While I abruptly spoke my mind,

           Rejecting the courtesan's role.

           Oh, a fool cannot learn to be smart!

           A fool cannot learn to be smart!

           I blame my mother's womb:

           Why don't I have a grain of sense in me!

Deng: Those two other boors were disgusting, and I
don't wonder that you despised them, but Master Hou ranks
high on the list for talent and looks. How is it that he
didn't appeal to you? Do you mean to say that the clients
you've been seeing are all superior to him?

Wang: My dear Miss Deng, I'm afraid you don't understand. The choice I was given tonight was quite different
from the way we normally accept clients. A great deal
depended on it. Normally we have no choice; even if the
client is not to our liking, we have to make the best of
things. But this time I was asked to choose a man myself,
which was tantamount to choosing a husband. Once I had
accepted him, he would have considered himself just like
a husband, not as a brothel client. "Husband"—the title
is not one to be loosely bestowed. Moreover, just such a
husband was placed there before my very eyes. How could
I pass him over in favor of anyone else?

Deng: Who was this husband? Not the one who ran away from the party?

Wang: That's right.

Deng: You're not fated to marry him, so don't get any wild ideas.

Wang: Why do you say that?

Deng (sings):   What use is all his talent
        If he lacks the romantic touch,
        Behaves like a moral prig,
        And avoids the street of flowers?
        They say his ancestor left rules
        Now printed as a document
        That forbid all marriage to a beauty.

Wang: You've never been intimate with him, so how do you know what his secret thoughts are?

Deng (sings):   He sent me word
        He sent me word,
        He wants this ugly creature
        To take the famous beauty's place.

Wang: So he has sent you an invitation, has he? But you haven't got him yet, and you're afraid someone else will snatch away the fun you're looking forward to. That's why you've invented this story, to cool my feelings for him. Very well, if that's the way things are, I respectfully comply. From this moment on, I'll never mention the name Hua again.

Deng: Oh, don't be so sensitive, my dear. Let me be candid with you. He's in love with you, but he's afraid that after you have made love together, you'll be inseparable; therefore it would be better not to meet at all. That is why he is looking for someone barely tolerable to amuse himself with for the time being, someone it will be easy to part from when the time comes. Master Hou recommended me, and I happened to meet his need for a stopgap. It is all arranged that I join him tomorrow as his mistress.

Wang: Ah, now I see. He really is an honest gentleman, after all. I respect him all the more for it. If we are careful how things start in this life, we can guarantee they will end safely. With a man like that as a husband, there'd be no sorrow in old age. For me, this is the end of my hopes. But you mustn't miss the chance, my dear Miss Deng; if he has a shred of true feeling for you, cling to him as tightly as you can. On no account must you lose an opportunity that is right before your eyes.

(sings):   True love's not easy to meet with,

           Events must conspire in its favor.

           Let him go, and your lover will not come back.

           Ill-fated were we, the sash was sewn in vain,

           My sorrow's dispelled before the knot is tied.

           This fool's unlucky, meets misfortune,

           Wants to join him, but is pushed away.

Deng: He's treating me as a stopgap now, before we've even met. Obviously, after we've been intimate, I'll still be nothing more than a stopgap. And since he looks at me that way, I shall do the same with him. You can hardly call that true love! And I have another reason, too. Master Hou and I have taken a vow to be husband and wife one day. How could I possibly betray my promise to him and favor someone else?

    Wang: You're right.

    Deng (sings):   Since he set the chilly tone,

           I'm sure no heart will catch on fire.

           My breast contains another love;

           I fear to sell as he fears to buy.

           My shop's a facade, devoid of wares.

           Our commerce will be in words and

              not in goods.

Now I've told you how I feel. My dear, if you really love him, confide your true feelings to me, and let me try to find a solution for you over time. Who knows, perhaps your chance will come.

    Wang: I'd be grateful to all eternity. But there is just one problem. A truly honest man like this can be taken only by deception, not by telling the truth. If you tell him

I want to marry him, he'll take fright and be even more reluctant to see me. We shall have to come up with some scheme that will bring us gradually closer together. Once I'm with him, I have my own ways of making bricks without straw.

      Deng: What scheme do you have in mind?

      Wang: Let me explain.

(sings):   His latest poems are a rare delight.

           Say how deeply I admire his gift,

           And wish to greet him as a female literary friend.

           If my visit is allowed,

           There's a poetry debt I'll have to pay.

      Deng: I understand. I'll tell him just as soon as I see him. I feel sure you'll be in luck.[50]

Miss Wang's and Miss Deng's differing attitudes to love have been set out in a lengthy discussion in Scene 3. The former's recommendation of "cool" lovers has prepared us for her reaction in this scene. Miss Deng, who prefers impetuous, "hot" lovers, undergoes her own disillusionment about the fickle Hou in Scene 27, the beautifully constructed counterpart to Scene 10. (It is also the tenth-to-last scene, mirroring its counterpart's position in the play.) In Scene 10, Miss Deng has consoled Miss Wang through the night as she agonizes over her love for Hua. In Scene 27, it is Miss Wang's turn to console Miss Deng as she waits sleeplessly for a summons from Hou, who has just succeeded in the examination. The latter scene, however, has a far greater degree of tension. Miss Deng is alone when Miss Wang and her mother knock on her door, and she at first mistakes their arrival for the joyous summons she has been expecting. She cannot sleep for excitement, and so Miss Wang sits up with her and they resume their old argument about hot and cool lovers, with Miss Deng insisting that Hou is the better lover, and that Hua is unemotional. Miss Wang expounds Li Yu's philosophy of low expectations, and then nods off. At dawn a second knocking is heard, and this time it is truly Hou's messenger, but the message he brings for Miss Deng, as the audience already knows, is one of rejection. Miss Wang, somewhat heartlessly under the circumstances, resumes her now triumphant argument against hot lovers.

As antiromantic thinking dominates *Be Careful about Love,* so the art world dominates *Ideal Love-matches.* Dong Qichang and Chen Jiru are gentlemen amateurs, hence esteemed; Miss Yang and Miss Lin are professional artists, hence despised. Each kind has its tribulations, which are set forth, with Li Yu's symmetry, in the first two scenes following the prologue. In Scene 2 Dong and Chen are shown suffering the consequences of their fame; they feel harassed, in return for a paltry recompense, by requests from colleagues and friends for paintings, inscriptions, poems, and prefaces, but especially for paintings, which take longer to complete. To escape the pressure, they decide to enjoy a vacation incognito at the West Lake, and at the same time to seek out artists capable of copying their respective styles. (The paintings can be touched up by Dong and Chen before delivery.) They prefer this solution to alternatives such as reclusion or the priesthood.

Scene 3 is a nearly complete contrast. We are introduced, through the calculations of a rascally art dealer, to the Hangzhou artist Yang Yunyou, daughter of an impoverished scholar. Enter Miss Yang, worried about how to settle the year-end debts, but in receipt of a modest commission from the art dealer for a painting in the manner of Dong Qichang. What shall she paint? She decides to paint herself in her present surroundings. Here is her tumbledown cottage, set in a bleak winter landscape. Her father is dragging himself home after another day's fruitless search for a tutor's job. The bridge over the stream has been deliberately broken, to keep their creditors at bay. And in the doorway of the cottage stands a girl, the artist, chanting a poem with her frozen breath. She signs Dong Qichang's name to the poem she inscribes on the picture, wondering briefly what kind of man he is. By this means Li Yu has handily described his heroine through her own painting.

The autobiographical painting serves another purpose in Scene 5, when Dong Qichang himself comes upon it at the art dealer's and realizes that it tells its artist's own story. His sympathy and admiration—why is she so obscure and he so famous?—engender love for her.

Li Yu is still not finished with Miss Yang's profession. In Scene 21, in a tour de force, he shows her giving a public demonstration of her art. A rumor has been circulating, concocted by young men curious

Miss Yang depicts her own situation in the style of the famous artist Dong Qichang, as her father returns home. Woodcut illustration from *Ideal Love-matches* (the Yishengtang edition of *Liweng chuanqi shizhong*).

about her beauty, that she gets male artists to do her painting for her. The demonstration is her response, precisely as the rumormongers have calculated. When the audience has assembled, the curtain above the table is drawn.

> *Yang:* Take a seat, gentlemen. If you have any orders, please give them to us now.
> A: I would like a fan.
> B: And I an album leaf.
> C: I would like a hand scroll, please.
> D: And I a kerchief.
> (*Miaoxiang, the maid, gathers their requests and gives them to Yang.*)
> *Yang:* Miaoxiang, grind up the ink, please.(*She does so.*)
> *Yang:* I know I'm making a spectacle of myself doing this. I hope you won't laugh at me.
> *All:* Not us.
> (*She draws. The audience praise her looks to each other.*)
> D: Her face and voice are stunning. But there's one other thing I'm suspicious about—her feet may be too big.
> *Others:* What makes you think so?
> D: If she had small feet, why would she hide the lower half of herself behind that table?
> C: You're absolutely right.
> D: Let me see if I can trick the maid into removing it.
> (*to Miaoxiang*): Oh, Miss, everyone says there's a man hidden under the table who is giving her tips on how to paint. Can you tell us if it's true?
> *Miaoxiang:* Of course it isn't! And I know very well what it is you're after. All right, since I've drawn the curtain, why do we need the table screen? We might as well take it away and let you see her feet.
> (*The table screen is removed.*)
> *Audience (peeping):* What tiny feet! Less than three inches! Now that we know she's perfect in every way, there's nothing more to be said.[51]

Dong Qichang comes upon Miss Yang's painting, attributed to himself, in the art shop. Woodcut illustration from *Ideal Love-matches* (the Yishengtang edition of *Liweng chuanqi shizhong*).

The scene goes on at great length to describe her four paintings (which caricature the individuals who request them), the money offered, and the obnoxious persistence of D, the *jing* character, who thinks Miss Yang favors him. Rebuffed, he threatens to use his power—he has recently purchased a position—to bend her to his will. She retorts that she will buy a similar position for her nominal husband, the eternally drunk Huang, so that he can protect her.

The private side of Miss Yang's life, as distinct from the professional, consists of one long search for a suitable husband. In the course of the play she undergoes three marriages, the third and last of which is the "ideal" match to Dong Qichang. The other two are both false. In the first of them, the art dealer, who covets Miss Yang for himself, pretends that Dong Qichang, having fallen in love with the girl's painting—this much is true—wants to marry her. To impersonate Dong at the wedding, he engages Huang the Natural Eunuch, an impotent debauchee. Later, when the real Dong Qichang offers marriage through an intermediary—he is now in Beijing and Miss Yang in Hangzhou—she is too suspicious of the offer to accept it. One of Dong's friends proposes a second false marriage, to a proxy husband who will deliver her to Dong in the capital. The proxy is Miss Lin, the other woman artist, now in disguise as a man. After the wedding, Miss Lin proposes they not be bound by convention but wait for an auspicious day before consummating the marriage. She is unaware that this is the same pretext for stalling that Huang used after the first wedding.

> *Yang (aside, to the maid):* Miaoxiang, there's something odd about what he's saying!
> *Miaoxiang:* You're right. Don't say he's another Natural Eunuch!
> *Yang:* One way or another, I'm going to get to the bottom of this tonight. Come over here, there's something I want to ask you. *(Miaoxiang approaches, and Yang whispers to her.)*
> *Miaoxiang:* Marvelous! I'll go and tell him. *(to Lin):* Master, the mistress says that since today is not an auspicious day, would you please order a sedan-chair and send

her home for the time being. When you have selected a good day, she'll return and complete the marriage.

Lin: Come now! Once you're married, you can't turn around and go home again. For my sake, do try to talk her out of it.

Miaoxiang: The mistress is a very determined person. Once she's made up her mind to go, she'll go. There's no talking her out of it.

Yang: Miaoxiang, hurry up and urge him to get the chair. Don't waste time.

Lin (aside, in panic): What shall I do? There's nothing else for it; I'll just have to counter her move by telling her everything.

(to Yang): Very well then, let's consummate the marriage tonight. There's no need for you to go home.

Yang: Hardly suitable, on an inauspicious day.

Lin: As the saying goes: better to take a chance than wait for a lucky day. Since I met your approval at the viewing, today must be a good day; there's no need to be too formal. Let me undo your sash and take off your gown.(*Undoes her hairpins.*)First we undo the hairpins and earrings.(*Undresses her.*)

(sings):   I loosen now her sash,

           And sense a rare perfume,

           And sense a rare perfume,

           That ravishes my heart and soul.

Miaoxiang: Master, would you please take off your gown, too?

Lin: What? I undress?

Miaoxiang: What else? Would you have the bride undress while the groom sleeps with his clothes on?

Lin: Since you put it like that, I daresay I shall have to.(*Takes off his cap.*)

Miaoxiang (peers, aside to Yang): Look, what a fine head of hair in a style just like yours!

Yang: You're right.

Miaoxiang (sings):   Why would a man put up his hair?

> When he doffs his cap, the tresses
> tumble down.

(Lin takes off his gown.)

Miaoxiang *(sings)*:   Look at his slender waist,
                       Fit to compare with your own!

Master, please sit down and let me take off your boots. *(Pulls off Lin's boots.)* *(astonished, aside to Yang)*: Oh Miss, with those black boots off, his feet are little "three-inch lotuses." It means he must be a girl!

(sings):   The girl's tresses, the slender waist, they're merely
              cause for doubt,
              But see the tiny feet revealed![52]

In *Sole Mates*, the key relationship is that of the actress Liu Jiangxian and her daughter. Jiangxian introduces herself in Scene 3, speaking in character—that is, not objectively—in one of Li Yu's long soliloquies, and, although she tries to put a good face on things, unwittingly revealing her nature. We notice her insistence on money and her pride in her beauty and acting skill, but when her thoughts turn to the effects of her beauty on the audience, we realize how her money is made.

Her daughter, in the sort of contrast Li Yu loves, is an intensely moral, idealistic girl, who has been well educated and is only now being introduced to acting. In Scene 3, her mother tries to pass on to her the secret formula for success, but the girl has scruples about acting, let alone prostitution. If she must be an actress, she says, she is determined to live by acting alone, at which point her mother chides her for "getting all moralistic." "What do women like us care about reputation and modesty, anyway," she says. "We have to make up our minds to it, and think of ourselves while making love as if we were acting in a play. The man may be in earnest, but we are just feigning. We take these sexual matters quite casually; in fact, that is what keeping oneself chaste really means. Why must you be so stubborn!" And she sings:

In courtesan houses,
Prudery has no place.

So fake a little feeling,
In exchange for wealth and favor.

She does not expect the girl to begin her career all at once, she says, revealing her three-part secret formula for staving off sexual intercourse:

>Let them look but not taste.
>Let them have the semblance but not the reality.
>Let them scheme but not succeed.
>*Girl:* What does that mean—"look but not taste"?
>*Mother:* While we're acting, the whole of our bodies is visible to the audience. Even when we're off stage playing or flirting with men, it is the same. The only thing is that we must not allow this goblet of fragrant wine to touch their lips. That's what it means.
>*Girl:* There's sense in that. What about "semblance but not the reality"?
>*Mother:* If some rich merchant or young nobleman wanted to do the real thing with me, I agreed, but kept putting him off on one pretext or another, and never let him get possession. That's what it means.
>*Girl:* I grant you that shows willpower. But what about "letting them plan but not succeed"?
>*Mother:* There were several of these infatuated youths who became attached to me and were prepared to put up large sums to buy me as a wife. I readily agreed, and let them scheme away from dawn till dark, heedless of what they had to pay for my friendship. In the end, their scheming came to nothing more than a spring dream. I was determined not to marry them. That's what it means.
>*Girl:* Since you can't bear to surrender yourself to them, why not tell them so directly instead of going in for all this trickery?
>*Mother:* The full expression of a man's love for a woman does not come as the result of the physical contact, but while they are still making eyes at each other. He's like a glutton at the sight of wine and food; you can let him smell,

but you can't let him start on it, for once he's done so, his desire will be gone. No more of that excitement, with him slavering at the mouth!

Notice how the mother has misunderstood her daughter's all too innocent questions. The girl then asks whether, if one is going to dissemble, it is necessary to do "that disgraceful act" at all.

> *Mother:* There you go again with your childish naïveté! The secret formulas are for the time before you get started, to make some money from the smaller spenders. If you are after a large sum, they'll never give you anything unless you do the real thing with them. Your only course is to choose the biggest moneybags of all, someone who scatters his money about like water, and take up with him. As for the smaller spenders, pay them back with a little verbal affection, but nothing more.[53]

Scene 13 is a diverting continuation of the disagreement between mother and daughter. The occasion is the suit of Qian, a caricature of the moneyed local gentleman, who lives by squeezing the debtors among his tenants. An old patron of the mother's, he is now infatuated with her daughter, and is prepared to offer the huge sum of one thousand taels for her hand as his concubine. He had originally invited the girl to visit him, but she refused, and her mother has come instead, grumbling about her daughter: "I must have committed some sin in a previous life to have given birth to such a little monster!"[54]

To her surprise, Qian says he understands the girl's reluctance to settle for anything less than marriage. In a long and crafty persuasion, he convinces the mother that marriage to someone like himself—rich, but not so high on the official scale as to be politically vulnerable— would be the best solution. Helped by the promise of money, the mother is wholly convinced—or *almost* wholly convinced. She has allowed herself to believe that the girl's future will be jeopardized if she continues as an actress while spurning the overtures of the noblemen who seek her, but she retains a slight, guilty concern. "Just one thing," she adds as an afterthought. "When you marry her, you must see that you treat her well."[55]

She breaks the news to the daughter in Scene 14, arriving with the case of money and asking the girl to guess what is inside. The first four guesses are wrong, and the daughter cannot utter the fifth. She refuses the match on the grounds that she already *has* a husband, at which her mother is aghast; how can she have married without her parents' approval? But they approved her "marriage" by hiring Tan to play opposite her, insists the girl. The debate covers most of the scene, with the girl sophistically arguing her case and the mother retorting with commonsense replies. Winning the debate but losing the argument, the girl resolves on a public suicide during the next day's performance.

The suicide scene is echoed in Scene 28, in which the mother, acting in the same play and on the same stage, breaks down in full view of her daughter. In the meantime, in Scene 17, Li Yu has given us his most savage satire of cupidity at all levels, as officials and commoners alike try to profit from the girl's suicide. Her mother, Liu Jiangxian, tries to extort money from the rich suitor, as do the local authorities. The suitor retaliates by telling the yamen clerk of the thousand taels he has already given Jiangxian. Finally, the clerk's superior, a rapacious magistrate, hears of the case and demands all the extorted money for himself. The commentator's note remarks: "This scene is not part of a play, but a brilliant examination essay on the topic 'High and low fighting over the spoils.' "[56]

What Jiangxian is to *Sole Mates*, Aijuan, the ugly half-sister, is to *The Mistake with the Kite*, but while Jiangxian's motive is money, Aijuan's is sex. She is introduced briefly in Scene 3, where she is shown to have the same quarrelsome and jealous nature as her mother, the concubine Miss Mei. In Scene 11, she retrieves the kite Han had intended for Shujuan and makes an assignation with him. Her earthiness—indeed, her crudeness—together with her ignorance are amply demonstrated in the assignation, in Scene 13. From the first moment, she pulls the pedantically protesting Han over to sit beside her. (Note that Han has signed Qi's name to the poem.)

> *Aijuan:* Oh, Master Qi! I've been dying of love for you these past few days.(*Embracing him.*)
> *Han:* Miss Zhan, it is an unexpected pleasure for a mere student like myself to approach your precious person, but since we formed our friendship through the medium of

The heroine leaps off the stage into the river. Woodcut illustration from *Sole Mates* (the Yishengtang edition of *Liweng chuanqi shizhong*).

The heroine's mother breaks down in the middle of her performance, as her daughter surreptitiously observes. Woodcut illustration from *Sole Mates* (the Yishengtang edition of *Liweng chuanqi shizhong*).

poetry, and without entertaining the motive of sexual de-sire, I hope you will calm yourself a little, lest you transgress the bounds of good taste.

Aijuan: I'd rather be calm later. At the moment I can't relax at all.

Han: Did you write a poem to match my unworthy effort?

Aijuan: I have replied to your unworthy effort.

Han (surprised): Won't you please read me your fine composition?

Aijuan: For the moment my fine composition has slipped my mind.

Han (surprised again): How could you have forgotten your own poem after just a few hours? Do try to remember.

Aijuan: My thoughts have been so much on you that I've forgotten the poem. Let me think. *(Thinks.)* Ah, now I have it!

Han: Please enlighten me.

Aijuan (recites):   A few clouds, a breeze, and the sun overhead,

Past the flowers and willows and across the stream I go.

They'll say I'm like a young man taking life easy;

But the joy that's in my heart they'll never know.

Han (astonished): That's from the *Anthology of Poems!* How can you say it's yours?

Aijuan (alarmed): Er . . . er . . . er . . . you're right, it *is* from the *Anthology.* I recited it just to test your knowledge. But you did remember the poem, and that shows that you really are a man of talent.

Han: Won't you please enlighten me with your real poem?

Aijuan: This is a golden opportunity, and we haven't the time to recite poetry. When our serious business is done with, there'll be time enough for that. *(Tries to pull him onto the bed, but he stands his ground.)*[57]

In Scene 16 Han has a nightmare, part of which I have translated earlier, in which Aijuan renews her assault on his virtue, not to speak of his sensibilities. After Qi is forced into marriage with her, on condition that he be allowed to take a concubine, we find her calculating, in Scene 24, how best to monopolize him. Better to let him go to brothels than to share him with a concubine, and better still to encourage him in adultery. Her reasons? Because an adulterous affair will inevitably run its course. And anyway, the difficulties in meeting his paramour will cause him to "vent" his passion on his own wife! In a devilish scheme, she fosters his infatuation with her half-sister, the virtuous and beautiful Shujuan, first in order to have something to blackmail him with, and second, to humble someone whom she has always envied and resented. When the attempted rape, aided and advised by Aijuan, fails, she is nonchalant before Shujuan's accusations of treachery.

The final scene, Scene 30, which is by convention a joyous reunion, is in this play a tour de force of patched-up quarrels. The girls' father has been away on military service, from which he is expected back at any moment, and the members of the divided household assemble to await his return. There are delicious moments as they eye—and in some cases recognize—each other after their complicated adventures. Han, newly married to Shujuan, recognizes Aijuan as the girl who tried to seduce him. She, unrepentant, admires his looks and complains about her nurse for interrupting them at the critical moment. Shujuan sees Qi for the first time since his attempted rape. She tells Han and is about to tell her fiery-tempered mother, Miss Liu, but Han prudently tries to dissuade her. Qi sees them talking in undertones and realizes they are discussing him. Miss Liu gets the gist of the story, and begins to curse Aijuan for her complicity in the rape, at which Han and Qi cravenly decide to retreat to the city outskirts to await the Master. Miss Liu denounces Aijuan to her mother, Miss Mei, who is driven to acknowledge that her daughter was in the wrong. However, she also shrewdly points out that some blame adheres to Miss Liu, for surrendering the kite with her daughter's poem attached. Shujuan, unable to forgive the attempted rape, relents only when her personal maid, in a desperate attempt to make peace, threatens to throw herself down the well. The last quarrel is patched up just as the Master walks in.

The Li Yu play strikes the reader with the comic originality and brilliant enactment of its ideas, but equally impressive are its artistic qualities, qualities that serve practical thematic needs but also go well beyond them. There is a dimension of gratuitous artistry that is part of the experience of reading a Li Yu play, and, to a lesser degree, a Li Yu story. In particular, the play can be analyzed as a set of intricate correspondences of character, event, circumstance, and text (ranging from the scene down to the word) that may underline, directly or figuratively, its theme but also contribute to a variety of additional aesthetic effects.

Li Yu the dramatist is a virtuoso in this regard. Although correspondence was a fetish of the Southern (*chuanqi*) drama, especially with regard to the variation and repetition of scenes, he goes far beyond the conventional bounds. His grosser correspondences, several of which have already been mentioned, concern character and event. In *The Kite*, for example, there are the two contrasting pairs of half-sisters and "brothers" involved in sexual imbroglios with each other. The repetitive elements are deception and error—the play is a "comedy of errors." There are two wedding nights and three attempted rapes, one of which is a nightmare. Even the initial deceptions, which cause the imbroglios, are similar; it is Aijuan's nurse who suggests that she pretend to be her half-sister, just as it is Han's servant who suggests that he take his "brother's" name. In *Ideal Love-matches*, a comedy of deception more than of error, two famous artists meet and marry two obscure forgers of their art. Scene 2 is devoted to the harassment of the former by colleagues and acquaintances and Scene 3 to the dunning of Miss Yang and her father by their creditors. Miss Yang endures two false weddings in which there are numerous minor parallels of incident and wording. There are even resemblances between the matchmakers: in the first case a phony Buddhist priest, in the second a Taoist nun. And the play contains no fewer than three literary examinations: Miss Yang tests the debauchee, the bandits test Miss Lin (in this case, it is they who are incompetent), and Miss Yang tests her suitors.

In some plays, the theme mandates correspondence, as in *The Jade Clasp*, which has two look-alike heroines, or *The Ingenious Finale*, in which the actions of good-hearted humans reflect Heaven's will, but in each case Li Yu goes far beyond the amount of correspondence required. *Sole Mates* is an example of a complex theme elaborated with the aid of an exceptional number of correspondences. It is set in the theater, and the theater and simulation in general prove to be necessary means for telling the truth. But correspondence also extends beyond this particular theme. The god, who is divine, corresponds to the rebel leader, who is half animal. Furthermore, the god is a water god, while the rebel is a "king of the mountains." There is correspondence also between the rebel and Murong, the recluse: Murong impersonates the god for a worthy purpose, and the rebel gets a henchman to impersonate Murong for an unworthy one. Murong and the rebel also represent different aspects of nature; Murong is the wise and gentle recluse, while the rebel is nature red in tooth and claw. The grasping materialism of the actress (and the rest of society) is, of course, contrasted with the idealistic morality of her daughter. But there is also a significant contrast between the actress as would-be mentor of her daughter and Murong as mentor of Tan, the young hero. The actress is unable to persuade her daughter to pursue an acting career, let along the after-hours career of courtesan, although it is worth noting that she returns to it herself rather than enjoy the life of leisure offered her. Murong, using the theater as a metaphor for public life, is successful in persuading the hero to abandon his career of public service in favor of a wise reclusion.[58]

Eight. Specialist in Idle Pursuits

Since discourse is so vital a part of his fiction and drama, one is not surprised to find that Li Yu specialized above all in the essay form. The word "essay" is itself a misnomer, of course, because in his time there was no general word that would cover both the formal, tightly structured essay and its more informal, personal counterpart. Nominally, some of Li's essays are assigned to minor prose genres such as the *lun* (discussion) and the *bian* (argument).[1] In a few cases, their genres have been flippantly bestowed; "A Deed of Sale for My Hill," for instance, is to be found under "deeds" in his collected works. But most of his essays, and notably those in *Casual Expressions*, his main collection, are given no generic title at all.

Even so, the word cannot be dispensed with. Many of his prose pieces fit our vague notion of the genre more fully than those of any other premodern Chinese writer. Using "essay" for them is at least as appropriate as applying the word "novel" to the longer forms of Chinese fiction, a usage that is almost universally accepted.

How much of Li Yu's writing falls into this category? The whole of *Casual Expressions*, obviously, although one might quibble that the chapters on drama are a segmented treatise rather than a series of essays. In addition, he has a number of short pieces that happen to include some of the finest personal essays in Chinese. *Discussions of the Past* also has a claim to be considered a volume of essays, for its interpretations are elaborated with the same love of paradox and the same deft twists and turns of argument as we find in the other works. I shall treat them here as belonging to a separate, though related, form.

Li Yu's essays are often described by literary historians as part of the so-called *xiaopin* ("short version" or "short piece") literature that flourished from the middle of the sixteenth century to the end of the seventeenth. *Xiaopin* is a vague term denoting not a genre but an aesthetic quality, a mood, attitude, or spirit that may be present in a number of short forms such as the *ji* (descriptive account), the preface, the letter, the biography, or the diary.[2] Its common features are best exemplified in the literary theory of Yuan Hongdao, in the light of which, since good literature is an expression of the author's personal nature, truth-to-self is prized above all other qualities.[3] Works classified as *xiaopin* do not seek to transcend the individual self in the search for some general or normative truth. Indeed, their most prominent characteristic is a refusal to acknowledge any didactic links between the world of the individual self and the larger social and moral world— an attitude that results in an often lyrical emphasis on the minor and private experiences of life. (The word often means something like "literature in a minor key.") There are endless discussions, growing ever more refined, of teas and tea making, of art, of the artist's and writer's materials, of antiques, even of literature. Little in the subject matter of *xiaopin* literature was taboo—except the major themes of moral and political discourse.

Yuan Hongdao had two other requirements of good literature: *qu*, spontaneous vitality or zest, and *yun* ("tone"), the refinement of *qu*, a quality that induces aesthetic pleasure. A contemporary writer, Shen Shouzheng, brings all three concepts together with *xiaopin* in the following remarkable passage. Given Yuan Hongdao's view of literature as self-expression, it is not surprising to find Shen applying *yun* to people as well as to the aesthetic object.

> A towering crag in the mountains, a pebble that will fit into one's hand, the "bird and insect" style of calligraphy, the painting of Wen Tong and Ni Zan, the poetry of Wei Yingwu, Meng Haoran, Meng Jiao, and Jia Dao—the fact that these things drive the observer almost wild with delight is due solely to the remarkable quality of their *qu*. However, people who do not understand belittle them as strange, marginal, and *xiaopin*. Now, anyone who possesses a bold, uncompromising spirit of *yun*, being ashamed to be like others, will refuse to say what his peers say and will delight in saying what they either dare not say or else cannot say.

He prefers the strange to the ordinary, the marginal to the
central, and the small and true to the large and phony.[4]

The "minor key" literature was also a low-key literature, its prevailing
manner light-hearted and its tone mild and unassuming.

It is obvious that Li Yu owes much to Yuan Hongdao's ideas and
to the *xiaopin* movement in general. He is concerned with the self,
with things near at hand, and with sensuous and aesthetic feeling. He
does sometimes link his concerns to moral and political themes, but
the linking is mostly for humorous effect. However, his divergence
from the *xiaopin* aesthetic is as striking as his allegiance to it. He uses
the word *qu* to mean stylistic liveliness, but without the meaning of
spontaneous self-expression that Yuan assigns to it.[5] In general, Li Yu
is more concerned with the powers of invention and analysis than with
emotional self-expression, and he engages most often in exposition
and debate, which were only minor forms in *xiaopin* literature.

His demotic attitudes also contrast sharply with the aesthetic
exclusivism implied by the word *yun*. The *xiaopin* writers seem to vie
with one another in sensitivity, creating a mystique about the conventionally aestheticized aspects of daily life, whereas Li Yu, whether
or not we believe his claims about having joined the vulgar fashion in
order to lead it in the right direction, consciously takes on the role of
the plain man's guide in aesthetic as well as practical matters, as a
kind of demotic connoisseur. This approach accounts for his expository
stance; his discursiveness; his simple, humorous, yet vivid language;
and the range of commonplace topics he turned his mind to.

The Li Yu essay takes more than one form even within *Casual Expressions*. The essays that introduce the eight main fields and, within these
fields, the thirty-six major sections are noticeably more theoretical, in
a humorous manner, than the rest. They often begin with a broad
statement that is successively refined, by thesis and antithesis, through
the course of an intricate argument that culminates, generally, in some
reference to Li himself. It was clearly his intention to mimic—and
also, to a degree, to parody—the classical (*guwen*) essay. In these
pieces he is likely to link his immediate subject to the overarching
themes of Confucian thought—again, in the classical manner. The

fact that the quotations from the canonical texts are humorously mis-applied, and that the argument is often carried beyond the reasonable into the outrageous, is one source of his comedy. The organization of these introductory essays is noticeably tighter than in the others, and their style less free and expansive. Allowing for the difference in language, we can see in their qualities, especially the misapplied quotations and the farcically extended arguments, the same features that distinguish the prologues to Li Yu's fiction.

The essay "Enjoying Oneself," translated earlier in Chapter 4, is an example of a standard opening essay without the parodic element.[6] Li's essay on walls, which I have mentioned before, parodies the classical essay. At the end of this terse and cryptic piece, he notes that walls are our one possession that is shared with others and is of mutual benefit:

> Thus the things in a state that ought to be strong are its walls and moats, for only if they are strong will the state be strong. Similarly, in a house it is the wall that ought to be secure, for only if the wall is secure will the house be secure. In fact, serving others' interests means serving your own interests, too. If people could devote to their minds and bodies a fraction of the thought they devote to walls, they would be successful wherever they go.
>
> People mock my exclusive concern with idle feeling and my reluctance to discuss Chan religion or neo-Confucian philosophy. That is why I have casually developed this argument—to defend myself from the charge. It is not clear, though, whether my argument is acceptable to both the neo-Confucian savants and also to our Buddhist friends.[7]

His more informal essay is difficult to characterize. It may begin in almost any fashion; the personal element plays a larger part in it; its language is more expansive, and there is less attempt at parallelism; its tone is conversational, like that of his family letters; its homely images, subtly adapted, are much more frequent and its verbal exaggerations more pronounced; it has little or no linkage to the great themes; and it proceeds by association as much as by logic. His essay on the narcissus, translated in Chapter 4, is a fine example of the type.[8]

I will analyze one of these freer essays, the one on antiques.[9] Li Yu has begun by declaring that antiques will not be treated thoroughly in his book. The main points of the argument are as follows:

1. People worship antiques, which command high prices.
2. Those who buy them claim that it is not the objects as such that they value, but rather the sense they get of being in the presence of the ancients.
3. But if the ancients themselves were still alive, would people want to buy *them* at such high prices and bring them home?
4. Anyway, books are the best means of communing with the ancients.
5. Antiques—those that have charm—are of value to the rich, who need them as a relatively secure and compact way of preserving their wealth.
6. The problem is that poor people now copy the rich until collecting becomes second nature to them. Some men would sooner part with their wives and children than with their prize antiques.
7. Li Yu's book sets out to promote thrift.
8. Anyway, he is too poor to buy new things, let alone old.
9. Perhaps he is just using his poverty to excuse his ignorance of antiques.

The essay's subject is really his decision not to treat antiques, and he begins and ends with that decision, offering the reader the final possibility that the whole argument may be a ploy. In the course of the essay he mingles general and particular, personal and impersonal, plausible and outrageous.

His essay on beds has similar qualities. Next to their womenfolk, he says, men spend more time with their beds than with anything or anyone else.

> Of the hundred years in a man's life, half are spent in the daytime and half at night. Our days are spent in a variety

of places—in this room or that, on a boat, in a carriage—but our nights are spent in only one place, in bed. Thus, beds are our constant companions for half of our lifetimes—they surpass even our wives in that respect—and we ought to treat them more generously than anything else. I fault my contemporaries for throwing themselves heart and soul into finding a house and yet studiously neglecting the sleeping quarters. The reason they do so is that their beds are not seen by anyone else, only by themselves. But by that reasoning, since wives, concubines, and maids, the human counterparts of beds, are also seen only by us, would these men allow them to go about like hags, with unkempt hair and dirty faces, and not do anything about it?

I am quite different. Every time we move, I plan the sleeping quarters first, before seeing to anything else, because if wives and concubines are the human counterparts of beds, beds are the inanimate counterparts of wives and concubines. If I were to make a new design for a bed, I would have trouble paying the carpenter, but I have always done my best to decorate the bed and bed-curtains and to arrange the sleeping quarters. It is like a poor man's taking a wife. He cannot change her rustic look into that of a classic beauty; he merely sees that she is conscientious about washing and combing and that she makes liberal use of oils and creams. What are my methods? The first is to Make the Bed Bloom with Flowers; the second is to Provide a Frame for the Bed-curtain; the third is to Supply a Lock for the Bed-curtain; and the fourth is to Put Skirts on the Bed.[10]

At one point in *Casual Expressions*, Li Yu divides his essays into *lun* (discussion or theory) and *fang* (method or prescription), that is to say, into theoretical and practical discourse.[11] He disdains, however, to give directions for recipes or prescriptions (medical "cookbooks"),[12] let alone alchemical formulas, in which he has little or no faith. He even claims in the Guidelines that "the benefit of theory outweighs that of prescription."[13] In reality, of course, he offers countless tips, many of which are supported by theory; theory and practice are constantly intermingled in his essays.

In either case, he rarely quotes authorities, preferring instead to argue by other means. On taking hot baths, for example, one of life's pleasures, he reports that some Taoist experts advise against the practice, in the belief that it saps the vital forces.[14] Li has two counterarguments. First, by analogy; rain and dew are good for plants, hence bathing will not be harmful to humans. Second, he has tested it himself and observed his own reactions. Although at first he felt a little enervated, he continued his experiments until he found a suitably gradual process of increasing the heat. Analogical, experiential, and also teleological arguments are standard usage in his essays.

Four or five of the earliest essays deal with Li Yu's life in the 1630s and 1640s. The "Hui sha bian" ("Argument about the Returning Sha Spirits") was occasioned by his father's funeral in 1629.[15] A diviner had suggested that he and his family move out of their house to avoid his father's ghost as it revisited its earthly home in the company of two *sha* spirits. Denouncing the belief as superstition, Li Yu proceeds to rout the diviner in debate.

"A Deed of Sale for My Hill" treats his departure from his beloved Mt. Yi. Like most of his early prose pieces, it contains a statement—in this case an address rather than a debate.[16] He begins by arguing that, even if a hill can be bought, its mere purchase does not guarantee the new owner full possession. Money may buy its trees and rocks, but not the essence or spirit of the place, which is preserved in its name. Only virtuous deeds and brilliant writing will suffice to give one possession, in which case the name will change, the spirit and essence will be gone, and the hill can be taken over. Thus the great hills and mountains each have their "owners," the famous men who once lived there and still possess the names and spirits of the hills. Li Yu now turns to his own Mt. Yi:

> Mt. Yi, situated on the western border of Jinhua, is not mentioned in any gazetteers or local histories. It is little more than three hundred feet in height, and in area does

not exceed fifteen acres. It has no ancient pines or lush bamboos, no fantastic rocks or flying streams that would delight the eye and ear, and it was only because the members of my clan lived nearby that we bought it and settled there. We are little people, with no virtues worth recording, nor any ability in literature. But the hill has few outstanding views, anyway, and tossing some worthless phrases at it would not slight its value too greatly. Mistakenly, we assumed that we would keep possession of it forever. How could we have foreseen that the ravages of war would be followed by famine? While the eight members of my family were crying with hunger, I recorded all of my property and transferred it to others.

Alas! Did the hill forsake us, or did we forsake the hill? How hastily we parted, how sadly we took our farewells! But having sold it, we had no business lingering there. Then, in addition to the deed specifying the boundaries, I also wrote this piece to give to the buyer:

I have received from you the string of copper coins in payment for the physical substance of the hill, its rocks and trees. But you will have to wait before you can obtain the spirit of the place and change its name. When people nowadays are preparing some article for use, they write in one corner of it: "Bought by so-and-so on such-and-such a date." That way, no one else can steal it from them and claim it as his. How vastly more applicable this is to a fifteen-acre hill! What's more, I once wrote a poem about my Mt. Yi retreat, and published it in my collected poems, which circulated quite widely. Some day, if a visitor remarks, "This is Master Li's hill," will you not be angry? Openly receiving payment for something while covertly retaining possession of its name—that is sharp practice indeed. However, it is not anything that a former owner can prevent. If you wish to "change the dynasty," there is an easy solution open to you. Quickly climb up to a high point and compose a rhapsody. Make a tour around the hill, and wait for a poem to strike your mind. Try to render both of them novel and distinctive beyond the reach of my poetry. Confer long life on them by printing, and then let them circulate as rapidly as possible, so that people, on reading them, will say: "Mt. Yi doesn't belong to Master Li anymore. It has been sold to this man." In that case, even if I wished to retain covert possession of its name, who would believe me? If you do not take this advice, mark my words well. Don't complain that I failed to make things clear to you at the outset and gave you a bad name behind your back.

In this essay we see a novel idea, a striking gesture, and some ingenious twists and turns of argument, all of which are characteristic of Li Yu's essay style. In addition, the essay brings together two of his themes: his love of his property and his concern for literary immortality.

Li has two essays on family pets from the Mt. Yi days, "Burying the Dog" and "Expelling the Cat."[17] In the former he uses the debate format again, this time between the master (obviously Li Yu) and a visitor. His beloved dog, Divine Hound, a "big, black, docile yet courageous" animal, has been poisoned by burglars planning to rob the house over which he stood guard. The master mourns him extravagantly, and has to defend himself against his visitor's criticism.

"Expelling the Cat" begins with a comparison of the usefulness of the various domestic animals. Why are cats not classed with oxen and horses, chickens and dogs? Li Yu's answer is that the service the cat contributes is not disinterested, for it not only catches mice, it enjoys eating them. If it will not even perform that service, a cat is not to be tolerated.

> I once had a cat that had a black jacket and a white skirt—Black Clouds over Snow, as the common expression goes. Her looks gained her her master's favor, and he petted and stroked her and skimped on his own food in order to give her tidbits. As a sign of his affection, he even shared his sleeping quarters with her. As her natural instincts developed, she came to look on mice as the enemy. There were some mice she did not chase, but those she did chase, she always caught. But before long she grew bored with this routine and longed for something different. She took to climbing up to precarious places like an ape and to running about in the open like a dog. She found her food among

the bird life and was ashamed to be ranked with the domestic animals any longer. By day she went hunting outside, while at night she slept soundly at home. She thought nothing of it if the creatures who had once been her enemy now shared her sleeping quarters. The situation grew so bad that the mice were going about publicly in droves; no container in the whole house was safe from them. Then, just as the master was about to pronounce her guilt, she happened to get pregnant. Shall I wait a while, he wondered. Before long, she bore two kittens and spent all day suckling them, which left her no time to forage in the fields. When she caught sight of the young chicks and puppies, she drooled with desire and sprang into action, at which the chickens and dogs set up a great clamor and lodged an accusation with the master. He flew into a rage, and said: "If I don't put a stop to this menace, the two species could be wiped out. Moreover, the reason I delayed before was the hope that the kittens might compensate for their mother. But now the kittens, in their innocence, will see their mother as the fount of wisdom. If they should imitate her behavior, they will think it normal to eat chicks and puppies and deviant to catch mice. In that case, what was still an emotional drive in the mother will become instinctive in the kittens. I cannot imagine where it will lead!"

The family suggested selling her, but the master objected. "That would be a lucky break for the seller, but what crime has the buyer committed?" "Shall we put her to death, then?" The master replied: "Her crimes merit execution, but her past contributions cannot be ignored. Moreover, there are her two kittens. How can we fail to preserve their mother? 'Executing the father and employing the son'— that is a practice that could be employed once, but that cannot be followed very often." He then proceeded to draw up her sentence: "You failed in your responsibility to catch mice, which amounts to dereliction of duty and comes under the statute of expulsion. You terrorized the meritorious, which is 'preventing good men from serving the state' and carries the penalty of exile. Several *li* from here, there is a great crossroads. Let it serve as your Northern Wilderness."

The master sends the boy off with the cat, which departs contritely, but with a brilliantly apt quotation from the *Poetry Classic* on her lips. He then warns the kittens: "As you follow your innate abilities, see that you are not affected by your mother's prenatal influence, but that you cover up her misdeeds with your good behavior. That would be the filial thing to do in your case." He addresses the other animals, too, which are awed, presumably, by his drastic action. Then the boy returns. He has taken the cat to a wood that is full of birds. "It was just as if she were waiting for something. Then, with a single bound, she sprang up and showed off her old tricks." The master sighs deeply over the cat's failure to repent and change her ways.[18]

The essay shows Li Yu's gentle domestic humor. It is not an allegory, although officials are sometimes represented in Chinese literature as cats (appointed to catch mice and thus keep order), and although there is constant reference to administration and officialdom.[19] It is true of this essay, as of much Chinese humor, that the official references are there to add an extra dimension; the constant use of examination images in Li's fiction fulfills a similar function.

The early essays, fresh and lively as they are, give only a hint of what was to come. Except for their personal reference, their concern with the domestic, and their humor, they hardly prepare us for *Casual Expressions*.

Li Yu himself set great store by this book, as I have mentioned; it was to be his best hope for immortality, and his letters at the time of publication are full of his pride in it. To one friend he writes that "its novelty is even greater than that of my other books," and he advises him to start with the Women and Houses sections; "perhaps it will break the solitude of your journey for ten days or so." The first chapters are on playwriting; they can be put off till later. "Why not read them after you've come to the end?" To another he gives similar advice: "Please begin by reading the Women and the Health and Pleasure sections, because you, my dear sir, have long been a past master with regard to such matters." When the friend's letter returns full of praise for his book, Li Yu compares the praise to a massage; it "scratches me just where I itch," and "can make a man die and then bring him back to life again."[20]

Li Yu also used the book, as I have discussed, in his quest for patronage. By this time he had heard that President Gong was buying the City Recluse Garden, and he looked forward to advising him on its renovation, claiming a talent for ordering nature: "Unfortunately, I have not been able to develop my talent, and no one has seen fit to employ it. Should I die with my ambitions unfulfilled, so that the Creator has borne me entirely in vain, it will be one of the greatest tragedies of all time! That is why I felt compelled to write the book *Casual Expressions of Idle Feeling,* relying on empty words to reveal a little of the knowledge I possess."[21] You Tong's comment on this letter runs: "Those who enter the Mustard Seed Garden see things they have never seen before, just as those who read *Casual Expressions* hear things they have never heard before. If he gets charge of the City Recluse Garden and is able to develop fully his intricate ideas, it is quite impossible to anticipate what remarkable scenery he will devise. Reading this whets one's interest."

Unlike most authorial hopes, Li Yu's were realized. In scope and subject matter, the book has no parallel; the numerous Chinese works on the scholar's studio furnishings and the recluse's pleasures do not come near to matching it.[22] Its organization and analytical approach, its style and humorous manner set it apart from other books. It is more than connoisseurship, more than know-how; it is, as it professes to be, a reflection of the tastes, interests, and thoughts of its author.

Formally speaking, *Casual Expressions* is a system of 300 essays, many of substantial length, in eight fields, roughly translatable as follows: Writing Plays; Putting on Plays; Women and Beauty; Houses and Gardens; Furniture, China, and the like; Food and Drink; Flowers and Trees; Health and Pleasure. The eight fields are divided into 36 sections, which are, in turn, subdivided into 264 topics. The sections and topics, 300 in all, each have titled essays.

Attached to the essays are 67 notes by two dozen different commentators, the most frequent being the writers You Tong and Yu Huai, both of whom also wrote prefaces for the book. There are also 20 unsigned notes. From the distribution of the notes, it would seem that Li Yu wrote the book in much the order we have it. All of You Tong's notes, for example, are in the Drama and Women fields, as are Yu Huai's, except for a single comment on furniture. The comments on Houses and Furniture are largely by friends residing in Nanjing, including Du Jun, Wang Gai, and Wang Zuoju. The latter parts, Food and Drink, Flowers and Trees, and Health and Pleasure, have fewer notes by fewer people; one of these note-writers is Shen Xinyou, Li Yu's son-in-law. No doubt these notes were finished last, when there was no time to send the essays away to friends.

The book is equipped with an elaborate, pretentious set of seven Guidelines, four of them labeled "aspirations," that is, things Li Yu aims to do, and three labeled "prohibitions," things he prides himself on not doing. The four aspirations may be seen as addressed to the authorities, especially the emperor; they are an attempt by Li Yu, not entirely serious, to ingratiate himself. What links the aspirations to the prohibitions is his prime value of novelty. Li Yu strenuously asserts his own devotion to the new, but he also says that the craze for the fashionably new cannot be stopped, and that the only solution is to channel it in the right direction. This leads him into the prohibitions, all of them about newness, in which he gives his usual diatribe against plagiarism, and even against imitating others and repeating oneself.

But the Guidelines are, as one might expect, an inadequate guide to a book whose justification is that it deals with Li Yu's own pleasures, pursuits, and ideas in detail and with a fresh wit. All eight fields are intimately connected with his own experience. He claimed to possess two skills to a superlative degree: writing plays and building gardens and pavilions, and thus this book is largely about his two main talents. His training of Miss Qiao and Miss Wang for the stage lies behind Putting on Plays, just as the education and advice he gave them informs Women and Beauty. The opinions in Food and Drink, Health and Pleasure spring from his lifelong interest in the sensuous pleasures and—a corollary—the preservation of physical and mental health.

In literary terms, the book is unified by his invented self and its simulated talk, and to a great extent it is actually written around his own ideas and inventions. Even when he has no invention to offer, he approaches his subject as if he had, and once launched on a topic, he is quick to brush aside the points he regards as established in order to concentrate on those on which he has his own ideas. There is a touch of comic posturing about his accounts of his own inventions which, if it were to be taken seriously, would qualify as megalomania. The Furniture field, for example, is really just a string of his inventions.[23] There is the Warm Chair, which I have mentioned, and the Cool Stool, which uses evaporation to cool the writer's seat. There is the flower-stand for his bed, which provides the scent of flowers throughout the night. There is his idea for making locks on trunks invisible, or at least unobtrusive. There is his device for tamping down the ashes in an incense-burner, as well as a technique for getting a crackleware effect on screens, and a way of combining poetry and painting more effectively. There are two methods of trimming the lamps hung at outdoor theatricals; one is his "long scissors," the other a device that lowers the lamps on a cord and allows them to be trimmed behind a curtain, so that the audience will not be distracted. He reports his experiments, and also, as in the last case, the occasions on which he lacked the money to try them out: "I merely suspend this brilliant idea here to await someone else's experiment."[24]

He frequently gives us the course of his invention. He had wanted to build a pleasure boat for the West Lake, but could not afford to do so, and in any case he soon moved away to Nanjing. The boat's original feature was to have been a fan-shaped "window," that is, an opening in its side through which the passengers could admire the scenery as they sipped their tea. (The book has an illustration.) We hear in detail of how Li Yu improved upon the idea in his house in Nanjing. Then in 1669, when a couple of his trees drowned in the floods, he found a use for their curved limbs as an artistic frame for his window.[25]

The essays do not deal with the major subjects of aesthetic appreciation, such as poetry, painting, and calligraphy, nor with the conventional minor subjects and pursuits, such as antiques, inkstones, seals, tea, wine, and the like, nor with the common subjects of playful writing, such as games, pastimes, and visits to courtesans.

One of Li's problems was economic. Since good objects cost money, was he to become merely an interior decorator for the rich? He claims to be writing for the man of humble means—he has to do so, he says, being poor himself—while refusing to cede a higher value to things that only the rich can afford. For him, it is not an object's rarity or the cost of its material that makes it valuable, but its practical usefulness and artistic quality. Contemporary porcelain is as good as that from the best Ming kilns.[26] Precious metals are of no account, and there is no cachet pertaining to antiques. Design is the great equalizer: quite ordinary modern objects may be well designed and beautiful, just as ancient or expensive things may be ugly.

Of course, his book was meant to be savored by the rich and eminent—why else should he send copies to Gong Dingzi and the others?—but it was also addressed to the literate public. It contains very few aesthetic shibboleths. At one point, the word *wenren* (literati) is even defined as "anyone who can read." [27] Like Li Yu's own fiction and plays, *Casual Expressions* was intended for a fairly broad readership.

Li Yu's chapters on drama constitute the most novel and systematic treatment the genre ever received in premodern times. His main innovation, apart from his systematic, analytical approach, is in upsetting the traditional priorities. He prides himself on beginning with plot construction,[28] a subject that in earlier treatises was rarely, if ever, mentioned. By construction he means the choice, first, of new subject matter, and second, of an initial plot conjuncture, his so-called "governing element," which will result in a unified play.[29] Construction displaces music and aria prosody, the subjects that dominate earlier discussions of the drama. In justifying the innovation, Li Yu claims that there are guides available for aria prosody, but none for construction. As for music, it is a technical matter, distinct from, and inferior to, literary composition.[30] For the prosody of aria-writing, he claims no authority either; his advice is simply to follow the rules, lest you be ignored by the public.[31]

His second emphasis is on speech, which he puts on a par with song—a revolutionary idea. But even speech is not without its rules, for certain prosodic criteria apply to it also. Li Yu vigorously defends the notoriously large amount of speech in his work, while admitting that in his earlier plays he may have gone to excess. He includes a debate over the merits of his dialogue in which an admirer says: "In the past, dialogue was always regarded as speech. It was casually spoken, and that was that. But Liweng's dialogue is to be regarded as literature. One must fathom the meaning of every word. In the past, dialogue need only be intelligible on the page, and no one cared whether it was smooth or awkward."[32] In his own plays, it appears that speech meant at least as much to him as song, and he has advice in plenty to offer drama teachers and actors on its enunciation and delivery, including the subjects of emphasis and rhythm. "As I look around at the acting profession, there must be 20 percent to 30 percent who sing well, but only 1 percent or 2 percent who deliver speech well."[33]

The third emphasis is precisely that: dramatic training and performance. Two of his chapters are on these subjects, including the selection of drama teachers, the choice and adaptation of plays, the training of actors, and certain aspects of performance. Most previous treatises had dealt only with texts, not performance; if they refer to performance at all, it is merely to correct faults in singing. But Li Yu was a man of the theater as well as a playwright, and he constantly talks of plays in terms of their effect on the audience.

Whereas most earlier treatments had been addressed to the writer's peers, this work, with its humorous personal reference and lively wit, is directed specifically to the novice playwright and to the prospective owner of a private dramatic troupe, and, through this highly restricted audience, to the broad mass of readers, a fact that some occasionally simple explanations make clear.

Since the drama chapters have little to say of old plays except how to renovate them, and nothing to say of contemporary plays except what is wrong with them, we are led to ask whether they apply best to Li Yu's own work. The answer is yes, at least with regard to his interest in an original plot, rationally but ingeniously organized; in the subtler structural qualities he calls "fine stitching"; in the characters' motivation; in dialogue and comic byplay; and in theatricality. The chapters are angled to his own interests and strengths, which is not to say that they lack self-criticism. On the other hand, they do not give due emphasis to his love of social paradox, his play of ideas, his internal patterning, or his ribaldry. They show us Li Yu analyzing the Southern drama with a bias toward some, but not all, of his own concerns.

Li's chapters on women are entitled *Shengrong* (voice and facial expression), signifying feminine beauty.[34] Actually, his concern was not with women in general but with concubines, and particularly with how to choose, train, and treat them, for concubines, unlike wives, were the choice of their husbands.

The modern reader will undoubtedly be discomfited to realize that the concubines Li Yu is speaking of are girls of no more than fourteen or fifteen. (Miss Qiao and Miss Wang were twelve when he acquired them). Even the thought that this guilt-free Humbert Humbert was living in a China of like-minded men will not ease the reader's embarrassment, any more than the knowledge that Li Yu himself was relatively considerate of women both in precept and practice. There is a cultural gap between him and ourselves that cannot be bridged.

Much of his advice is on the practical matter of how to pick the most pleasing girl with regard to her complexion, the shape of her eyes and eyebrows, and the softness of her hands and feet, as well as the ineffable quality of *taidu*, of which the nearest English equivalents are "charm" and "grace." Other essays include hints on beauty care (washing and combing, hairstyling, perfume, cosmetics); on hair ornaments; on dresses, shoes, and stockings; and on accomplishments such as poetry, music, and singing. The advice is detailed, but not so detailed as to deter the general reader. Oddly, little is said about temperament, except that the shape of a girl's eyes gives an indication of her disposition.

There is nothing overtly erotic about the writing, except in the passage on fondling women's feet, translated earlier in Chapter 4.[35] Beauty is valued for its suggestiveness, for its power to induce an erotic mood. It is not true passion in a girl that is being celebrated—the emotions implied lack the reciprocity of love—but a naive, unsophisticated charm that induces in her husband moods ranging from aesthetic admiration through piquant enjoyment to the onset of erotic feeling. It is certainly not mere sensuality; Li Yu detests girls who make up for their lack of accomplishment by fawning on their husbands.[36]

These are young girls that he writes of, doubly subordinate as women and as concubines, and they induce in him a certain sympathy. In a trivial case, he urges every household to provide flowers so that the girl can choose her own ornaments:

> If a poor man marries a beautiful woman, he, too, ought to plant trees and flowers in any vacant space beside his house, in order to provide adornments for her hair. Other things may be skimped on, but not this. How long will her youth last? It is rare for a man to meet with beauty. Even

some of the noblest and richest of men have been thwarted by a niggardly fortune or else an empress's jealousy and have lived out their whole lives without ever making love to a beautiful woman. What sort of a fellow am I, you should ask, to claim such happiness for myself? If I fail to get one or two things to delight her heart and adorn her beauty, what a waste of heaven's bounty! It would be like emptying fine rice on a dungheap! Even the poorest of men, without a scrap of land on which to plant flowers, ought to beg some from a famous garden or else buy them at a stall. Even if it costs him a few cash a day, that will only mean one less cup of wine. How much greater the benefit, if the flowers not only delight the girl's heart, but please his own eye![37]

More important, Li Yu takes up the cause of the education of women, especially concubines, and attacks the vicious notion that equated education for women with immorality.

"If a woman is without talent, it is a virtue." Even if this statement seems reasonable, it was not made without a special point in mind: because many intelligent women have lost their chastity, women without talent are to be preferred. Presumably, it was somebody's *cri de coeur,* but it belongs in the same category as considering study and public service dangerous—and leaving a deathbed testament forbidding your descendants to study or serve—just because your son got into trouble as an official. Both re-actions are based on the principle of "giving up eating because you have seen someone choke on his food." Can study really be given up? Can all public careers be abandoned? I hold that talent and virtue are not incompatible. Not all talented women have been unchaste, any more than all lecherous women have been educated. The only essential is that the woman's husband have an appreciation for her talent and the skill to direct it.[38]

He goes on to advocate the education of concubines in both literary composition and musical performance, and not merely to advocate it, but to describe the steps by which it is to be undertaken. His description is practical and highly original, revealing his own experience in educating Miss Qiao and Miss Wang, but it is also sympathetic to the girls' interests. He is trying to educate his readers into an awareness of a girl's feelings, partly from kindness, but also for the sake of the tender eroticism such an awareness will evoke.

I will pass rapidly over the next four fields—Houses, Furniture, Food and Drink, Flowers and Trees. The sheer variety of the topics dealt with in each field is indicated by this rough list of the contents of Houses:[39] the direction a house should face, paths, the slope of the site, eaves, ceilings, paving, sprinkling and sweeping, trash disposal, windows and latticework, inner and outer walls, tablets and couplets, rockeries and grottoes. Illustrations and diagrams are attached. A good deal of the advice is quite specific; the essay on the best way to sprinkle and sweep, for example, is surely the most detailed treatment that subject has ever received.[40] Li's approach is not analytical in the sense that the drama chapters are analytical; it resembles that of his chapters on women in focusing on the new ideas he is contributing.

His last field is that of *yiyang*, which means recuperation and relaxation, although the chapter's contents make it clear that his real subject is physical pleasure and health.[41] (Pleasure is the key to health, in Li Yu's opinion.) The essays contain his views on the instinctual basis of pleasure and on hedonism itself, together with the best mental strategies for enhancing pleasure and minimizing pain, as discussed earlier in Chapter 4.[42] What they omit is fully as remarkable as what they include. One looks in vain for any ideal of service or duty as the proper function of man. One's duty, at least in this book, is to oneself: to maximize one's pleasure in a prudent and rational way.

Here is the opening essay of Section 6, "On the Treatment of Illness":

> "Take no medicine for your illness, and the results will be the same as if you had consulted the average doctor." How many endangered lives have been saved by this twenty-word elixir! If the advice is offered to someone just after he has contracted an illness, it will be condemned as im-

practical. But when all the treatments have been tried and every effort exhausted and the patient is still critically ill, he will have no choice but to follow it. It will be a case of heaven and man both forcing him to consult the "average doctor." Then, should his illness vanish without further treatment, he will at last be convinced of the truth of what the elixir says.

As I see it, the world contains only those who are afraid of death; it contains no medicine capable of restoring them to life. "Medicine cures only non-fatal illnesses, just as Buddhism claims only predestined converts." How true that is! It must not be regarded as a mere commonplace. But we find it as hard to refrain from treating an illness as we do to refrain from prayer in a time of drought. We know full well that the moisture is up there in the heavens and that no amount of praying is going to bring it down, but how can we sit idly by and let the crops wither? So we simply throw ourselves into prayer.

All my life I have been prone to illness, but now in my old age I take no medicine at all. I have tried every herb in existence—I'm practically Shen Nong incarnate—but, apart from rhubarb for the relief of constipation, I have found nothing that works effectively and reliably. All my writings and ideas throughout the course of my career have been completely of my own invention, and the same thing holds true for my methods of treatment. When I get an illness, I immediately study its origins, and only after identifying the cause do I proceed to treat it and prescribe for it. By this, I do not mean the kind of treatment found in the medical texts, but something improvised and ad hoc. Nor do I mean the sort of prescription given in pharmacopoeias, but anything I fancy that happens to be close at hand. I am well aware that I ought not to be offering unsubstantiated advice, but let me just talk uncritically here, to suit the public's penchant for uncritical listening. Readers of this book should accept the theories they find worthy of belief, and ignore any facts that seem questionable. "Not to allow the words to obscure the sentence, nor the sentence to obscure the intended meaning"—that is the attitude expected of all who read Liweng's books.[43]

One of the items under "On the Treatment of Illness" is this astonishing but entirely characteristic essay, "Curing the Patient with the Aid of Someone He is Passionately in Love with."

Third: Someone the patient is passionately in love with can serve as a remedy. Private passion will always find its love object. Rulers have often been denied the loyalty of their officials and fathers the affection of their sons, with the result that the most alien and incompatible people, those least worthy of love, have become the focus of their thoughts and the be-all and end-all of their existence— that is to say, the objects of their love. Whether it is a pretty young wife or a beautiful concubine, a dissolute crony or a catamite, a close relative or friend, in every case the longing to possess one's beloved or the lack of an opportunity to make love to him or her may result in illness. Even if the cause of the illness was not related to love, once the patient is enduring its pain and frustration, his thoughts will inevitably turn to the one he is in love with, and if he is now brought together with his beloved, he will be like a fish returning to water. In such cases, the patient's looks and spirits will always show a sudden improvement, as if the demons of illness had departed.

Of all the remedies I am proposing, sex is the most powerful; the majority of illnesses suffered by young people are caused by it. Parents, in their ignorance, make the mistake of heeding the doctors' warnings against sex. Little do they realize that the notion of sex as harmful applies to the normal case, while the notion of sex as therapeutic applies to the variant. People may be dying of love, but no one treats them with love! If someone were dying of starvation, we would hardly forbid him to eat, just so that he could keep Bo Yi's and Shu Qi's fast! Any boy or girl, past puberty but not yet married, who gets ill and does not immediately respond to treatment, can be cured by this means and no other. If the patient's health is too delicate to allow him to make love, a mere visit to his bedside will assure him that his beloved is his and thus allay most of his lovesickness. It is the same as inhaling a medicine instead of taking it; it still penetrates the fibers and strengthens the physique. If the patient's beloved is from outside the women's quarters, it will be much easier to bring her in and arrange a congress. Having her approach the sickbed and make love is not so much a matter of inviting him to bear her company, as of paying for a remedy and getting him to try it. Good-hearted, filial sons taking care of their parents, as well as stern fathers and indulgent mothers who cherish their sons, are enjoined to provide this remedy well in advance, to guard against illness.[44]

The whole book is deeply personal, first in that Li Yu's tastes and ideas form its subject matter, and second in that his personae are omnipresent. Some of the latter include the humorous veteran dispensing his hard-won know-how; the brilliant conversationalist, outrageous and incorrigible; the poor scribbler mocking his own poverty; the sane and sensible hedonist. Much humor is extracted from the author's various guises. Here is Li Yu, the servant of his public, with the usual self-mockery and perhaps also a rare hint of self-contempt, at the end of his essay on winter pleasures: "Alas! What does other men's pursuit of pleasure have to do with me, that in its service my mind has become dulled, my tongue is on fire, and my hand is about to come off at the wrist? Can it be that I have a compulsion to curry favor, and that I use paper and ink instead of a smooth and subtle approach?"[45]

Finally, a good deal of *Casual Expressions* is actually about Li Yu. There are his travels, his narrow escapes from death (in an essay on turtles), his idyllic sojourn in the mountains during the fighting (in an essay on summertime pleasures), his passions (narcissi, crabs), his dislikes (garlic, turnips, turtles), and his illnesses.[46] And there is also the oath he once published to the effect that he never had attacked, and never would attack, anybody in his plays. If he has broken the oath, he asks, why has the Creator not punished him during the twenty years that have elapsed since he swore it? His answer shows a rather

different self from the one he presents to us in the patronage letters
with which this book began:

> Let us put aside the question of what happens after my
> death, and talk of my life now. I am nearly sixty, and if I
> should go to my coffin any time soon, it would not be an
> early death. I used to feel "Bodao's anxiety," but now I
> have five sons and two daughters, plus more than one wife
> who is pregnant or who has just delivered and expects to
> be pregnant again. Although my sons are all as unworthy
> as "Liu Biao's pigs and dogs," at least I have someone to
> comfort me in my old age; I do not share the pauper's fears
> of having nobody to turn to. And although I may be old,
> my strength has not diminished. I cross rivers and climb
> mountains so vigorously that often the young men can't
> keep up with me. My face may be drawn, but my semen
> and blood have not dwindled; visiting the pleasure quarters,
> I feel my sexual powers as strong as ever. What I am con-
> cerned about is poverty, but at least poverty is not illness.
> What I lack are honors, but honors are not something
> everyone has the good fortune to obtain. From all this, one
> might conclude that the pity shown me by the Creator has
> been great indeed. And he has taken pity on me, not be-
> cause of my talent, nor yet because of my virtue, but because
> I harbored no ulterior motives. The books I have written
> in the course of my life, although of no benefit to either
> conscience or morality, would, if piled one on top of the
> other, stand almost as tall as the "rice-eating Cao Jiao." If
> there were even a trace of malice secreted in their pages,
> if there were a stiletto or two planted here and there in
> them, do you suppose for one moment that the Creator
> would have been too busy to snatch me away, and that he
> would let a man who had sown the seeds of his own ruin
> survive to old age and go on living this mock-crazy, reckless
> life in the world of letters?[47]

Notes

A Note on the Sources of Li Yu's Biography. There are two main biographical sources for Li Yu: his own poetry and prose, and the clan genealogy. Li Yu collected his poetry and prose in *Liweng yijia yan* (*Liweng's Independent Words*) and *Liweng yijia yan erji* (*Liweng's Independent Words, Second Collection*). The former appeared probably in 1673, the latter in late 1678 or early 1679. After Li's death in 1680, the printing blocks of the two editions were used again several times in a combined edition. Then, in 1730, there appeared *Liweng yijia yan quanji* (*Complete Collection of Liweng's Independent Words*), a new edition by the Jieziyuan that integrates the first and second collections and makes various important substitutions and additions. Details of the textual history will be found in the section "Editions of *Independent Words* (*Yijia yan*)" following the Notes.

Ideally, the first and second collections (the second survives only in the combined reprint) should be the editions of reference. But they are extremely rare, whereas the 1730 edition has been republished several times and is accessible in most of the larger sinological libraries. It has also been reproduced in the fifteen-volume *Li Yu quanji* (*Complete Works of Li Yu*) edited by Helmut Martin and published by the Chengwen Chubanshe in Taipei in 1970. The copy reproduced is that in the Literature Department of Kyoto University. Unfortunately, it is illegible at a number of points, and rather than give its superimposed pagination, I have chosen to cite the original pagination, which should hold true for the other editions that are labeled Jieziyuan. Note that all the passages translated in this book have been checked against the combined reprint, also entitled *Liweng yijia yan quanji*, in the Library of Congress.

The *Xianqing ouji* (*Casual Expressions of Idle Feeling*) was first published separately by the Yishengtang in Nanjing in sixteen *juan*, and then republished in the 1730 edition in six. Reference is made here to the edition edited by Shan Jinheng and published by the Zhejiang Guji Chubanshe in Hangzhou in 1985. Translated passages have been checked against the Yishengtang edition in the Harvard-Yenching Library at Harvard University. In the case of Li Yu's plays, reference is to the Shidetang edition reproduced in *Li Yu quanji*. (The copy reproduced is that in National Taiwan University.) In the case of the story collections *Wusheng xi* (*Silent Operas*) and *Shi'er lou* (*Twelve Structures*), reference is also to the editions reproduced in *Li Yu quanji*. (The copies reproduced are in the Sonkeikaku in Tokyo and Academia Sinica in Taiwan, respectively.)

The existence of a genealogy of Li Yu's clan was brought to light in two articles by Zhao Wenqing, "Li Yu shengping shiji de xin faxian," *Xiwen* (1981.4): 49–52, and "Youguan Li Yu shengping de jige wenti," *Zhejiang shifan xueyuan xuebao* (Social Sciences Edition, 1981.1: 58–63). The genealogy is the Dunmutang filiation (one of four) of the *Longmen Lishi zongpu*. It is a block-print edition, last revised in 1923, which is preserved in Xiali Village of Lanqi County in Zhejiang. The genealogy has not been republished, and my knowledge of it is drawn from Zhao Wenqing's articles as well as from Jiang Feng's "Li Yu jiashi ji qita," *Xiwen* (1982.3): 63–64, which is a critique of Zhao's use of oral lore in the first-mentioned article. Yuan Yizhi's "Li Yu shengzunian kaobian," *Wenxue pinglun congkan* 13 (1982): 200–205, criticizes the genealogy itself as to the date of Li Yu's birth—1610, whereas Li Yu himself believed that he was born in 1611. The same critical attitude toward the genealogy is found in Xia Xieshi's "Li Yu shengping chutan," *Xiqu yanjiu* 10 (Sept. 1983): 162–181. However, most scholars have tended to accept the genealogy's statements even when they clash with Li Yu's assertions.

The pioneer, and still the outstanding, biographical study is Sun Kaidi's "Li Liweng yu *Shi'er lou,*" which was first published in *Tushuguanxue jikan* 9.3–4 (1935): 379–441, and which then, in adapted form, served as the introduction to the Yadong Tushuguan (Shanghai) edition of the *Shi'er lou* in 1949. A slightly revised version of the original article appears in Sun's *Cangzhou houji* (Beijing: Zhonghua, 1985), pp. 151–205. Gu Dunrou's "Li Liweng nianpu," an unpublished, undated manuscript preserved in Beijing University Library, differs from Sun's account in several respects. Huang Lizhen amplifies and, in a few cases, corrects Sun's account in her *Li Yu yanjiu* (Taipei: Chun Wenxue, 1974), pp. 1–46. She also corrects Li Yu's own mistaken chronology of his 1673 journey to Beijing.

The works just listed are the most important contributions to Li Yu's biography before the discovery of the genealogy. Among those that have appeared since, in addition to Zhao Wenqing's articles, the following seem to be the most significant: Shan Jinheng, "Li Yu nianbiao," *Zhejiang shifan xueyuan xuebao* (Social Sciences Edition, 1982.4): 36–46; Xia Xieshi, "Li Yu shengping chutan"; and Xiao Rong, *Li Yu pingzhuan* (Hangzhou: Zhejiang wenyi, 1985). When these half-dozen studies agree on a point, I have not given the evidence in specific notes.

1. Making a Living

1. Gong's generosity was legendary. Li Yu's elegy "Dazongbo Gong Zhilu xiansheng wange," *Liweng yijia yan quanji*, 5:47ab, asserts that Gong went into debt to help others. He had a talented mistress, Meisheng, who traveled everywhere with him. His character as bon vivant is vilified in later Qing attacks; see *Qingdai jinhui shumu buyi* (Shanghai: Commercial Press, 1957), II, 273. Note that Li Yu has some defensive poems about his own habit of taking his concubines with him on his patronage journeys; see, for example, "Yu xi funü chu you you xiao qi shi ji zhe shi yi jie chao," *Liweng yijia yan quanji*, 6:26a. People criticize his journeys as resembling a cavalcade, but he prefers that criticism to being labeled an itinerant monk. The story of the journey is told in the prologues to the set of ten poems he wrote on the death of Miss Wang; see "Hou duanchang shi shishou you xu," ibid., 6:51b–56b.

2. See "Yu Gong Zhilu dazongbo," *Liweng yijia yan quanji*, 3:4a–6a. The four *jueju* sent with this letter are to be found in ibid., 7:50a–51a. Li Yu may have met him for the first time in Hangzhou in 1657, when Gong traveled there with Meisheng; see Dong Qian, "Gong Zhilu nianpu," part 2, *Zhonghe yuekan* 3.2 (Feb. 1942): 68, on Gong's travels. Visiting Nanjing on the same journey, they lodged in the Garden of the Urban Recluse (Shiyinyuan). Li Yu met Gong in Beijing in 1666; see *Xianqing ouji*, 1:26. Gong wrote the name tablet for Li's Mustard Seed Garden (Jieziyuan); it is pictured in *Xianqing ouji*, "Lianbian," 4:176. The date given on the tablet's picture is summer 1669, but Gong could not have written it in the Mustard Seed Garden; he was in Beijing at the time. (See "Gong Zhilu nianpu," part 3, *Zhonghe yuekan* 3.3, March 1942: 79–88.) He must have written the name in Beijing and sent it to Li Yu.

3. "Yu Chen Xueshan shaozai," *Liweng yijia yan quanji*, 3:6a–9a. Li Yu enjoyed "twenty years of friendship" with Chen; see "Ji da Chen Xueshan shaozai," ibid., 6:31ab. (It is one of the two poems that Li Yu sent with this letter in reply to Chen's letter and poems.) Note that the other vice-president of the Board of Civil Office at the time was Li Zhifang, who had held minor office in Jinhua in the late 1640s and who was also a friend of Li Yu's. The "great beauty" is my paraphrase for Xishi, the legendary beauty whose every mannerism, even her frown, was imitated by other women. The reference to "lived in the same age as he" is to the Han emperor Wudi, who is said to have uttered this regret on reading a rhapsody by the poet Sima Xiangru. (Sima *was* his contemporary.) For Li Yu, Sima Xiangru was the prime example of the properly appreciated writer. The reference to "seven or eight years old" is actually expressed in an allusion to Tao Qian's poem "Ze zi." All translations of Li Yu's writings are my own.

4. "Yu Ji Bozi," *Liweng yijia yan quanji*, 3:9a–10b. Li Yu sent a poem also—see "Ji Ji Bozi," ibid., 6:30b–31a—in which he refers to Ji's old house as near the Mustard Seed Garden. On Gong's patronage of Ji, see Deng Zhicheng, *Qingshi jishi chubian* (Shanghai: Shanghai guji, 1984), I, 19–20.

5. "Fu Ke Yanchu zhangke," *Liweng yijia yan quanji*, 3:41b–43a. Gifts of cloaks and chicken and millet dinners refer to archetypal stories of patronage and friendship, respectively.

6. "You fu pianzha," *Liweng yijia yan quanji*, 3:43b. Ke's letter is appended.

7. "Fu Chen Xueshan shaozai," *Liweng yijia yan quanji*, 3:39ab, and "You yu Yanchu zhangke," ibid., 3:44ab. For Li Yu's contacts with Songgotu, see "Ti Suo xiangguo yuanting erlian," ibid., 4:13ab; "Zeng Suo Yu'an xiangguo," ibid., 4:18ab; and "Cheng Suo Yu'an xiangguo ershou," ibid., 8:79b–80a.

8. "You yu Yanchu zhangke."

9. Li Yu could be disingenuous when the occasion required. See "Yu Wei Danzu zhizhi," *Liweng yijia yan quanji*, 3:2a–3b, in which he writes that he is leaving Nanjing to avoid embarrassment, since everyone assumes he will benefit from his friend Wei's appointment. With one stroke, he appears virtuous and also delivers a subtle reminder to his friend. Li Yu's poems occasionally reflect compunction at having to ask for patronage; see "Lü kuang," ibid., 5:89b.

10. See "Nan gui daoshang sheng er zi he ershou," *Liweng yijia yan quanji*, 6:56b–57a.

11. See especially the letters. "Jian Cong Muxu," *Liweng yijia yan quanji*, 3:25a,

suggests that the eminent person Li Yu is going to see may not even know what "pure talk" is. "Fu Tang Junzong," ibid., 3:25b, complains of nausea after eating rich food and asks for simple fare and "pure talk" instead. Of course this may be a polite gesture to an impecunious host, but it is repeated elsewhere, for example, in "Yu Li Renshu," ibid., 3:35b. For the sharp distinction that Li Yu drew between his patrons, whom he called *dizhu*, and his friends, see "Sizitie ci Wulin zhuqinyou zhi zhao," ibid., 3:29b–30a.

12. "Yu Zhao Jieshan," ibid., 3:25ab: "I won't take this cheap merchandise again!" His accounts of the failure of his journeys come in his patronage letters, and are therefore suspect, but he says much the same in his letters to his family. Note that he made many shorter patronage journeys, even during these years: to Hangzhou in 1664, to Suzhou in 1671, and again to Hangzhou in 1674. Li Yu himself claims that he could not afford to buy the site of his long-desired garden even on his return from the northwest in 1668; see "Qin you po zhuang gui hou jin chang jibu yi san wu yihan er fu ci," ibid., 5:88ab. But he had evidently bought it by the sixth month of that year. See Fang Wen, "Li Liweng zhaitou tong Wang Zuoju yu su," *Tushanji* (Shanghai: Shanghai guji, 1979), III, 1037. Fang Wen was a friend who spent even more time traveling than did Li Yu.

13. On Li's friendship with Ji Yuan, see "Qiu sheng lu xu," *Liweng yijia yan quanji*, 1:26a–28b. For the 1666 invitation, see "Jixie Jia Jiaohou dazhongcheng," ibid., 3:12ab. Li Yu is said to have designed Jia's Banmu Garden in Beijing; see J. L. Van Hecken and W. A. Grootaers, "The Half Acre Garden, Pan-mou Yüan," *Monumenta Serica* 18 (1959): 360–387. The claim is made in Linqing's (1791–1846) autobiography, *Hongxue yinyuan tuji*; see "Banmu ying yuan" in part 1 of the third collection in the Yangzhou, 1847 edition. It is very dubious; Jia was not even in Beijing during Li Yu's first visit, in 1666, and there is no mention of Jia or of the garden during Li's second visit, in 1673. An even higher degree of skepticism should be accorded the claims that Li Yu had anything to do with the various Mustard Seed Gardens in Beijing. On Jia and Liu Dou, see Li Yu's joint biography of his two concubines, Miss Qiao and Miss Wang, "Qiao Fusheng Wang Zailai erji hezhuan," *Liweng yijia yan quanji*, 2:37b–46b.

14. See Guo Chuanfang's preface to the play *Shen luanjiao*, *Li Yu quanji*, XI, 4792–4793. For the suggestion that Li Yu revise the *West Chamber*, see "Yin lü," *Xianqing ouji*, 1:26. Some of Li Yu's patrons were occasional dramatists; on a play by Gong Dingzi, see Zhuang Yifu, *Gudian xiqu cunmu huikao* (Shanghai: Shanghai guji, 1982), II, 1191.

15. See "Yizhong qing," *Quhai zongmu tiyao* (Beijing: Renmin, 1959), II, 995: "People regarded him as a comedian (*paiyou*)." The question of the ambivalence of Li Yu's peers toward him, and of his own ambivalence toward the personae he used, is dealt with in Chapter 2.

16. For the girls' lives with Li Yu, see his combined biography, "Qiao Fusheng Wang Zailai erji hezhuan." As he passed through Pengcheng (Tongshan in Jiangsu) on his return journey from the northwest, he was invited by two officials, Subprefect Ji Yuan, a friend from his days in Hangzhou, and Director of Studies Li Shenyu, to stay and celebrate the New Year. On the performance given in honor of the birthday of Li Shenyu's wife, see the couplet "Li Shenyu kunjun shoulian," *Liweng yijia yan quanji*, 4:2a. Miss Qiao had fallen ill by the sixth month of 1672;

see Gu Jingxing's poems, "Yuehu da Li Yu wushou," *Baimaotang ji* (Qing edition), 12:15b, as well as Li Yu's letter, "Da Gu Chifang," *Liweng yijia yan quanji*, 3:47ab. There is plenty of evidence that the girls accompanied Li Yu to Suzhou in 1671 and Hanyang in 1672, but none that they accompanied him to Fuzhou in 1670, except for the inclusion of Fujian in a somewhat hyperbolic list of places visited as given in the combined biography.

17. Li Yu lists several distinguished littérateurs with an interest in the drama in his "Qiao Fusheng Wang Zailai erji hezhuan," where, of course, he is putting the performances in as respectable a light as possible, claiming that the two girls were frequently likened by guests to the concubines of the poet Bai Juyi. But except for the New Year's performance in 1668, all the evidence we have confirms the point. Fang Wen, an itinerant friend even poorer than Li Yu, brought an out-of-town visitor to see a play in Li Yu's Mustard Seed Garden on a festive occasion in 1669, taking care to bring the refreshments with him; see *Tushanji*, III, 988–989. The Shandong poet Du Chuang visited the Garden in spring 1670, and evidently saw a play performed; see his poem "Li Liweng Fuboxuan" in his *Meihu yinji* (Qing edition, 1680 preface), 7:4b. There are records of two performances given for the poets You Tong, Song Wan, and Yu Huai, as well as for Yu's family, in Li Yu's rented lodgings in Suzhou in 1671. See "He You Hui'an guan jiaji yan ju ci yuanyun," *Liweng yijia yan quanji*, 8:91a. Yu Huai's poems are preserved in Xu Qiu, comp., *Benshi shi* (Qing edition), 11:16a–18a, together with You Tong's poems in response. Their poems were offered instead of the presents (*chantou*) customarily given to actresses. Yu Huai also has a lyric on a performance in the Garden, probably in 1669; see "Tong Shaocun Xingzhai ji Lihong Fuboxuan ting qu ershou," *Yuqinzhai ci* (Guoxue tushuguan, 1928), pp. 57a–58a. (Shaocun was the celebrated poet Chai Shaobing.) Zhou Lianggong attended a performance in the Garden at the beginning of 1672; see the note to "Hou duanchang shi shishou you xu," *Liweng yijia yan quanji*, 6:51b–52a. According to Gu Jingxing's "Yuehu da Li Yu wushou," Li Yu brought four concubines with him to Hanyang in 1672. Li Yu has a poem about hosting a performance for his literary friends, none of whom was a patron, in the second or third month of 1672; see "Du Tianzhu, Xiong Xunshu, Xiong Yuanxian, Li Renshu . . . ," *Liweng yijia yan quanji*, 7:46ab. Of course, even to have one's concubines perform a play under such circumstances was a risqué thing to do. The *Benshi shi* contains several other cases, but in none of them is the husband named.

18. One comment describes Li Yu not merely as a pornographer but as a pander; see Dong Han's *Chunxiang zhuibi* (in the 1868 expanded edition of the *Shuo ling*), 2:21a. The *Chunxiang zhuibi* is a gossipy, censorious collection of jottings by an early Qing official. Essentially the same item, using much of the same text, is attributed in another work, the *Nuoru shanfang shuo you*, to Li Yu's contemporary, the playwright Yuan Yuling; see the text as quoted in Aoki Masaru, *Zhongguo jinshi xiqushi*, trans. Wang Gulu (Beijing: Zuojia, 1958), I, 333. Shizue Matsuda, "The Beauty and the Scholar in Li Yu's Short Stories," *Studies in Short Fiction* 10.3 (Summer 1973): 280, discredits the attribution for this reason. If Yuan ever wrote the comment, he must have done so at the very end of his life, for it refers to Li Yu's *Independent Words* (*Yijia yan*), the first collection of which cannot have appeared before the middle of 1673, while Yuan died in 1674. It is noteworthy

that the *Chunxiang zhuibi* has equally scathing comments to make about others, including Yuan Yuling. Under the circumstances, it is surprising that scholars continue to give the comment any credence. Li Yu was the kind of flamboyant, self-publicizing person about whom apocryphal stories collected even in his lifetime.

19. See "Shang dumen guren shu jiuzhuang shu," *Liweng yijia yan quanji*, 3:59b–63b. Mao's note appears on 3:60b.

20. See "Yue you jiabao zhi si," ibid., 3:28a–29a. On the birth of his third and fourth sons, see "Renyin ju disan zi fu ju disi zi," ibid., 6:24b. On the size of his household, see, for example, *Xianqing ouji* ("Tang"), 5:223, in which he describes himself as "a poor scholar with half a hundred mouths to feed."

21. For this information, I am dependent on Zhao Wenqing's two articles on the genealogy. It has been claimed by some that Li Yu was related to the famous Ming artist Li Liufang, apparently on the strength of Li Yu's reference to him as "Changheng of our family" in the (1679) preface to the *Mustard Seed Garden Manual of Painting* (*Jieziyuan huazhuan*). But Li Yu was given to referring to any celebrated person with the surname Li as "of our family." He refers thus to Li Bai and even to Lao Zi; see *Xianqing ouji* ("Guiren xing le zhi fa") 6:284. I think this is what he was doing in Li Liufang's case.

22. *Xianqing ouji* ("Zhidu"), 4:185.

23. See Li Yu's foreword (*bianyan*) attached to his *Yijia yan bieji*, as found in the combined reprint of his first and second collections of the *Liweng yijia yan*. (Full details are given in the section "Editions of *Independent Words*" following the Notes. There are several other references to his poverty. In *Xianqing ouji* ("Fangshe"), 4:144, he says he has been poor and lowly all his life. His New Year poem for 1642, "Renwu chuxi," *Liweng yijia yan quanji*, 5:77a, contains the line, "Young and obscure, I've sampled every hardship," and another, the "Song of Dire Poverty" ("Qiqiong ge"), ibid., 5:31b–32b, has the line, "Our poor bones were shaped by Heaven."

24. The preface to the *Jade Clasp* (*Yu saotou*) by Huangheshan Nong; see *Li Yu quanji*, X, 4361. Zhao Wenqing, "Youguan Li Yu shengping de jige wenti," p. 61, suggests that the preface writer is trying to raise Li Yu's position.

25. According to Li Yu's "Hui sha bian," *Liweng yijia yan quanji*, 2:56a–58a, his father was buried in 1629, but he must have died several years earlier. Xia Xieshi, "Li Yu shengping chutan," p. 163, notes that Li Yu's New Year poem for 1627 gives thanks that his mother is still alive but does not mention his father.

26. "Ye meng xianci ze yu huangfei juye, xing shu zi cheng," *Liweng yijia yan quanji*, 5:77a. On Li's ambivalence, see the poem he wrote after his failure in 1639, "Banghou jian tongshi xiadizhe," ibid., 6:2b–3a. He continued to regard the examinations and the civil service in this light; see "He zhuyou cheng shang xi ci lai yun," the fourth poem, ibid., 6:29b, which contains the lines "Slaving away at writing will keep me alive, / I'd never be willing to dream the dangerous dream of going to Handan." I do not think this should be interpreted as anti-Manchu, as many scholars believe; at the time he wrote it he was escorting his two sons to the examinations, a venture about which he felt many reservations. The 1637 date for his admission comes from the genealogy; see Zhao Wenqing, "Li Yu shengping shiji de xin faxian."

27. "Ji Fujian jingnan xunhaidao Chen Dalai xiansheng wen," *Liweng yijia yan quanji*, 1:64a–67a, and "Ji Fujian jingnan zongdu Fan Jingong xiansheng wen," ibid., 1:67a–71b. These were notional elegies; Li Yu had not seen the corpses, but felt he could wait no longer before writing. Frederic Wakeman is mistaken in asserting that Li Yu was the main speaker at the funeral ceremonies in Beijing; see *The Great Enterprise* (Berkeley: University of California Press, 1985), II, 1116. The Bannermen from whom Li Yu received patronage include Chen and Fan, as well as Fan's father, Fan Wencheng, and also Cao Xi, silk commissioner in Jiangnan. He also exchanged poems and letters with several members of the Tong clan of Liaodong. Li Yu's stories contain bitter criticism of the rebel leader Li Zicheng. An indication of his contempt for the Southern Ming is found in the second prologue story of "Qi'er xing haoshi, huangdi zuo meiren," which was the third story of the *Lianchengbi* collection; see Yu Wencao, ed., *Li Liweng xiaoshuo shiwuzhong* (Hangzhou: Zhejiang renmin, 1983), pp. 40–41. For laudatory references to the Manchus, see this same prologue, as well as the tenth story of *Twelve Structures*, "Fengxianlou."

28. The dates 1644 to 1646 are tentative. Li Yu himself says he was two years with Xu, and Jinhua fell to the Manchu army in the seventh month of 1646. Xia Xieshi, "Li Yu shengping chutan," suggests that it was the local revolt led by Xu Du that made Li Yu seek protection. He believes that, from 1643, when the revolt began, Li Yu alternated between the Lanqi countryside and Jinhua, evading both the rebels and the troops in pursuit of them (whom he characterizes as more predatory even than the rebels).

29. For example, his friends Sun Zhi and Bao Xuan; see "Zeng Sun Zi Yutai," *Liweng yijia yan quanji*, 6:70b–71a, and "Zeng Bao Yeshan," ibid., 5:93a. For some of the options open to the ambitious, educated man in the seventeenth century, see Willard J. Peterson, *Bitter Gourd: Fang I-chih and the Impetus for Intellectual Change* (New Haven: Yale University Press, 1979).

30. For example, "Ci yun he Xu Donglai zeng bie," *Liweng yijia yan quanji*, 6:41a; "Gu Liangfen dianji, yi ren zeng suguo jian yi, dai jian fuxie," ibid., 6:64b; and "Ci yun he Wu Xiuchan shijun guofang ershou," ibid., 6:34b–35a.

31. They include Wang Zuoju and his sons Wang Gai and Wang Shi; Huang Yuanjie and Wang Duanshu, both women; Fan Qi and Wu Hong, two of the so-called Eight Masters of Jinling (Nanjing); Ji Yingzhong; Li Yu's cousin Jiang Zhengxue; and a number of others. There were only a few professional playwrights among Li Yu's friends. His career may be compared with that of his friend Fang Wen, who was born in 1612. Fang, who may have given up all thought of office for loyalist reasons, traveled even more often than Li Yu, living from patronage, from selling fortunes, and from practicing medicine. His copious poems are notorious for the simplicity of their syntax and diction, but they are not in the vernacular. He was not a professional author in the same sense as Li Yu.

32. "Ni gou Yishan bieye wei sui," *Liweng yijia yan quanji*, 6:2a. The information about Mt. Yi comes partly from his poems, but mainly from his essay "Mai shan quan" ("A Deed of Sale for a Hill"), ibid., 2:64a–66a. The dates of purchase and sale have never been determined; scholarly opinion varies, for the purchase, from the late 1630s to nearly 1650. In the autobiographical prologue to the last story in *Twelve Structures*, which was written probably in 1658, he speaks of

retreating to the country twenty years before and living ten years there as "Prime Minister of the Mountains." (*See Li Yu quanji,* XV, 6541.) This suggests a period of ownership from the late 1630s to the late 1640s. In his essay "Mai shan quan" he mentions the devastation of war followed by the famine as the reason for selling; presumably he bought it at some time before, say 1643. The poem "Guangling gui zhi jiaci danri," *Liweng yijia yan quanji,* 5:74a, mentions returning from his trip to Yangzhou to a country place, which might be Mt. Yi. Huang Lizhen sets the return in 1640; see *Li Yu yanjiu,* p. 5.

33. "Da Jiang Cisheng wen shanju jinzhuang," *Liweng yijia yan quanji,* 5:77ab. Zhao Wenqing, basing himself presumably on the genealogy, says that friends and relatives helped Li to buy Mt. Yi; see "Li Yu shengping shiji de xin faxian." On the pleasures of his life there, see "Yi yuan shibian," ibid., 7:30a–31a.

34. For example, the poem "You sui," ibid., 5:81b. For the dispute, see the two articles by Zhao Wenqing.

35. On its destruction in the fighting, see the poem "Xu ke 'Wutong shi'," ibid., 5:1ab.

36. See *Liweng yijia yan quanji, juan* 2. The essays are discussed in detail in Chapter 8.

37. The dates of his arrival in Hangzhou and departure for Nanjing are both uncertain; estimates by scholars vary from 1647 to 1654 for his arrival and from 1657 to 1664 for his departure. The earlier set of dates, which were suggested by Sun Kaidi and which have been accepted by most other scholars, are based on Li's own statements that he spent twenty years in Nanjing (which he left in 1677) after ten years in Hangzhou. The later set of dates, which were proposed by Gu Dunrou in his "Li Liweng nianpu," are based on the prologue to a poem Li Yu wrote in 1674 saying that he had been away from Hangzhou ten years; see "Zeng niexian Guo Shengzhou xiansheng," *Liweng yijia yan quanji,* 6:68b–69a. Apparently, Li Yu did not count his visit in 1670. Two kinds of new evidence affect these estimates. One is the genealogy, which prints the rules of the ancestral temple as drawn up by Li Yu, its director, in 1651; presumably he was still living in Lanqi, or at least in Jinhua. The other kind of evidence is found in two poems. One is by Fang Wen, written in 1659 in Hangzhou, in which Fang refers to Li Yu's return from Nanjing and his purchase of another residence in Hangzhou. See "Fang Li Lihong," *Tushanji,* II, 19b. The second is by the Shandong writer Ding Yaokang, author of the *Xu Jin Ping Mei* (a sequel to the *Jin Ping Mei*), who visited the West Lake at the beginning of 1660 and enjoyed an excursion with Li Yu and others. See his "Wang Zhongzhao Sun Yutai Zhang Shijiu Li Liweng . . . ," *Jianggan cao,* 1:12ab. (The *Jianggan cao* is included in *Ding Yehao xiansheng shicigao,* of which the Beijing Library has the original, early-Qing edition.) Thus it seems that Li Yu left Hangzhou for Nanjing in the late 1650s, returned, and then left again. When he left for the second time is hard to say. It is perhaps worth noting that Qian Qianyi's preface to Li Yu's plays was written in Hangzhou in summer 1661.

38. "Yu Zhao Shengbo wenxue," *Liweng yijia yan quanji,* 3:10b–11b. Zhao was Zhao Shiji. Li Yu's reasons do not make obvious sense. Why would the pirates cease to plague him merely because he had moved from Hangzhou to Nanjing?

Dai Bufan suggests that Li Yu may have gotten into trouble over something he had written; see "Li Liweng shilüe," *Juben* (1957.3): 95. Several possibilities come to mind. There was the Zhang Jinyan case, which may have involved his *Wusheng xi erji*; see n. 78 below. This occurred in 1660. There is at least a possibility that his erotic novel, *Rou putuan*, was somehow involved. There is a striking change in the kind of works that Li Yu began to publish in 1660. On the other hand, it has also been suggested that his move had something to do with the seaborne attacks of the revanchist general Zheng Chenggong (Coxinga), who almost reached Nanjing in autumn 1659 before being defeated. (See Sun Kaidi, "Li Liweng yu *Shi'er lou*," p. 159.) There may also have been other reasons. The last years of the Shunzhi reign were dangerous for Chinese intellectuals; Li Yu's friends Lu Qi, Fan Xiang, and Zha Jizuo were implicated in the Ming History case and imprisoned. See L. C. Goodrich, "Chuang T'ing-lung," in Arthur W. Hummel, ed., *Eminent Chinese of the Ch'ing Period* (Washington, D.C.: Government Printing Office, 1943–1944), p. 206.

39. See n. 75 below.

40. "Fu Wang Zuoju," *Liweng yijia yan quanji*, 3:20b–21a. For an explanation of the *ying zhai*, literally "camp loan," see Sun Kaidi, "Li Liweng yu *Shi'er lou*," p. 165.

41. Li Yu was probably partly dependent on patronage, even in these years. A likely patron was Wang Ruqian, known as "Mr. West Lake" because of the various improvements he had made in the lake at his own expense. Wang died in 1655. Li Yu has two poems written on occasions on which Wang entertained him: "Yuanxiao wu yue ci Wang Ranming fengweng yun," *Liweng yijia yan quanji*, 5:88b, and "Qingmingri Wang Ranming fengweng zhao yin hushang," ibid., 6:17ab. Wang's *Chunxingtang shiji* (*Congmu Wang shi yishu* edition), 5:27b, 28b, contains two poems by Li Yu in praise of Wang and the West Lake, alongside poems by the woman artist Huang Yuanjie.

42. On Shen's age, see "A Qian Shen Yinbo sishi chudu shi ban yu ke Tiaochuan shiri chu zhi," *Liweng yijia yan quanji*, 5:26a–27a. On Li Yu *in loco parentis*, see his reply to Shen's grandfather: "Fu Shen Zemin taiqinweng," ibid., 3:11b–12a. A second son-in-law later joined Li Yu in the editing work. On Li Yu's notepaper, see his 1663 New Year poem, "Guimao yuanri," ibid., 6:24b–25a. Li Yu was not yet living in the Mustard Seed Garden, which he did not acquire until the middle of 1668. At the time, he was living near the Jinling locks; see "Xiti Jinling zha jiuju," ibid., 4:7a.

43. "Jianjian," *Xianqing ouji*, 4:210. When the *Xianqing ouji* was included in the 1730 revised edition of Li Yu's works, the shop's address was changed to "the Nanjing bookshop quarter." I have followed the original (1671) edition of the *Xianqing ouji*. It is a mistake to assume, as scholars often do, that the Mustard Seed Garden (Jieziyuan) editions were edited or published by Li Yu. Apart from the famous painting manual, *Jieziyuan huazhuan*, which carries Li Yu's preface dated 1679, I do not know of any Jieziyuan edition that is associated with him. The Jieziyuan editions are evidently all later than Li Yu's death, that is, later than 1680. Note that the works we know Li Yu to have published carry the names of other publishers, such as the Yishengtang, or else none at all. Li Yu's anthology

of parallel prose, *Siliu chuzheng*, was published in 1671 by the Yishengtang, while the Guidelines are signed by Shen Xinyou, whose address is given as the Jieziyuan. See the Bibliography for details of editions.

44. See *Li Yu quanji*, VII. Note that by 1655 Li Yu was well enough known to be included in the list of readers of the leading handbook of Southern drama prosody, the *Chongding Nanjiugong cipu*, ed. Shen Zijin. See the modern facsimile edition (Shanghai: Commercial Press, 1936).

45. See Sun Kaidi, "Li Liweng yu *Shi'er lou*," p. 177.

46. "Na ji," *Liweng yijia yan quanji*, 7:38ab, and "Xian nei yin," ibid., 7:37b–38a.

47. See "Neizi yu ceshi bing buyi nan . . . ," ibid., 5:77b–78a.

48. It is tempting to link the oath with *Women in Love*, but there is a problem with the chronology. Repeating the oath in *Xianqing ouji* ("Jie fengci," 1:6), Li Yu says that he first swore it twenty-odd years before, that is, in the late 1640s. But if the genealogy is to be believed, he was still in Lanqi or Jinhua in 1651. Perhaps his movements were more complicated than we suppose.

49. For Li Yu's admiration of Wu Bing, see "Ji su'e" and "Xuan ju" in *Xianqing ouji*, 2:51–52 and 2:60–61, respectively. Wu had a reputation for ingenuity of structure, attention to dialogue, and an emphasis on the comic byplay of the base characters, all of which are recognized features of Li Yu's drama. *Lü mudan* (*The Green Peony*) is his representative comedy. Ruan Dacheng's famous *Yanzi jian* has often been likened to *The Mistake with the Kite*. For the latter, see *Li Yu quanji*, VII.

50. *Li Yu quanji*, VIII.

51. Huang is known to have moved to Hangzhou after the war, and in the preface she says she has been there ten years.

52. *Li Yu quanji*, VIII, 3380.

53. *Li Yu quanji*, VIII.

54. See "Tuo kejiu" and "Jie huangtang" in *Xianqing ouji*, 1:8–9 and 1:12–13, respectively. It is based on the Yuan plays *Liu Yi chuan shu* and *Zhang sheng zhu hai* by Shang Zhongxian and Li Haogu, respectively. The former is itself based on the Tang tale "Liu Yi zhuan."

55. This is the only evidence that Li Yu belonged to this society. But our main knowledge of it comes from the anthology *Xiling shizi shixuan* edited by Chai Shaobing and Mao Xianshu, in which Mao's preface is dated 1650, a time at which Li Yu may not even have arrived in Hangzhou. (See the original edition in the Beijing Library.) On the other hand, it is odd that Shen Qian, one of the founding members, failed to mention Li Yu in his anthology *Dongjiang jichao*, which has a preface by Mao Xianshu dated 1655. (See the original edition in the Academy of Sciences Library, Beijing.)

56. *Li Yu quanji*, X.

57. *Li Yu quanji*, IX. The play is based on the first story in *Silent Operas*, "An Ugly Husband Fears Marriage to a Pretty Wife but Gets a Beautiful One."

58. *Li Yu quanji*, XII, 5047.

59. For *Bimuyu*, see *Li Yu quanji*, X. The story is based on "Tan Chuyu xili chuan qing, Liu Maogu quzhong si jie," which was originally published in *Wusheng*

xi erji, then republished in *Liancheng bi;* see n. 75 below. The text of the story may be found in *Li Liweng xiaoshuo shiwuzhong,* pp. 1–24.

60. For the play, see *Li Yu quanji,* IX. The story it is based on is entitled "Guafu she ji zhui xinlang, zhongmei qi xin duo caici" in *Liancheng bi.*

61. For the play, see *Li Yu quanji,* XI. The official was Guo Chuanfang, who also wrote comments on Li Yu's *ci* lyrics in his *Liweng yijia yan* (the first collection, preserved in the Academy of Sciences Library, Beijing).

62. See *Li Yu quanji,* XI, 4864–4865.

63. "Heguilou" ("Hall of the Homing Crane"). See *Li Yu quanji,* XV.

64. See *Li Yu quanji,* XI, 4623.

65. "Shengwolou" and "Nü Chen Ping ji sheng qichu," in *Li Yu quanji,* XV and XII, respectively.

66. *Li Yu quanji,* XI, 4778. In the text, the scene is incorrectly numbered as 33.

67. New versions of parts of *Pipaji* and *Mingzhuji* are given under "Bian jiu wei xin" in *Xianqing ouji,* 2:68–75. Li Yu also adapted other plays, including *Nan Xixiang, Yuzanji,* and *Youguiji.*

68. See "Da Gu Chifang," *Liweng yijia yan quanji,* 3:47ab. It was written in 1672.

69. See "Suo chang wei duan," *Xianqing ouji,* 2:64–65.

70. "Li shi wuzhong zongxu," *Sun Yutai ji,* 7:6a–7a. The *Sun Yutai ji* is preserved in the Naikaku Bunko. Sun related that he was impressed by seeing a performance of *Lianxiang ban,* then obtained a copy of *Fengzheng wu,* and finally got his hands on three more plays. The preface testifies to the excitement Li Yu's plays aroused at the time, but it is not clear that it served as the preface for a collective edition.

71. "Li Liweng chuanqi xu," in Qian's *Muzhai waiji,* 6:13a–14b. The *Muzhai waiji* is a manuscript preserved in Beijing Library. Qian lauds Li Yu as being responsible for a revolution in drama comparable to the earlier one by Tang Xianzu. "The *Jin Ping* [Mei] cannot compete with the plays' sensuality, nor can Yuming (Tang Xianzu) exhaust their ingenuity." He traces both vernacular fiction and drama from the Song, and may well be referring to Li Yu's fiction as well as to his drama. The *Muzhai waiji* also contains what is clearly another version of the preface, entitled "Li Liweng chuanqi xiti," ibid., 25:6a–7a. It makes the same points in almost the same language, and closes with the same date and place. (It omits the first part of the preface, and may well be a reworking of it.) It refers to "several tens of Liweng's plays, earlier and later," which may be a reference to the title of the Li Yu anthology. Note that Qian Qianyi, like Gong Dingzi a bon vivant with a famous and talented mistress, commented on a number of Li Yu's earlier poems and essays. One of the comments is on Li Yu's birthday poem in 1660. Qian's association with Li Yu may have been confined to the 1660–1661 period.

72. See Guo Chuanfang's preface to *Shen luanjiao* (*Li Yu chuanji,* XI). He speaks of the earlier anthology's having created a stir in the capital for some ten years, but it is not clear whether he is speaking as of 1667 (when he met Li Yu) or as of the time he wrote the preface (conceivably several years later). In a note to Scene 10, he refers to *Four Plays, Earlier and Later,* which is presumably a slip.

(See pp. 4864–4865.) In *Xianqing ouji*, Li Yu refers to the later anthology as unpublished; see "Yin lü," 1:28.

73. See "Ao ju nan hao" and "Ci bie fan jian," *Xianqing ouji*, 1:34 and 2:45, respectively.

74. Even the earliest edition, by the Yishengtang, has no general preface, just the prefaces to the individual plays as published previously. Strange as it may seem that Li Yu would let the anthology be issued without a general preface, it is clear that it was published in his lifetime. The *Ten Plays* are mentioned in Huang Zhouxing's *Zhi qu zhiyu*, which served as a preface to his play *Rentian le*, of which the second preface is dated 1678. For the *Rentian le*, see the *Guben xiqu congkan*, third series.

75. See the original edition in the Sonkeikaku, as reproduced in *Li Yu quanji*, XII, XIII. The term *wusheng shi* ("silent poetry") had long been applied to Wang Wei's paintings. In fact, a history of painting entitled *Wusheng shi shi* appeared in the Shunzhi period and may have inspired Li Yu's title. For the history, see *Siku quanshu zongmu* (Beijing: Zhonghua, 1965 rpt.), p. 977. The complex problems surrounding the *Wusheng xi* and *Liancheng bi* editions have been largely solved by Itoh Sohei in "Ri Gyo no shōsetsu 'Museigeki' no hampon ni tsuite," *Chū tetsubun gakkaihō* 9 (June 1984): 126–133, and "Ri Gyo no shōsetsu no hampon to sono ryūden—'Museigeki' wo chūshin to shite," *Nihon Chūgoku gakkaihō* 36 (1984): 191–206. Itoh describes the complete eighteen-story *Liancheng bi* edition in the Saeki Municipal Library in Japan, and argues convincingly that the twelve-story *Wusheng xi* edition in the Sonkeikaku is in fact Li Yu's first edition, not a later anthology as is commonly supposed. It was followed by a *Wusheng xi erji* that no longer exists. Then came the *Wusheng xi heji*, a twelve-story anthology drawn from both earlier collections. In a later edition entitled *Liancheng bi*, the six stories omitted in the *Wusheng xi heji* were added as a supplement (*waibian*). My brief account is based upon Itoh's articles.

76. See the story discussed in Chapter 5, "A Male Mencius's Mother Educates His Son and Moves House Three Times."

77. See Itoh Sohei, "Ri Gyo no shōsetsu no hampon to sono ryūden," p. 205, n. 29. We cannot be sure that it contained precisely six stories.

78. First noted by Sun Kaidi, "Li Liweng yu *Shi'er lou*," pp. 183–184. See also Itoh Sohei, "Ri Gyo no shōsetsu no hampon to sono ryūden," p. 198. Zhang's biography, which contains an excerpt from Xiao Zhen's memorial, is found in *Erchen zhuan*, *Guoshi liezhuan* (*Man Han dachen liezhuan*), 12:17a–21a. See also the 1747 *Xinxiang xianzhi*, 33. (His publications are listed in *juan* 22.) The purged Grand Secretary was Liu Zhengzong. The most natural interpretation of the passage taken from the memorial is that the words "busi yingxiong" occurred in the *Wusheng xi erji*, and this is how Sun Kaidi took it; see p. 184. It is Itoh's suggestion that Zhang may have written the preface to *Silent Operas*.

79. That is, the *Liancheng bi* story referred to in n. 27 above.

80. See the meeting referred to in "Yin lü," *Xianqing ouji*, 1:26, and also a letter recommending one of his book engravers to Wei for employment: "Yu Wei Zhen'an xiangguo," *Liweng yijia yan quanji*, 3:14ab.

81. A fragmentary edition is preserved in Beijing University Library (Ma Lian Collection).

82. For example, between stories one and two, three and four. If there is a principle behind Du's choice, it seems to be a preference for romance over ribaldry. The source story of *Sole Mates* replaces the source story of *You Can't Do Anything about Fate* at the beginning of the collection, while three of the most ribald stories are excluded.

83. The original preface can only be reconstructed, as Sun Kaidi has done, from the prefaces in the *Wusheng xi heji* edition and from the *Liancheng bi* (Sun had only the sixteen-story manuscript in the Lüda Municipal Library). The former removes all reference to a second collection, while the latter alters references to Li Yu to general expressions such as "my friend." See Sun Kaidi, *Riben Dongjing suo jian Zhongguo xiaoshuo shumu* (Beijing, rev. ed., 1958), pp. 155–159.

84. Itoh Sohei believes that this was done to stave off the challenge of the pirates; see "Ri Gyo no shōsetsu no hampon to sono ryūden," pp. 199–200. "Liancheng bi" is an allusion to the fifteen towns that were to be exchanged for a famous jade disc in Warring States times. There is also a different anthology of twelve stories drawn from both the first and second collections that is entitled *Wusheng xi hexuan*. Until recently, it was in the possession of Kong Xianyi; see his account of it, "Guanyu Li Yu de *Wusheng xi* canben," *Wen shi* (Zhonghua shuju) 9 (June 1980): 245–248. Itoh believes it to be a pirated edition, perhaps the very one Li Yu was so exercised about.

85. See the edition in *Li Yu quanji*, XIV, XV.

86. The only editions widely available are those printed in Japan, which tend to abridge the text and omit the critiques, and the tiny lithographic editions of the late Qing, which occasionally inflate the text. The edition of reference is a block-print edition in the Harvard-Yenching Library with a 12-column, 21-character format, which has illustrations of the novel's main figures. Nevertheless, it is a careless edition, with numerous miswritings.

87. The story is "Guizhenglou," the fifth one in the collection. On its connection to the *Rou putuan*, see Patrick Hanan, *The Chinese Vernacular Story* (Cambridge, Mass.: Harvard University Press, 1981), p. 185. To the best of our knowledge, Li Yu wrote only one classical tale, "Qinhuai jian'er zhuan," which is highly derivative, unlike his vernacular stories. (Although they may share motifs with other works, Li Yu's stories do not have sources in any significant sense of the word; in this he differs from his predecessors in the genre.) The tale appears to be based on the "Liu Dongshan" of the late-Ming writer Song Maocheng; see his *Jiuyueji*, ed. Wang Liqi (Beijing: Zhongguo shehui kexue, 1984), pp. 263–266. The same source was also used by Ling Mengchu, in the third story of his *Pai'an jingqi* (Hong Kong: Youlian, 1966). Li Yu's tale has been translated by Conrad Lung under the title "The Strong Kid of the Ch'in-huai Region" in Y. W. Ma and Joseph S. M. Lau, eds., *Traditional Chinese Stories: Themes and Variations* (New York: Columbia University Press, 1978), pp. 110–114.

88. See his preface to the *Zizhi xinshu erji*, dated 1667.

89. For example, he returned from his journey to the northwest with a sheaf of cases given him by the governors of Shaanxi and Gansu, Jia Hanfu and Liu Dou, who had been two of his principal hosts.

90. "Yu Fang Shaocun shiyu," *Liweng yijia yan quanji*, 3:49a. Li Yu was soliciting comments for his essay on the *ci* lyric, "Kui ci guanjian."

91. See Mao Xianshu's crushing rebuke of someone who had dared to fabricate his (Mao's) comments and print them with his "masterpiece:" "Yu ren qi qu pingyu," *Xiao kuang wenchao (Sigutang shisizhong shu*, manuscript, Naikaku Bunko), 1:20a–21a.

92. Editions are preserved in the Academy of Sciences Library in Beijing and also in the Library of Congress.

93. See a letter to Li Yu in *juan* 3 praising *Silent Operas* and another in *juan* 1 praising *Lianxiang ban, Fengzheng wu*, and other plays.

94. The *Chidu xinchao*; see the Shanghai zazhi gongsi edition of 1935. Zhou's Guidelines are dated the sixth month of 1662. The *Chidu xinchao* was followed by at least two sequels.

95. See "Yu Du Yuhang," *Liweng yijia yan quanji*, 3:18a; "Yu Wu Meicun taishi," ibid., 3:23b; and "Fu Cao Gu'an taishi," ibid., 3:17b–18a. In the second letter the title is given as *Chidu xinpian*; in the third, as *Chidu xingao*.

96. See the edition by the Wenjintang in the Academy of Sciences Library in Beijing. It has the characteristic publisher's blurb on the title page. (Note that the book is nowhere described as a "First Collection.") The same library also possesses a second impression by the same publisher but with a new title, *Xinzeng Zizhi xinshu quanji (A Newly Expanded, Complete New Aid to Administration)*. In fact, it contains no new material. The essays are entitled "Xiang xing moyi" and "Shen yu chuyan," respectively.

97. See "Xiang xing moyi."

98. The Harvard-Yenching Library has a Jingyetang edition with *Xinzeng* ("Newly Expanded") prefixed to the title on the title-page. It contains nothing extra. (See n. 96 above.)

99. See "*Qiu sheng lu* xu," *Liweng yijia yan quanji*, 1:26a–28b. The book has not survived.

100. The first edition in the Harvard-Yenching Library has the title *Xin siliu chuzheng* on the title-page, but plain *Siliu chuzheng* in the rest of the book. On the strength of the title-page, this edition has sometimes been listed as a separate work. This is the least original and enterprising of all the compilations associated with Li Yu. The Naikaku Bunko has a *Siliu xinshu guangji* by a different compiler; it has a preface dated 1670, a year earlier than this book's preface. Several of the same authors, for example, You Tong and Yu Huai, are represented in both works.

101. The anthology, which is not extant, is referred to in several letters, especially "Yu Xu Dianfa," *Liweng yijia yan quanji*, 3:50b–51b, which solicits some of Gong Dingzi's lyrics from the man who is editing his posthumous works. Its prefaces, by You Tong and Li Yu, survive in their respective collected works. The anthology was still not finished when Li Yu wrote the preface to his *Naige ci* (see n. 121 below) in the autumn of 1678.

102. The one independent edition that survives was formerly in Fu Xihua's possession. Its present whereabouts are unknown; it is not among the books of Fu's that the Zhongguo Xiqu Yanjiuyuan in Beijing has so far catalogued. According to Sun Kaidi's report of it (see "Li Liweng yu *Shi'er lou*," pp. 173–174), its full title was *Liweng zengding Lun gu (Liweng's Expanded and Revised Discussions of the Past)*, and it had prefaces dated 1664 and 1665. It may not, of course, have really been a revised edition; cf. n. 96 above. This was the work that Li Yu drastically

abridged and rewrote as part *(bieji)* of the second collection of his works *(Liweng yijia yan erji)*; see his foreword *(bianyan)*, in which he refers to it simply as *Liweng lun gu.* The editors of the 1730 *Liweng yijia yan quanji* evidently replaced the abridged and rewritten version with the original work. If this assumption is correct, we have the original *Liweng lun gu* in *juan* 9 and 10 of the accessible collected works, while for the abridged and revised version we must turn to the few surviving copies of the combined reprint of the first and second collections of *Liweng yijia yan* in Beijing University Library, in the Library of Congress, or in the possession of Itoh Sohei and Wu Xiaoling. In the original work there are a few items that Li Yu refers to as juvenilia. I think he means only that he wrote them long before the rest, not that they formed part of some earlier collection.

103. See Chapters 2 and 3. A chronicle history entitled *Gujin shilüe (Outline of History)* that is preserved in the Naikaku Bunko is attributed to Li Yu, using his commonest pseudonym. It is a dry and inept chronicle, with sparse notes and none of the distinctive qualities of Li Yu's writing—a palpable fake.

104. A commentator actually compares Li Yu favorably to Li Zhi; see "Lun Dongfang Shuo jian na Dong Yan zhi jiu xuanshi," *Liweng yijia yan quanji,* 9:50a–52a. Yu Huai's comment on another section compares Li Yu's history favorably to Zhong Xing's *Shi huai,* of which there is a late-Ming edition in the Academy of Sciences Library in Beijing. But the two works are not comparable. The *Shi huai* treats works of history rather than historical problems, and its interpretations are literary as well as historical. Yu's comment is attached to "Lun Cao Cao zi chen gongfa ji rang huan sanxian," *Liweng yijia yan quanji,* 9:85b–87b. Most of Li Yu's peers included a section of *shilun* (historical discussions) in their collected works, but none resembles Li Yu's; they are serious rather than humorous, often with scholarly pretensions, and there is little that is personal about their style or manner. For Sun Zhi's, see *Sun Yutai ji,* 10; for Mao Xianshu's, see *Sigutang ji,* 1.

105. See "Lun Yao rang tianxia Xu You Tang rang tianxia yu Bian Sui Wu Guang," *Liweng yijia yan quanji,* 9:2a–3a.

106. See "Lun Tang bing san bian Tang wen san bian," ibid., 10:49a–51a.

107. See "Lun Wei Jiang gui Jin Hou yi an le si zhong," ibid., 9:9a–10b. Li Yu repeats the idea, but without the chess metaphor, in "Zhi Xuanzi Zhao Jianzi zhi lihou," ibid., 9:16b–18b. One of Li Yu's methods is to interpret a person's speech as ironic.

108. See "Lun Cheng Ying li gu er si," ibid., 9:12b–15b.

109. See "Lun Yang Xiong Tao Qian chu chu," ibid., 10:20b–22b.

110. "Lun Han Xin ci piaomu guan shaonian," ibid., 9:25b–27b. Heroes act according to their *xingling* (personal natures), and hence often from self-centered motives; see Li's piece on Lin Xiangru; "Lun Lin Xiangru qu yu Lian Po," ibid., 9:20b–21a. Jie Zitui (Zhitui), however, is castigated for excessive self-sacrifice; see "Lun Jin Wengong shang zongwangzhe er buji Jie Zitui," ibid., 9:5a–7b.

111. On legitimacy, see "Lun Tang Taizong Zhou Qin xiuduan zhi yi," ibid., 10:29b–31a. Taizong raised the question of legitimacy in order to galvanize his successors. The implication is that the Manchus may have won China by subversion, but that they had established moral authority after taking power. Note also Li Yu's praise for Wei Zi, a Shang official who transferred the Shang sacrificial vessels to the succeeding dynasty; see "Lun Wei Zi xian bao jiqi gui Zhou," ibid.,

9:4a–5a. On Li's impatience with recluses, see "Lun er Shu qing lao," ibid., 9:63a–64a; "Lun er Shu bu yi cai lei zisun," ibid., 9:64a–65a; "Lun Yin Hao ni Guan Ge," ibid., 10:9a–10b; "Lun Xie Fei He Dian He Yin shu you," ibid., 10:23b–24b. Several other items show a strenuous opposition to Buddhism, which was often associated with Ming loyalism in the early Qing dynasty.

112. "Lun Yuan Shizu zhi dai Wen Tianxiang," ibid., 90b–91b.

113. It carries a preface by Yu Huai dated autumn 1671. You Tong also wrote a preface, which was not used; it is found in his *Xitang zazu* (*Xitang quanji* edition), second collection, 3:11a–13a. The original title has been translated in several different ways, from "the arts of living," a paraphrase, in Lin Yutang's *The Importance of Understanding* (Cleveland: World, 1960) to "a temporary lodge for my leisure thoughts" in Nathan K. Mao and Liu Ts'un-yan, *Li Yü* (Boston: Twayne, 1977). *Ji* on its own may mean an avocation, an absorbing interest, while *ji qing* may mean to express one's feelings in writing. Li Yu never explains the title, but he does use its components in ways that may be suggestive. In *"Xiangcaoting chuanqi xu," Liweng yijia yan quanji*, 1:44a–45b, he uses *ji qing* in a parallel formation to *tuo xing*; it clearly means "to invest one's feelings in, to attach one's interests to." However, the most direct use of the two terms *xianqing* and *ouji* occurs in "Zhi fu," *Xianqing ouji*, 3:119. After bolstering his argument with a quotation from *The Great Learning*, he issues a mock apology: "I once presented this argument in fiction, and now I am including it among idle feelings *[xianqing]*. Goodness! How could one expect anyone who is fond of idle feelings or who writes fiction to be capable of an explication such as this? Let me just casually express *[ouji]* it here." I base my interpretation of the title on this passage, while sincerely hoping that Li Yu was not merely playing a verbal game. Note that *xianqing* means idle sentiments, as distinct from serious matters of moral concern; it carries the suggestion of frivolity, and even, occasionally, of sexual indulgence. Li Yu did use the quotation from *The Great Learning* in his fiction; it appears in the story "Shengwolou" in *Shi'er lou*; see *Li Yu quanji*, XV, 6481–6482.

114. The edict was issued in the tenth month of 1670, according to *Qing shi gao*, Basic Annals. (This was after Li Yu had begun writing *Xianqing ouji*.) It was not printed until later, when it appeared under the title of *Shengyu xiangjie*. The fifth maxim counsels moderation and thrift, and forbids lavish expenditure and waste. Li Yu's use of it is pure opportunism, with a dash of humorous self-mockery.

115. "Qi jingti renxin," *Xianqing ouji*, introduction, p. 4.

116. In "Jie piaoqie chenyan," *Xianqing ouji*, introduction, p. 5, Li Yu compares this book to a tree and all his previous works to annuals. He spent his sixtieth birthday (in 1670) in Fuzhou, and it was then that he persuaded Li Changxiang and Bao Xuan to write prefaces for his collected works. His own preface, "Yijia yan shiyi" ("An Explanation of the Meaning of 'Yijia yan' "), was written on his birthday in 1672. (His birthday was on the seventh of the eighth month.) No one has been able to reconcile the difference between the genealogy and Li Yu himself as to the year of his birth. In "Youguan Li Yu shengping de jige wenti," Zhao Wenqing suggests that Li Yu simply reckoned his age in a different manner. But Fang Wen, Li Yu's friend, who was born in 1612, tells us that he was one year younger than Li Yu; see the note attached to the poem "Fang Li Liweng" mentioned in n. 37 above.

117. See "Ou xia jian canshu fen qi keyi bu du zhe," *Liweng yijia yan quanji*, 5:100a.

118. The term goes back at least to Sima Qian's preface to the *Shi ji*. It was in quite common use. Li Yu explained his own use of it several times: in "Ci bie fan jian," *Xianqing ouji*, 2:45; in his preface to his collected works, "Yijia yan shiyi"; and in the preface to his rhymebook of *shi* poetry, "Shiyun xu," *Liweng yijia yan quanji*, 1:31b–33b. It means independence from the bonds of tradition—he does not imitate—as well as boldness in ignoring criticism. He also declares his wish that people not imitate him.

119. On these and the following editions, see the Bibliography.

120. See n. 102 above. The comments in the revised version recognize the book's humor far more than those in the original, which tended to make a case for Li Yu as a historian. Zhang Zhou comments on an added item: "The humor of his writing often makes one break the silence with a burst of laughter." See *Liweng yijia yan* (the combined first and second collections), "Bieji," 3:16a.

121. The rhymebooks are the *Liweng shiyun*, published in 1674, and the *Liweng ciyun*, published probably in 1679. (In his introduction to his *Naige ci*, he declares his intention of compiling the second book.) Both books are extant, as is *Liweng piyue Sanguo zhi*, his annotated edition of the famous historical novel. Although the annotations to the last work are of interest, it is noteworthy that Li Yu suppresses his normally ebullient persona in writing them. It would be difficult to show from the annotations themselves that Li Yu was their author, and the likelihood is that someone else may have written them for him. The *Qiangu qiwen* has not been accessible to me. The only known copy was among Fu Xihua's books; Sun Kaidi reported briefly on it in "Li Liweng yu Shi'er lou," pp. 176–177. Li Yu's preface, written in 1679, explains that the book was a revision and abridgment of Chen Baifeng's *Nü shi* (*History of Women*), presumably a collection of model lives, and that it was intended in the first place for the instruction of his own daughters. The *Naige ci* has a preface by Li Yu dated autumn 1678. This whole work was included by the editors in the 1730 *Liweng yijia yan quanji* as *juan* 8, displacing the much slimmer collection of Li Yu's *ci* in the first collection of *Liweng yijia yan*. There were no *ci* in the second collection, because Li Yu was occupied at the time he compiled it in preparing the more specialized *Naige ci*. The introduction to *Naige ci* is entitled "Kui ci guanjian" ("A Modest Glance at the Lyric"). It is a major piece of criticism, second only to the drama chapters of *Xianqing ouji* among Li Yu's critical writings. Li Yu in the 1671 *Xianqing ouji* and Shen Xinyou in the *Siliu chuzheng* of the same year both announce numerous future publications, including sequels to Li's collection of letters as well as another anthology of plays, but to the best of our knowledge none of them ever appeared.

Several works, in addition to the *Gujin shilüe* already mentioned, are spuriously attributed to Li Yu. One is the *Gijin chidu daquan*, an anthology of letters Li Yu is supposed to have collected. (See the 1688 edition in the Beijing University Library.) The statement attributed to Li Yu has none of the characteristics of his mind or style. Two collections of medicinal cures, expressed in ditties, are also attributed to him; see the *Yiqingji* and the *Changxingji*, of which Wu Xiaoling has copies. Several works on parallelism and rhyme are also attributed to him with little credibility; see the *Gujin liansou* (Beijing University Library), the *Liweng duilian* (Beijing Library, plus several recent annotated editions), and the *Jieziyuan zalian* (referred to by Dai Bufan in his "Li Liweng shilüe"). Reservations should also be expressed about his actual editing of the *Sanguo zhi* (see above) and far stronger reservations about his editing of the *Shuihu zhuan* and other novels. I have suggested that the Jieziyuan editions are all later than Li Yu.

2. Creating a Self

1. I am using "self" to mean a created self, or persona. "Persona" is to be taken in its broadest meaning, the sense in which literary and other expression is scarcely conceivable without it, at anything above the instinctive level of behavior. Cf. Erving Goffman, *The Presentation of Self in Everyday Life* (London: Allen and Unwin, 1959), and other works. Within this broad meaning, numerous distinctions can be made; see Robert C. Elliott, *The Literary Persona* (Chicago: University of Chicago Press, 1982). I refer here to an author's self-projection in his work, and particularly to his self-reference. Note that notions like "sincerity" and "truth to self" are not negated by a theory of personae unless they are taken naively.

2. Namely, Tang Xianzu and Wu Bing.

3. "Shou qu," *Xianqing ouji*, 2:83.

4. "Ci bie fan jian," *Xianqing ouji*, 2:43–44.

5. "Dian ran," *Xianqing ouji*, 3:117.

6. "Bie," ibid., 5:233.

7. "Chuang zhang," ibid., 4:192–193.

8. "Xie," ibid., 5:234.

9. Scene 19, *Li Yu quanji*, XI, 4919–4920.

10. "Ci bie fan jian," *Xianqing ouji*, 2:44, and "Yu qiu xiaosi," ibid., 2:43.

11. See, for example, Guo Shaoyu, *Zhongguo wenxue pipingshi*, rev. ed. (Shanghai: Commercial Press, 1947), II, 264–283, and James J. Y. Liu, *Chinese Theories of Literature* (Chicago: University of Chicago Press, 1975), pp. 78–82. More specialized studies include John C. Y. Wang, *Chin Sheng-t'an* (New York: Twayne, 1972), pp. 13–52; Richard John Lynn, "Alternate Routes to Self-realization in Ming Theories of Poetry," in Susan Bush and Christian Murck, eds., *Theories of the Arts in China* (Princeton: Princeton University Press, 1983), pp. 317–340; and Jonathan Chaves, "Self in the Kung-an School," in Robert E. Hegel and Richard C. Hessney, eds., *Expressions of Self in Chinese Literature* (New York: Columbia University Press, 1985), pp. 123–150.

12. Wang Shizhen's theory of *shenyun* (spirit and tone), developed in the mid-seventeenth century, took account of the poet's persona; see Liu, *Chinese Theories of Literature*, p. 45.

13. "Gujin xiao shi xu," *Liweng yijia yan quanji*, 1:23ab; italics mine.

14. "Yu qiu xiaosi," *Xianqing ouji*, 2:42–43.

15. "Guo Ziling diaotai," *Liweng yijia yan quanji*, 8:99b.

16. See "Budeng gao fu," ibid., 1:8b.

17. "Jixie Liu Yaowei dazhongcheng," ibid., 3:13ab.

18. "Zeng Wulin Li Liweng," in Cheng Maoheng and Yang Xuehang, eds., *Wu Meicun shiji jianzhu* (Shanghai: Shanghai guji rpt., 1983), 10:653.

19. "Yuehu da Li Yu," *Baimaotang ji* (Qing edition), 16:5a. Gu was also a protégé of Gong Dingzi.

20. For Sun Zhi's preface to five of Li Yu's plays, see Chapter 1, n. 70. Li Changxiang's preface is to the first collection of his *Liweng yijia yan* (Academy of Sciences Library). Bao Xuan's was originally written for the second collection; it was then incorporated as the second preface in *Liweng yijia yan quanji*. Li Yu was not alone in presenting an obtrusive and distinctive persona in his work, although he was more consistent in the practice, and took it to greater extremes, than anyone else. Jin Shengtan presents a parallel, although he was by no means as thoroughgoing as Li Yu. Li's friend Mao Xianshu presents a pronounced and distinctive persona, but only in his more relaxed works, such as *Kuang lin* (*Mao Zhihuang shi'erzhong shu* edition).

21. See his defense of Dongfang Shuo, *Liweng yijia yan quanji*, 9:50b. It is Sun Zhi who makes the explicit comparison.

22. See Chapter 1, n. 104. Li Yu, by contrast, compares himself to Chen Jiru on several occasions.

23. "Liuzhi zi shou sishou," *Liweng yijia yan quanji*, 6:27b–28b.

24. See "Guo Ziling diaotai," ibid., 8:99b, and "Yu Sun Yutai," ibid., 3:53ab.

25. For Qian Qianyi's preface and "appreciation," see Chapter 1, n. 71.

26. See Chapter 1, nn. 16, 17.

27. In addition to the works by Mao Xianshu, Sun Zhi, Yu Huai, You Tong, Fang Wen, Du Chuang, and others that I have cited, letters and poems to Li Yu are to be found in Lu Qi's *Weifengtang wenji* (preface dated 1666), Wang Rigao's *Huaixuan shiji* (preface dated 1668), and Liang Yunzhi's *Tengwu shiji* (preface dated 1678). Original editions of the first two works are preserved in the Academy of Sciences Library; the original edition of the third is in the Beijing Library. What is surprising is that there are no poems or letters to Li Yu in the works of Du Jun, Zhou Lianggong, Hu Jie, Ding Peng (although his preface to *Liweng yijia yan erji* is reprinted), Gong Dingzi, Chai Shaobing, or Wang Ji.

28. "Yiwu," *Xianqing ouji*, 4:191.

29. "Qu jing zai jie," ibid., 4:159.

30. "Pinjian xing le zhi fa," ibid., 6:286–287.

31. "Shuixian," ibid., 5:262–263.

32. "Huai A Qian Shen Yinbo ji wu nü Shuzhao," poem 2, *Liweng yijia yan quanji*, 5:9b.

33. "Ji'an," *Xianqing ouji*, 4:186.

34. "Ye xing," *Liweng yijia yan quanji*, 6:24ab.

35. "Liuzhi zi shou sishou," poem 3, ibid., 6:28a.

36. See his preface to the first collection of *Liweng yijia yan* which is preserved in the Academy of Sciences Library. Li Yu himself, in "Tan," *Xianqing ouji*, 6:299, quotes the saying: "An evening of talk with you is better than ten years of reading."

37. "Kui ci guanjian," no. 12, *Liweng yijia yan quanji*, 8:9a–10a.

38. "Zhong ji qu," *Xianqing ouji*, 1:19.

39. "Qi guizheng fengsu," ibid., introduction, p. 4. In his preface to his own *ci* collection, *Naige ci*, Li Yu says that the strength of his *ci* is that they are intended for the voice; see *Liweng yijia yan quanji*, 8.

40. "Lun Dongfang Shuo jian na Dong Yan zhi jiu xuanshi," ibid., 9:50a–

52b. He objects to people's characterizing Dongfang as a "comedian" or "actor," terms that some of his contemporaries applied to him.

41. Note that Li Yu only once ventured to write a classical tale, a genre in which the narrator's voice is comparatively unobtrusive. For the tale, see Chapter 1, n. 87. One reason is surely that the tale was not suited to Li Yu's approach to writing.

42. For the four works just listed, see *Liweng yijia yan quanji*, 2:56a–58a, 2:73a–74b, 2:64a–66a, and 2:74b–76a, respectively.

43. See "Shui," *Xianqing ouji*, 6:294–295, and also "Ci bie fan jian," ibid., 2:43–44.

44. "Kui ci guanjian," no. 12, *Liweng yijia yan quanji*, 8:9a–10a.

45. "Yue you jiabao," ibid., 3:26b–29b.

46. "Sheng wu kengchiang," *Xianqing ouji*, 2:41.

47. "Kehun," ibid., 2:50.

48. "Ji Fujian jingnan xunhaidao Chen Dalai xiansheng wen," *Liweng yijia yan quanji*, 1:64a–67a. For obvious reasons, there were fewer works written by Li Yu in the last half-dozen years of his life that show his exuberant humor. For an exception, see his "Nai bing jie" ("Putting Up with Illness"), which was written in late 1677, after an illness that he thought would prove fatal. See *Liweng yijia yan quanji*, 2:89b–91a.

49. "Qiao Fusheng Wang Zailai erji hezhuan." For the poems of grief for each girl, see *Liweng yijia yan quanji*, 6:17a–19b and 6:21a–22b, respectively. The poems were written before the biography.

50. The outstanding example of a moving biography of a concubine is the *Yingmei'an yiyu* by Li Yu's contemporary, Mao Xiang. The concubine died in 1651, and he wrote the account the following year. See the *Yingmei'an yiyu* (*Rugao Mao shi congshu* edition).

51. "Zhu Jingzi zhuan," *Liweng yijia yan quanji*, 2:46b–49a.

52. Ibid., 1:7a–9a.

53. "Jinyouyuan shiji xu," ibid., 1:35a–36b.

54. "Kui ci guanjian," no. 17, ibid., 8:12b–13a.

55. "Yiren zhiji xing, zeng Tong Bimei shijun," ibid., 5:70a–71a. The idea of writing being as distinctive as the writer's face echoes Yuan Hongdao; see *Yuan Hongdao ji jianjiao*, I, 284, "Qiu Changru."

3. The Necessity of Invention

1. On Li Zhi's independence from traditional thought, see K. C. Hsiao, "Li Chih," in L. Carrington Goodrich and Chaoying Fang, eds., *Dictionary of Ming Biography: 1368–1644* (New York: Columbia University Press, 1976), I, 810–813, and William Theodore de Bary, "Individualism and Humanism in Late Ming Thought," in de Bary, ed., *Self and Society in Ming Thought* (New York: Columbia University Press, 1970), pp. 189–203. A commentator on Li Yu's *Discussions of the Past* compares him with Li Zhi; see Chapter 1, n. 104. Zhu Yan, compiler of the *Jinhua shilu* (*Notes on Poets and Poetry of Jinhua*), whose Guidelines are dated 1773, mentions both Li Zhi and Chen Jiru as comparably innovative authors; see the 1883 reprint in the Academy of Sciences Library, 48:12ab. Chen does indeed

place a value on *qi* (the unusual) in his collection of apothegms, *Xiaochuang youji* (Shanghai: Zhongyang shudian, 1935 rpt.), but it is hard to see him as a particularly inventive mind. Li Yu himself, however, invokes him frequently as an inventor of practical things, usually in a comic context. See "Zhu" and "Lu ping" in *Xianqing ouji*, 5:227 and 4:200, respectively. Gu Yanwu (1613–1682) places a stress on originality that sometimes almost resembles Li Yu's. In his "Yu ren shu shi," *Gu Tinglin shiwenji* (Beijing: Zhonghua, 1983 rpt.), p. 93, he is scathing about the lack of originality of his contemporaries (they "polish up old coins"), and goes on to explain his slow progress on his *Rizhi lu* as due to his more exacting standards. He strikes the same note in the short passage before his table of contents to the latter; whenever he found that one of his ideas had been anticipated in earlier writings, he discarded it. See the *Rizhi lu* (Shanghai: Commercial Press, 1933). In "Zhu shu zhi nan," Gu Yanwu asserts that the early philosophers were independent thinkers, using the term *yijia yan* that Li Yu later took as the title of his collected works; nowadays most authors, he claims, because of their eagerness to make a name for themselves, are essentially compilers. In "Wenren mofang zhi bing" he attacks imitation in literature, particularly imitation of the superficialities. See ibid., 7:3–4, 11–13, respectively. Some trends in seventeenth-century painting offer a comparison to these literary developments; they, too, can be linked to the theories of Yuan Hongdao and his circle. See James Cahill, *The Compelling Image: Nature and Style in Seventeenth-Century Chinese Painting* (Cambridge, Mass.: Harvard University Press, 1982), p. 216: "A belief underlying these chapters has been that seventeenth-century Chinese painting reveals a greater awareness of these problems [i.e., the "burden of the past"] . . . than any other passage in world art before the nineteenth century in Europe. And the most interesting attempt of all, I think, is Tao-chi's." For some Ming antecedents, see Richard Barnhart, "The 'Wild and Heterodox' School of Ming Painting," in Susan Bush and Christian Murck, eds., *Theories of the Arts in China* (Princeton: Princeton University Press, 1983), pp. 365–396, especially p. 391 on the suggested parallel with the theory of Yuan Hongdao.

It is important to note that Li Yu was not part of a movement in seventeenth-century literature; even his own friends were critical of the desire for novelty. See Chai Shaobing, "Li yan dang jin shuo," *Yiwang shanren wenchao* (Qing edition, Nanjing Library), 2:29a–32a. Mao Xianshu, "Zhi you zuo chuanqi shu," *Sun shu (Mao Zhihuang shi'erzhong shu* edition), 6:12a–14b, is a letter written to a friend urging him to stop writing the classical tale. Several writers condemn the corrupting effect of fiction on prose; see Deng Zhicheng, *Qingshi jishi chubian*, I, 322, under "Wang Wan." Nothing comparable to Li Yu's advocacy of the new for its own sake can be found in European literature before the late nineteenth century, with the exception of Edward Young's *Conjectures on Original Composition* and the *Romantische Welt* of Novalis, both eighteenth-century works; for a discussion of these works, see M. H. Abrams, *The Mirror and the Lamp: Romantic Theory and the Critical Tradition* (Oxford: Oxford University Press, 1953).

2. "Tuo kejiu," *Xianqing ouji*, 1:8–9. Li Yu did not regard this as inconsistent with the practice of training oneself by taking models, especially from Yuan drama. The first quotation is from the *Shang shu*, the second from Han Yu's "Da Li Yi shu," *Han Changli wenji jiaozhu* (Shanghai: Gudian wenxue, 1957 edition), p. 99.

3. "Tan," *Xianqing ouji*, 6:300.

4. "Tuo kejiu," 1:9.

5. Ibid.

6. "Bian diao," *Xianqing ouji*, 2:63.

7. "Xiao shousha," ibid., 2:57.

8. See *The Analects*, 7.1. D. C. Lau (*The Analects*, London: Penguin Books, 1979, p. 86) translates *zuo* as "innovate."

9. "Jie wangluo jiuji," *Xianqing ouji*, introduction, p. 6.

10. "Lun Tang Taizong yi gong shi jian wu yu zhi dao," *Liweng yijia yan quanji*, 10:31a–33a.

11. "Furen xiewa bian," appended to "Xiewa," *Xianqing ouji*, 3:129–130. This seems to have been the first time the essay was published. Yu's memoir of the courtesans of old Nanjing is the *Banqiao zaji*. Li Yu rarely indulged in the pleasures of reminiscence; one exception is his excursion about hiding out in the wilds to escape the rebels and soldiers. See "Xiaji xing le zhi fa," *Xianqing ouji*, 6:291–292. This sets him apart from contemporaries such as Yu Huai and Zhang Dai. On the power of the mode of reminiscence in Chinese literature, see Stephen Owen, *Reminiscences: The Experience of the Past in Classical Chinese Literature* (Cambridge, Mass.: Harvard University Press, 1986). As an indication of Li Yu's general attitude, note that he named all his sons with the word *jiang*, referring to the future. See "Ming zhuzi shuo," *Liweng yijia yan quanji*, 2:61ab.

12. For example, "Lun Yao rang tianxia Xu You Tang rang tianxia Bian Sui Wu Guang," *Liweng yijia yan quanji*, 9:2a–3a.

13. "Lun Jin Wengong shang zongwangzhe er buji Jie Zitui," ibid., 9:5a–7b, and "Yu Xu Donglai," ibid., 3.47a.

14. "Bian jiu cheng xin," *Xianqing ouji*, 2:66.

15. Ibid., p. 65.

16. "Ci bie fan jian," ibid., 2:44–45. The most extreme expression of his notion of the unending changeability of literary taste comes in the preface to his *ci* anthology; see "Mingci xuansheng xu," *Liweng yijia yan quanji*, 1:29a–31a.

17. "Geju," *Xianqing ouji*, 2:54.

18. "Qi guizheng fengsu," ibid., introduction, p. 4.

19. "Shoushi," ibid., 3:121.

20. "Jie piaoqie chenyan," ibid., introduction, p. 5.

21. "Fangshe," ibid., 4:144.

22. "Jie wangluo jiuji," ibid., introduction, p. 6.

23. "Jie zhili buzou," ibid.

24. Ibid.

25. "Xiang long qie si," ibid., 4:197.

26. "Jie huangtang," ibid., 1:12–13.

27. See Patrick Hanan, *The Chinese Vernacular Story* (Cambridge, Mass.: Harvard University Press, 1981), pp. 147–148.

28. Li Yu's robust skepticism could not be suppressed even in the colophon he wrote for a friend's book of medical remedies. See *"Shou shi qi fang* ba," *Liweng yijia yan quanji*, 2:71a–72b. Several times he declares himself a Confucian; see "Fori cheng shang ji," ibid., 2:15a, and "Lun Han zhao Liu Xiu dian ling wujing

suo zou qilüe jiuliu zhi yi," ibid., 9:67a–68a, in the last of which he objects to ranking Buddhism and Taoism alongside Confucianism.

29. "Jie huangtang," *Xianqing ouji,* 1:13.

30. Molière and Shaw represent the two kinds of comedy well. Molière treats social excesses and foibles such as hypocrisy and snobbery, while Shaw's is the comedy of emerging social ideas. Ling Mengchu's comedy is of the former kind.

31. "Shengwolou," *Shi'er lou.* See *Li Yu quanji,* XV, 6478–6479.

32. All of these stories are discussed in Chapter 5.

33. "Kui ci guanjian," no. 6, *Liweng yijia yan quanji,* 8:6ab.

34. Ibid. The former appears in "Jiegou" and "Gui xianqian," *Xianqing ouji,* 1:3 and 1:16, respectively.

35. "Yi qu jianxin," ibid., 2:47–48. The word he is avoiding is *xianqiao,* "exquisite."

36. It appears in *Xianqing ouji,* 2:42–43.

37. Several passages in *Xianqing ouji* should be viewed in the same light.

38. "Suchang le wei zhi yao," *Xianqing ouji,* 6:322.

39. "Yin lü," ibid., 1:23–24.

40. Ibid., 1:23.

41. See, for example, "Ting bi," *Xianqing ouji,* 4:169, in which he describes his invention of the living mural: "I racked my brains for a year and then with a flash of insight I came up with a good solution." He sometimes uses the following expression, ultimately derived from the *Guan Zi* ("Nei ye"): "Si zhi, si zhi, guishen tong zhi" ("Think, think, and the ghosts and spirits will communicate [an answer]"). See, for example, "Chugui," ibid., 4:195.

42. "Cang hou na wu," ibid., 4:151.

43. "Da shan," ibid., 4:181.

44. "Jiegou," ibid., 1:4.

45. "Binbai," ibid., 2:40–41.

46. Ibid., 5.

47. Ibid., 3.

48. See "Zhidu," ibid., 4:186.

49. James J. Y. Liu, *Chinese Theories of Literature* (Chicago: University of Chicago Press, 1975), p. 94, prefers to translate *zaowu* as "Nature," and argues against anthropomorphism. There is an obvious danger of confusing Li Yu's use of *zaowu* with the Western idea of the Creator. Still, Li Yu's *zaowu* is given some personal attributes and he is described as making and constructing, not as engaging in some mechanical process. The word was in common use as the author of a capricious fate, but no one, I think, used it as widely as Li Yu.

50. "Sushi," *Xianqing ouji,* 5:214–215.

51. See the comments on "Heyinglou," *Shi'er lou, Li Yu quanji,* XIV, 5883; the critiques to *Fengzheng wu* and *Bimuyu,* ibid., VII, 3221, and X, 4304, respectively; two critiques in *Rou putuan,* 12:18ab and 16:10b; and the comment on "Lun Zhao Pu zhi jian Taizu," *Liweng yijia yan quanji,* 10:82b. It is likely that some of the comments and critiques are by Li Yu himself.

52. "Tian ci yulun," *Xianqing ouji,* 2:59.

53. "Xiang long qie si," ibid., 4:197.

54. "Jie fengci" and "Jie huangtang," ibid., 1:6 and 1:13, respectively.
55. "Shan shi," ibid., 4:180.
56. "Yu qiu xiaosi," ibid., 2:43.
57. "Jie fufan," ibid., 1:21.
58. "Ci bie fan jian," ibid., 2:44.
59. "Chongchang," ibid., 2:56.
60. "Wen gui jiejing," ibid., 2:47. In one of his letters he tells of finishing the first half of a play and giving it to the players; see "Yu mougong," *Liweng yijia yan quanji*, 3:16b–17a.

4. The Primacy of Pleasure

1. "Xing le," *Xianqing ouji*, 6:282.
2. "Xuan zi," ibid., 3:100. Li Yu is quoting with approval a statement originally attributed to Gao Zi in *Mencius*, VI A.4. See *Mencius*, trans. D. C. Lau (London: Penguin Books, 1970), p. 161: "Appetite for food and sex is nature." Note that Yuan Hongdao, Qian Qianyi, and Gong Dingzi, as well as many of Li Yu's friends, could be described, to some degree at least, as voluptuaries. Cf. also Jin Shengtan's "Thirty-three Delights in Life," as discussed in John C. Y. Wang, *Chin Sheng-t'an* (New York: Twayne, 1972), p. 27.
3. "Xuan zi," *Xianqing ouji*, 3:100. The quotation is from *The Doctrine of the Mean*, 14.2. Li Yu several times makes the point that things were created for our enjoyment. See "Cao ben," *Xianqing ouji*, 5:259: "Everything in the world was established for mankind's benefit."
4. "Benxing kuhao zhi yao," *Xianqing ouji*, 6:318–319. The "wild strawberries" are actually the berries of the *Myrica rubra*, *yangmei*, known as the wild strawberry tree.
5. "Suchang le wei zhi yao," ibid., 6:322–323.
6. "Xing le," ibid., 6:283, and "Shui," ibid., 6:294–295, respectively.
7. "Jie longdong shengshu zhi yu," ibid., 6:313.
8. Ibid.
9. "Sizhu," ibid., 3:136.
10. "Dongji xing le zhi fa," ibid., 6:293.
11. "Pinjian xing le zhi fa," ibid., 6:286–287. For his "take a step backward method," see "Guiren xing le zhi fa," ibid., 6:284. Li Yu traces it back to Lao Zi.
12. "Jie youhuan shang qing zhi yu," ibid., 6:311.
13. "Suishi ji jing jiu shi xing le zhi fa," ibid., 6:294.
14. "Yisheng wei jian zhi yao," ibid., 6:321.
15. "Jiegou," ibid., 1:1.
16. See Chapter 2.
17. "Xin yu," *Liweng yijia yan quanji*, 5:18ab. The last lines refer to the attainment of a Taoist immortality.
18. "Muyu," *Xianqing ouji*, 6:300.
19. "Zhiyi fu," *Liweng yijia yan quanji*, 1:3ab.
20. "Xie," ibid., 5:235.
21. "Fu ju fu" and "Minzhong shi xian lizhi," *Liweng yijia yan quanji*, 1:16a–17b and 5:87b, respectively.

22. "Xun mei," ibid., 5:81b.
23. "Shuixian," ibid., 5:262.
24. "Fuyunlou," *Shi'er lou, Li Yu quanji*, XV, 6212.
25. "Gewu," *Xianqing ouji*, 3:142.
26. "Wenyi," ibid., 3:134.
27. Ibid., p. 135.
28. "Taidu," *Xianqing ouji*, 3:106. Cf. Yuan Hongdao's "Xu Chen Zhengfu Huixinji," *Yuan Hongdao ji jianjiao*, I, 463. Yuan's passage is translated in David E. Pollard, *A Chinese Look at Literature* (Berkeley and Los Angeles: University of California Press, 1973), pp. 79–80.
29. "Shouzu," *Xianqing ouji*, 3:105–106. On the practice of foot-binding and the erotics of small feet, see Robert H. Van Gulik, *Sexual Life in Ancient China* (Leiden: Brill, 1961), 216–222.
30. "Qu jing zai jie," *Xianqing ouji*, 4:164. The two previously quoted passages also come from this section, from pp. 164 and 158, respectively.
31. "Jinqian," ibid., 5:267.
32. "Lan," ibid., 5:260–261.
33. "Sizhu," ibid., 3:137.
34. "Ting bi," ibid., 4:170. As Li Yu describes it, the most important point is his friends' reaction: "Their expressions change; they are transported. In their astonishment, they see a divine hand behind it. Then, before their bewilderment has subsided, there is yet more fluttering and birdsong, and the birds appear about to fly up and down. They look closely, and then realize the truth. Is there anyone among them who does not clap his hands in admiration and declare that the mural's art matches Heaven's skill?"
35. "Ji'an," ibid., 4:186 (drawers) and 4:187 (guard-boards). Li Yu's ideas are generally sensible and practical. His crazier ideas often have something to do with sexuality, and should probably be regarded as ribald jokes. See his piece on the crape myrtle, the name for which is *hehuan* (lovers' union). He claims to have proved by his own experience that it flourishes best if watered with water in which a man and a woman have bathed together. (Ibid., 5:251.) See also his discussion of the apricot, whose name is a homonym of *xing* (sex). When a virgin's skirt was tied around a barren apricot tree, it bore fruit. "I tried it, and it worked. It means the tree has a lascivious nature." (Ibid., 5:243.)
36. "Chugui," ibid., 4:195.
37. "Xiang long qie si," ibid., 4:196.
38. "Tujing," ibid., 4:146.
39. "Lianbian," ibid., 4:174.
40. "Zhong ji qu," ibid., 1:18. "Fine stitching" refers to his section "Mi zhenxian," ibid., 1:9–11.
41. "Shoushi," ibid., 3:121. The preceding items are also taken from *Xianqing ouji*, as follows: vegetables, "Sushi," 5:215; perfume, "Xuntao," 3:114; lichee, ibid.; song, "Gewu," 3:139; natural authenticity, "Guanjie," 3:111; imitation flowers, "Shoushi," 3:121.
42. "Yishan," ibid., 3:125.
43. "Gewu," ibid., 3:139. For the passage on rocks, see "Xiao shan," ibid., 4:182–183.

44. "Xuan zi," ibid., 3:100.
45. "Zhi ti yi jian," ibid., 4:152, and also "Xiao shan," ibid., 4:182–183.
46. Ibid., p. 182.
47. "Gui huobian," ibid., 4:213. *Huajing* (the transformed state) is a common term in Chinese aesthetics. It refers to a union with the Dao or Nature, and comes to express the height of artistic naturalness. See James J. Y. Liu, *Chinese Theories of Literature* (Chicago: University of Chicago Press, 1975), pp. 40, 44.
48. "Fangshe," *Xianqing ouji*, 4:143.
49. "Ji pai'ou," ibid., 4:211–212.
50. Ibid.
51. "Dian ran," ibid., 3:115.
52. Ibid., p. 117.
53. "Xiewa," ibid., 3:128.
54. "Jianjian," ibid., 4:210.
55. "Lianbian," ibid., 4:173.
56. "Guanjie," ibid., 3:111–112.
57. See Chapter 1, n. 114.
58. "Tang," *Xianqing ouji*, 5:223, and "Gushi," ibid., 5:221.
59. "Tingbi," ibid., 4:169–170.
60. "Shufang bi," ibid., 4:171.
61. "Zhidu," ibid., 4:185.
62. For example, "Shufang bi," ibid., 4:172.
63. "Lu ping," ibid., 4:201.
64. "Jian touxu," ibid., 1:12.
65. "Yi qu jianxin," ibid., 2:48.
66. On Gong's play, see Chapter 1, n. 14.
67. "Yu Han Ziju," *Liweng yijia yan quanji*, 3:55a–56a, and the epilogue song of *Fengzheng wu*, *Li Yu quanji*, VII, 3220, respectively. See also his conception of his mission in life as that of comic entertainer in "Ou xing," *Liweng yijia yan quanji*, 5:19a.

5. Paradoxical Farceur

1. See "Fangshe," *Xianqing ouji*, 4:144.
2. Before the novel was widely accepted as being by Li Yu, Helmut Martin showed that elements of its style were close to the practice of Li Yu's stories. See *Li Liweng über das Theater* (Taipei: Meiya, 1966), pp. 295–301. Although the demonstration was not extensive enough to constitute a proof, it is persuasive.
3. *Li Yu quanji*, XIV.
4. In *Xianqing ouji*, juan 1 and 2.
5. *Li Yu quanji*, XIV, 6047.
6. Ibid., 6047. The word "images" has been added in the translation.
7. Ibid., 6005.
8. Ibid., 6009–6010.
9. Ibid., 6011.
10. Ibid., 6024.
11. Ibid., 5992.

12. Ibid., 5993.

13. Ibid., 5998. The reference is to the apocryphal meeting of the feudal lords at Lintong.

14. Ibid., 6048.

15. *Li Yu quanji*, XV, 6245–6248 (in chap. 3).

16. Ibid., 6278–6279.

17. Ibid., 6271–6272. "Impartiality and openness" (*zhengda guangming*) served as an imperial motto.

18. Ibid., 6272. Itoh Sohei suggests that this story may have belonged originally to the *Wusheng xi erji*. See "Ri Gyo no shōsetsu no hampon to sono ryūden," p. 199.

19. Ibid., 6290.

20. Ibid., 6291.

21. Ibid., 6292–6293. The quotation is from *Analects*, 16.1. See *The Analects*, trans. D. C. Lau (London: Penguin Books, 1979), p. 139: "once they have come one makes them content." Confucius is referring to the distant subjects of a ruler. Formally speaking, the pronoun can be understood as singular or plural, and Nenghong is taking it as singular. The quotation had (and has) a proverbial force. In the first story of *Wusheng xi*, it is quoted without the source; see *Li Yu quanji*, XII, 5130.

22. *Li Yu quanji*, XV, 6307.

23. Ibid., 6202.

24. Ibid., 6255.

25. *Li Yu quanji*, XIV. It is the opening story of *Shi'er lou.*

26. Ibid., 5868–5869. The hero's and heroine's poems had been collected in a volume called "Combined Reflections."

27. Ibid., 5920–5921.

28. Ibid., 5824.

29. "Qing fugui nüdan quan zhen." This story, presumably originally in the *Wusheng xi erji*, is preserved in the *Liancheng bi* anthology, where its title translates as "Tan Chuyu Declares His Love in the Play; Liu Maogu Dies for Honor's Sake after Her Song." The text of reference is *Li Liweng xiaoshuo shiwuzhong*, pp. 1–24. The title I have quoted is the presumed original title of the story, as it must have appeared in the *Wusheng xi erji*. It occurs in the variant, perhaps pirated, anthology entitled *Wusheng xi hexuan*, for a description of which see Kong Xianyi, "Guanyu Li Yu de *Wusheng xi* canben." I have taken my title from the list of surviving stories as given in Kong's article. Cf. Chapter 1, n. 84.

30. *Li Liweng xiaoshuo shiwuzhong*, p. 16.

31. For the three preceding quotations, see ibid., pp. 18, 20–21, and 24, respectively.

32. For the three preceding quotations, see ibid., pp. 2, 14, and 14, respectively. The examination image appears on page 5.

33. *Jingchaiji.* See the *Liushizhong qu* edition (rev. ed., Beijing, 1958.) The suicide scene is no. 26, the mourning scene no. 30.

34. *Li Liweng xiaoshuo shiwuzhong*, p. 2.

35. Ibid., pp. 3–4. Pan An and Cao Zhi were standard allusions for good looks and literary flair and facility, respectively.

36. Ibid., p. 9.

37. *Li Yu quanji*, XII, "Chou langjun pa jiao pian de yan." It is the first story of *Wusheng xi*.

38. *Caizi jiaren* stands for a thematic type, not a genre, although it is often applied to the rather formulaic, short novels of romance that were popular in the Qing. Here it is used as a thematic type, a type that was well defined by the time of the Song dynasty.

39. *Li Yu quanji*, 5076–5077 (all three quotations).

40. *Hongyan boming*, literally, "pink cheeks, wretched fate."

41. *Li Yu quanji*, 5079.

42. Ibid., 5083.

43. Ibid., 5082.

44. Ibid., 5159–5163. Pan An and Song Yu were standard allusions for good looks.

45. Ibid., 5095–5097. Xishi was a standard allusion for a beautiful woman.

46. Ibid., 5106.

47. Ibid., 5117.

48. "Guafu she ji zhui xinlang, zhongmei qi xin duo caizi." It is preserved in the *Liancheng bi*, a blockprint edition in Saeki Municipal Library, Japan, which is the text I have used, as well as in the *Liancheng bi* manuscript.

49. "Nan Meng mu jiao he san qian," *Li Yu quanji*, XIII. For earlier vernacular stories on homosexual love, see Patrick Hanan, *The Chinese Vernacular Story* (Cambridge, Mass.: Harvard University Press, 1981), p. 137.

50. *Li Yu quanji*, XIII, 5386–5387.

51. For the three references, see ibid., 5417, 5437, and 5382–5383, respectively.

52. *Li Yu quanji*, XIV.

53. Ibid., XV.

54. *Li Yu quanji*, XIII, 5427.

55. It means response or requital, in terms of either human or divine reward or punishment. For its use in fiction, see Hanan, *The Chinese Vernacular Story*, p. 26.

56. *Li Yu quanji*, XIV, 6134 (chap. 1). The poem is included in Li Yu's collected works; see "Huqiu maihuashi," *Liweng yijia yan quanji*, 5:71ab.

57. *Li Yu quanji*, XIV, 6137–6138.

58. Ibid., 6133.

59. Ibid., 6144.

60. Ibid., 6140–6141. The term translated, inadequately, as "artistic consultants" is *qingke*, which usually refers to friends of officials and rich men who help with advice and conversation and who receive hospitality in return.

61. Ibid., 6141 (both quotations).

62. Ibid., 6158–6160.

63. Ibid., 6173–6174. Chen Tuan, a legendary Taoist adept, could sleep for years at a time.

64. Ibid., 6175.

65. "Ren su ji qionggui su piaoyuan," *Li Yu quanji*, XIII. The story is no. 7.

66. The story appears in the *Xing shi hengyan;* see Hanan, *The Chinese Vernacular Story,* p. 138. Li Yu slips, giving the wrong collection.

67. "Ersun qi haigu tongpu ben sang," *Li Yu quanji,* XIII. For the original source see Tian Rucheng, *Tian Shuhe wenji* (1563 edition, preserved in Hōsa Bunko, Nagoya), 6:18b–19b. It has been frequently anthologized. For the vernacular story, see Hanan, *The Chinese Vernacular Story,* p. 123.

68. *Li Yu quanji,* XV.

69. Ibid., 6528.

70. *Li Yu quanji,* XIV. On this theme see Hanan, *The Chinese Vernacular Story,* p. 184. Ling's story is *Erke Pai'an jingqi,* no. 39.

71. "Nü Chen Ping ji sheng qichu," *Li Yu quanji,* XII.

72. "Yi qi huan qie guishen qi," ibid., XIII.

73. See the sole story that is contained in the *Liancheng bi* edition (Saeki Municipal Library) but not in either the *Liancheng bi* manuscript or the *Wusheng xi.* It is a long work, entitled "Duqi shou you fu zhi gua, nuofu huan bu si zhi hun."

74. *Li Yu quanji,* XIII, 5631. The story is no. 10.

75. Ibid., 5632.

76. *Li Yu quanji,* XII. The story is no. 3.

77. See *Li Liweng xiaoshuo shiwuzhong* edition. I have translated what is presumably the original title, drawn from the *Wusheng xi hexuan,* "Ao gongqing qi'er zhang yi."

78. *Li Liweng xiaoshuo shiwuzhong,* p. 35.

79. Ibid., p. 41.

80. Ibid., p. 35.

81. Ibid.

82. "Mei nanzi bi huo fan sheng yi," *Li Yu quanji,* XII.

83. Ibid., 5199. Shizue Matsuda, "Li Yü: His Life and Moral Philosophy As Reflected in His Fiction," Ph.D. diss., Columbia University, 1977, chap. 2, p. 59, makes the point that Li Yu anticipated Liu E.

84. *Liancheng bi,* preserved in Saeki Municipal Library, "Nüzi shou zhen lai yibang, pengchai xiang nüe zhi qiyuan."

85. *Li Yu quanji,* XV.

86. Ibid., 6349.

87. See Chapter 4, n. 11 above.

88. *Li Yu quanji,* XV, 6435.

89. Ibid., 6354, 6355.

90. Ibid., 6363 and 6369, respectively.

91. Ibid., 6407.

92. Ibid., 6434.

93. *Li Yu quanji,* XIV.

94. Ibid., 5944.

95. Ibid., 5947.

96. *Li Yu quanji,* XV. Matsuda, "Li Yü," chap. 2, p. 47, suggests that the relationship between the hero and his patron may be based on the friendship between Chen Jiru and Dong Qichang. Dong built a "lou" which he named for Chen in order to encourage his visits.

97. *Li Yu quanji*, XV, 6548–6549. The text contains several miswritings, the most serious of which is that of "true art."

6. Comic *Erotiker*

1. This is the explanation offered us by the narrator. See *Rou putuan*, chap. 2:4b. (The edition of reference is the Qing blockprint edition in the Harvard-Yenching Library.) The locus classicus for *weiyang* is the "Ting liao" poem in the "Xiao ya" section of the *Poetry Classic*. The term *weiyang* is traditionally glossed as either "not yet dawn" or "not yet midnight." The German word *erotiker* has been chosen for the title of this chapter because it is free of the legal and other connotations of "pornographer."

2. He appears in the Tang tale of that name by Pei Xing. The tale is preserved in the *Taiping guangji*. It is translated as "The Kunlun Slave" by Chi-chen Wang in his *Traditional Chinese Tales* (New York: Columbia University Press, 1944), pp. 93–97.

3. *Rou putuan*, chap. 6:6a–8a. The word translated as "endowment" is *ben-qian*, literally "capital." An aphrodisiac in the Chinese context is a medicine calculated to increase sexual capacity and stamina rather than sexual desire. There are several obvious miswritings, the most serious of which is of *shu* (number).

4. *Rou putuan*, chap. 6:8b–11a. The passage contains at least nine miswritings, most of them obvious. The word *piruan* occurs here in an obviously miswritten form, as *ba po ruan*.

5. Robert E. Hegel argues that the novel parodies the romantic comedy; see his book *The Novel in Seventeenth-Century China* (New York: Columbia University Press, 1981), pp. 173–176.

6. *Rou putuan*, chap. 9:1a–2a.

7. For *qing* in fiction see Patrick Hanan, *The Chinese Vernacular Story* (Cambridge, Mass.: Harvard University Press, 1981), pp. 49–50, 79–80, 96–97, and 161–162.

8. *Rou putuan*, chap. 11:6a.

9. Ibid., chap. 14:2a. At this point, the editions published in Japan include three lubricious images drawn from the *Chi pozi zhuan* that do not occur in the other editions I have seen. I believe that they were inserted, perhaps at the same time the text was trimmed.

10. There is a Meiji period Kyoto edition of the *Ruyi Jun zhuan*. An excerpt of a Ming version appears in a 1587 miscellany, *Zazuan xingshui bian*, compiled by Ye Rubi. (The Library of Congress has a copy.) The source of the excerpt is given as *Wu Zhao zhuan*. (Wu Zhao was the name of the empress Wu Zetian.) We know from Ming references that the title *Ruyi Jun zhuan* was the current one. The earliest known reference occurs in a 1561 work, *Du shu yi de*, by Huang Xun; see 2:27a–28a. (The *Du shu yi de* is preserved in the Palace Museum, Taiwan.) A Ming edition of the *Xiuta yeshi* exists, in the possession of Hatano Tarō. For the *Chi pozi zhuan*, there is a Qing edition as well as a Meiji period Kyoto edition.

11. See *Rou putuan*, chaps. 4:9ab and 17:4b.

12. *Li Yu quanji*, XIV.

13. This is Tony Tanner's thesis, in his *Adultery and the Novel: Contract and Transgression* (Baltimore and London: Johns Hopkins University Press, 1979).

14. *Rou putuan*, chap. 2:9a and 2:9b, respectively.

15. Ibid., chap. 19:9b. Note the stress Li Yu places on the crime of adultery in his introduction to *Zizhi xinshu*, arguing for stronger punishments. The critique is being disingenuous, of course, but it cannot be dismissed entirely.

16. *Rou putuan*, chaps. 2:8a, 2:10b, and 20.9a, respectively.

17. Ibid., chap. 17:17a.

18. Ibid., chap. 18:8b.

19. Ibid., chap. 1:1b.

20. Ibid., chap. 5:8b. *Re* ("hot") is miswritten.

21. Ibid., chap. 1:3b–4a. The notion of joining a trend in order to guide it occurs several times in *Xianqing ouji*. The reference to shooting a sparrow is from the *Zhuang Zi*. Burton Watson, *Chuang Tzu* (New York, Columbia University Press, 1968), p. 313, translates the passage as follows: "Now suppose there were a man who took the priceless pearl of the Marquis of Sui and used it as a pellet to shoot at a sparrow a thousand yards up in the air—the world would certainly laugh at him." "Southern Zhou" and "Southern Zhao" are the titles of the first two sections of the "Songs of the States" division of the *Poetry Classic*; as such, they stand for the songs as a whole, many of which are on love themes. Numerous attempts have been made to provide them with a moral purpose. "Fitting the action to the case and the treatment to the man" are both commonplaces. By his reference to Mencius, Li Yu means *Mencius*, 1A.7 and 1B.5, in which the philosopher gets King Xuan's attention by talking of the king's interest in war and sex, respectively.

22. Ibid., chap. 1:5a.

23. Ibid., chap. 1:5b.

24. Ibid., chap. 10:8a.

25. "Xuntao," *Xianqing ouji*, 3:114.

26. *Rou putuan*, chap. 18:3a.

27. The point is noted in Nathan K. Mao and Liu Ts'un-yan, *Li Yü*, (Boston: Twayne, 1977), pp. 100–101.

28. *Rou putuan*, chap. 7:10a. *Gu* ("leg") is miswritten.

29. The locations of the seven images are as follows: *Rou putuan*, chaps. 8:2b, 10:3b, 14:1a, 15:4a, 15:6b, 16:6a, 16:12a.

30. For the references to an author see ibid., chaps. 1:3a, 13:4b, and 18:3a, respectively.

31. Both quotations are in *Rou putuan*, chap. 16:10b.

32. Ibid., chap. 20:10a. Cf. *Mencius*, 1A.4. D. C. Lau translates: "The inventor of burial figures in human form deserves not to have any progeny." (See *Mencius*, p. 52.) The critique at the end of chap. 8 also refers to the burial images. Note that Li Yu refers to himself jestingly in *Xianqing ouji* as "the inventor of burial images"; see "Ci bie fanjian," 3:44. He is defending the quantity of dialogue in his plays, and blames himself, mockingly, as the initiator of a new fashion.

33. *Rou putuan*, chap. 20:10ab.

34. The quotation is from *Mencius*, 3A.9. D. C. Lau translates: "Those who

understand me will do so through the *Spring and Autumn Annals;* those who condemn me will also do so because of the *Spring and Autumn Annals.*" (*Mencius*, p. 114.)

35. *Rou putuan*, chap. 12:18a. Li Yu's treatment of chapters as acts was noted by Hegel, *The Novel in Seventeenth-Century China*, p. 182.

7. Virtuoso of Fine Stitching

1. *Huang qiu feng, Li Yu quanji*, IX, 3784–3785. References to Li Yu's plays are all to the *Li Yu quanji*, VII–XI. *Lianxiang ban* and *Fengzheng wu* are in VII; *Yizhong yuan* and *Shenzhong lou* are in VIII; *Huang qiu feng* and *Naihe tian* are in IX; *Bimuyu* and *Yu saotou* are in X; and *Qiao tuanyuan* and *Shen luanjiao* are in XI. The illustrations in this chapter to *Yizhong yuan* and *Bimuyu* are taken from Fu Xihua, ed., *Zhongguo gudian wenxue banhua xuanji*, Shanghai meishu, 1979. The illustration to *Shen luanjiao* is from the original edition in Wu Xiaoling's possession.

2. IX, 3918 and 4066, respectively.

3. IX, 3683.

4. See the *Yueyatang congshu* edition. It was originally a Song work.

5. VII, 2979.

6. VII, 2827–2828 (Scene 3).

7. VII, 2872.

8. "Li zhunao," *Xianqing ouji*, 1:7–8. Li Yu defines *zhunao* in general terms, as "the author's basic intent in writing," but in the examples he gives from drama, he seems to refer to a critical conjuncture of events that set the plot in motion, that is, something more of structural than thematic significance. There is a brisk controversy among scholars as to his intention. It seems to me that the thrust of the essay "Li zhunao" is toward the latter interpretation. I believe he gave the more general definition only in an attempt to universalize the term's importance by applying it to all genres.

9. VII, 2872. For Sakyamuni's remark, see p. 2840 (Scene 5).

10. "An Ugly Husband Fears Marriage to a Pretty Wife but Gets a Beautiful One" and "A Widow Hatches a Plot to Receive a Bridegroom, and Beautiful Women Unite to Seize a Brilliant Poet," respectively.

11. See C. T. Hsia, "Time and the Human Condition in the Plays of T'ang Hsien-tsu," in *Self and Society in Ming Thought*, ed. Wm. Theodore de Bary (New York: Columbia University Press, 1970), pp. 249–290. Tang Xianzu's *Mudan ting* (*Peony Pavilion*) is the outstanding representation of *qing* in drama.

12. VII, 2945–2946 (Scene 21).

13. See *The Peony Pavilion*, trans. Cyril Birch (Bloomington: Indiana University Press, 1980).

14. VII, 2947 (Scene 21). In the translated passages, I have replaced the names of the roles (*sheng, dan,* and so on) with the names of the characters represented. In the case of songs, I have also omitted the tune titles.

15. See X, 4140 (Scene 1) and 4165 (Scene 6), respectively.

16. X, 4174 (Scene 7).

17. VII, 3049 (Scene 2).

18. VII, 3067–3068 (Scene 6). Eric P. Henry made the point that Han was being slightly mocked here; see his *Chinese Amusement: The Lively Plays of Li Yü* (Hamden, Conn.: Archon Books, 1980), pp. 117–118. I believe, however, that Li Yu was well aware of the ironies involved.

19. VII, 3129–3130 (Scene 16).

20. XI, 4793.

21. XI, 4812.

22. XI, 4811–4812.

23. XI, 4835 (Scene 6).

24. See *Lianxiang ban,* Scenes 6 and 17, respectively.

25. VII, 2944–2945.

26. VIII, 3253 and 3250, respectively.

27. VIII, 3279–3280. *Qingke* is here translated as "disinterested friend."

28. That is, Du Guangting, "Qiuran ke zhuan," in which Red Duster (Hongfu) appears, and Guan Hanqing, *Zhao Pan'er fengyue jiu fengchen.* The former is translated by Cyril Birch in his *Anthology of Chinese Literature* (New York: Grove Press, 1965), pp. 314–322, under the title of "The Curly-bearded Hero"; the latter is translated by Yang Hsien-yi and Gladys Yang in their *Selected Plays of Kuan Han-ch'ing* (Shanghai: New Art and Literature Publishing House, 1958).

29. Scenes 10 and 14, respectively.

30. X, 4231 (Scene 14).

31. IX, 3780 (Scene 14).

32. XI, 4822 (Scene 4).

33. XI, 4905–4906 (Scene 17).

34. Scenes 6 and 13, respectively.

35. VIII, 3273 (Scene 6). Cf. "Ji su'e," *Xianqing ouji,* 2:51, where Li Yu remarks: "The beauty of comic byplay lies in its bordering on vulgarity, but the greatest pitfall is that it be too vulgar. If it is not vulgar at all, it will resemble the conversation of Confucian pedants, but if it is too vulgar, it will no longer be the work of a man of letters."

36. Scenes 28 and 10, respectively.

37. VII, 3180–3181 (Scene 26).

38. VIII, 3261 (Scene 5).

39. IX, 3704–3706 (Scene 3).

40. "Ji leng re," *Xianqing ouji,* 2:63.

41. VIII, 3481 (Scene 5).

42. X, 4387 (Scene 4).

43. XI, 4736. Note that the scene is misnumbered, as 27, in this edition. Li Yu uses the term "fine stitching," which was in occasional use before his time, to refer to intricate construction, to encompass psychological subtlety as well as structural pattern and correspondence, which is why I have employed it in the title of this chapter. He describes the "Enjoying the Mid-Autumn Moonlight" scene of *The Lute (Pipa ji)* as "the finest of fine stitching," precisely because of its psychological subtlety. See "Mi zhenxian," *Xianqing ouji,* 1:11. This is a case in which the feelings of hero and heroine determine their very different descriptions of the scene. Li Yu placed far more importance on the inner world of feeling and thought (*qing*) than on the outer world of phenomena (*jing*) in his criticism; see

"Jie fufan," *Xianqing ouji,* 1:20, in which he invokes the same scene from *The Lute.*

44. *Bimuyu, Li Yu quanji* X, 4306 (Scene 26). Note that much of his most general argument about drama, including what might be called psychological realism, is given in the section on dialogue.

45. VII, 2888–2889.

46. VII, 2869–2872. Liang Hong and Meng Guang were famous exemplars of marital affection.

47. VII, 3001–3002.

48. XI, Scenes 12 and 17, respectively.

49. XI, 4864–4865.

50. VIII, 4865–4870. In Miss Deng's song, standard allusions for beauty and ugliness in women have been paraphrased as "famous beauty" and "ugly creature."

51. VIII, 3381–3382.

52. VIII, 3427–3429 (Scene 28).

53. X, 4150–4153 (all four quotations).

54. X, 4219.

55. X, 4223.

56. X, 4265. The essay topic is drawn from *Mencius.* See *Mencius,* trans. D. C. Lau (London: Penguin Books, 1970), p. 49: "Those above and those below will be trying to profit at the expense of one another and the state will be imperilled."

57. VII, 3107–3109. The poem Aijuan quotes is the first item in the standard children's primer of poetry, the *Qianjia shixuan* (*A Choice of Poems from the Thousand Poets*), compiled by Xie Fangde of the Southern Song. It contains one hundred and more poems. This one was written by Cheng Hao, the famous philosopher. Eric P. Henry has suggested that Scenes 13 and 16 of this play may parody the typical meeting and dream scenes of the romantic comedy. See *Chinese Amusement: The Lively Plays of Li Yü,* p. 96.

58. X, 4356 (Scene 32). The hero's posing as an actor is the first case of simulation.

8. Specialist in Idle Pursuits

1. See *Liweng yijia yan quanji,* 2.

2. For an account of the *xiaopin* vogue, together with its twentieth-century revival, see Chen Shaotang, *Wan Ming xiaopin lunxi* (Taipei: Yuanliu chubanshe, 1982 rpt.; originally published by Bowen in Hong Kong in 1981). For a discussion of the *xiaopin* essay and its modern practitioners, see also David Pollard, *A Chinese Look at Literature* (Berkeley and Los Angeles: University of California Press, 1973), pp. 105–120.

3. On Yuan Hongdao's theory, see Chapter 2, n. 11. *Qu* is variously translated as "zest" by Lin Yutang (*The Importance of Understanding,* Cleveland: World, 1960, p. 112) and as "gusto" by James J. Y. Liu (*Chinese Theories of Literature,* Chicago: University of Chicago Press, 1975, p. 81). *Yun* is rendered by Liu as "tone, rhyme, rhythm, consonance, resonance" (ibid., p. 45).

4. "Ling Shizhong xiaocao xiaoyin," *Xuetangji* (original edition, with a 1630

preface, preserved in the National Central Library), 5:43b–44b. The piece is dated 1619. An annotated but slightly abridged version is to be found in Zhu Jianxin, ed., *Wan Ming xiaopinwen xuan* (Shanghai: Commercial Press, 1937), pp. 96–97. "Bird and insect" refers to an early style of calligraphy.

5. "Zhong ji qu," *Xianqing ouji,* 1:18–19.

6. "Xing le," *Xianqing ouji,* 6:282.

7. "Qiangbi," *Xianqing ouji,* 4:167.

8. "Shuixian," *Xianqing ouji,* 5:262.

9. "Gudong," *Xianqing ouji,* 4:198–199.

10. "Chuang zhang," ibid., 4:191–192. The capitalized expressions are the titles of the topics he proceeds to treat.

11. *Xianqing ouji,* 5:238.

12. "Xing le," ibid., 6:283.

13. "Jie zhili buzou," ibid., introduction, p. 6.

14. "Muyu," ibid., 6:300.

15. *Liweng yijia yan quanji,* 2:56a–58a.

16. Ibid., 2:65a–66a.

17. Ibid., 2:73a–74b and 2:74b–76a, respectively.

18. Ibid., 2:75a–76a. The cat's parting remark comes from the *Gu feng* poem: "Though for my person you have no regard, / At least pity my brood." This is Arthur Waley's translation; see *The Book of Songs* (New York: Grove Press, 1960 rpt.), p. 100.

19. However, it is conceivable, as Dr. Loh Wai-fong has suggested to me, that the passage, with its artful, allusion-laden style, is an allegory of an incident in Li Yu's own house, such as his expulsion of a concubine.

20. "Yu Liu shijun," *Xianqing ouji,* 3:51b–52a; "Yu Chen Duanbo shilang," ibid., 3:46b; and "Fu Chen Duanbo sikong," ibid., 3:35b, respectively.

21. "Yu Gong Zhilu dazongbo," ibid., 3:4b.

22. The *Kaopan yushi* (*Congshu jicheng* edition), attributed to the Ming writer Tu Long, treats furniture and objets d'art, but it is terse and impersonal. The *Zunsheng bajian,* by the Ming playwright Gao Lian, has been suggested as Li Yu's model in writing *Xianqing ouji*; see Jiang Xingyu, "*Yuzanji* zuozhe Gao Lian," *Yi xi dai yao* (Guangzhou: Guangdong renmin, 1980), pp. 65–66. The edition of Gao Lian's work in the Beijing Library has a preface dated 1591 by Tu Long. Like Li Yu's book, it is much concerned with health and pleasure, and it employs a prominent persona. But there are also substantial differences in the subject matter, in the nature of the persona, and in the method of argument. It was an antecedent of Li Yu's book, but I would hesitate to describe it as a model.

23. *Xianqing ouji,* 4:185–213.

24. "Deng zhu," ibid., 4:208.

25. "Qu jing zai jie," ibid., 4:158.

26. "Jiuju," ibid., 4:205.

27. "Yisheng wei jian zhi yao," ibid., 6:321.

28. "Jiegou," ibid., 1:4. *Juan* 1 and 2 of the 6-*juan Xianqing ouji* are devoted to drama. For a translation into German of most of the drama treatise, plus a study of Li Yu as a theorist of the drama, see Helmut Martin, *Li Li-weng über das Theater* (Taipei: Meiya, 1966). For an annotated edition of the drama treatise,

with useful comparisons with other Chinese treatises, see Chen Duo, *Li Liweng quhua* (Changsha: Hunan renmin, 1980).

29. See Chapter 7, n. 8.
30. "Jiegou," *Xianqing ouji*, 1:4.
31. See "Keshou ciyun" and "Linzun qupu," ibid., 1:28–29 and 1:30.
32. "Ci bie fan jian," ibid., 2:43–44.
33. "Jiao bai," ibid., 2:91.
34. Ibid., 3:100–142.
35. Ibid., 3:105–106.
36. "Xi ji," ibid., 3:131.
37. "Shoushi," ibid., 3:120.
38. "Xi ji," ibid., 3:131.
39. *Xianqing ouji*, 4:143–150.
40. "Sasao," ibid., 4:149–150.
41. Ibid., 6:282–323.
42. Ibid., 6:286–287.
43. "Liao bing," ibid., 6:316–317. The final sentence quotes from *Mencius*, 5A.4. D. C. Lau (*Mencius*, p. 142) translates: "Hence in explaining an ode, one should not allow the words to obscure the sentence, nor the sentence to obscure the intended meaning. The right way is to meet the intentions of the poet with sympathetic understanding." Mencius is talking about the proper interpretation of the *Poetry Classic* and arguing against a literal interpretation.
44. "Yixin zhongai zhi yao," *Xianqing ouji*, 6:320.
45. "Dongji xing le zhi fa," ibid., 6:293–294. The "mind" of "my mind has been dulled" is literally "point, cutting edge." In some texts, the character (*ying*) has been changed to *sang*, "throat," giving the meaning "my throat is worn out." *Zhiwei*, literally "oil and soft leather," has been translated as "a smooth and subtle approach," which is more comprehensible but lacks parallelism.
46. For these passages, see ibid., 5:233 (turtles), 6:291–292 (summertime pleasures), 4:219 (garlic), and 4:220 (turnips).
47. "Jie fengci," ibid., 1:6–7. The passage contains several allusions. Bodao (style of Deng You) lamented having no sons. Liu Biao's sons were characterized as "pigs and dogs," which thereafter became a self-depreciatory way of referring to one's own sons. Cao Jiao, a rice-eater, stood nine (Chinese) feet tall; see *Mencius*, 6B.2. The oath Li Yu swore twenty years before is printed in his *Liweng yijia yan quanji*; see "Qubu shici," 2:66a–67a.

Editions of *Independent Words* (*Yijia Yan*)

The only easily accessible early edition of *Independent Words* is the *Liweng yijia yan quanji* 笠翁一家言全集 published by the Jieziyuan 芥子園 in 1730, on which all modern editions are based. It was preceded, however, by three different kinds of editions that are distinct from the 1730 edition and that ought to be the scholar's primary recourse.

1. *Liweng yijia yan* 笠翁一家言. This edition, containing four *juan* of prose and eight of poetry, separately numbered, is preserved in the Chinese Academy of Sciences Library, Beijing. The title-page is missing, but the above title is found in most *juan* and other headings, and uniformly in the fishtail. The edition bears an undated preface by Li Changxiang 李長祥, in which he says that Li Yu showed him the manuscript of the book in Fuzhou. The preface must have been written during Li Yu's visit there in the summer and autumn of 1670. (He celebrated his sixtieth birthday, on the seventh day of the eighth month, in Fuzhou in 1670.) A second preface, by Bao Xuan 郎璿, is dated early autumn, 1670, also in Fuzhou. Bao's preface is followed by Li Yu's own "Yijia yan shiyi" 一家言釋義 ("Explanation of the term 'Yijia yan' "), dated on his birthday in 1672, which, we are told, serves as the author's preface. Because the title-page is missing, there is no indication of the publisher, but the book is advertised on the title-page of *Xianqing ouji* 閒情偶寄, and it was clearly published by the Yishengtang 翼聖堂. This book is the first collection of Li Yu's works. (It is not described here as a "first collection," and Li Yu may not have intended at the time to make a second collection. But note that the title-page is missing.) He was still editing the book in Hanyang in 1672, as Miss Qiao's consumption grew worse. The latest datable material in it seems to be his poems on returning to Nanjing, written at the end of 1672. Li Yu has little to say about the book in his letters, in comparison with his enthusiasm about *Casual Expressions* (*Xianqing ouji*). The book may well have been published in 1673, before he set off for Beijing.

2. *Liweng yijia yan erji* 笠翁一家言二集. In the autumn of 1677, Li Yu wrote to Sun Zhi and Mao Xianshu to tell them that he was engaged at the publisher's insistence on a sequel to what he calls *Yijia yan chuji* 一家言初集 and to ask their assistance. (See "Yu Sun Yutai Mao Zhihuang erhaoyou" 與孫宇台毛稺黃二好友, *Liweng yijia yan quanji*, 3:58a–59a). This second collection is not extant as an independent publication, to the best of my knowledge, but it was

evidently reprinted as part of an edition that combined the first and second collections (see below). Its title-page had a note by the owner of the Yishengtang explaining that he is bringing out the *Yijia yan erji* in the same format as the *chuji* to
satisfy public demand. The preface was by Ding Peng 丁澎, dated the seventh
month of 1678. The work was published probably late in that same year. It contained twelve *juan*, numbered consecutively, of which the first six were prose
genres, the seventh consisted of couplets, and the last five were poetic genres, ex-
cluding *ci*. (There had been a section of *ci* in the first collection, but at this time
Li Yu was compiling his own *ci* collection, *Naige ci*.) As in the first collection, the
upper margins contained numerous comments by Li Yu's friends and acquaintances.

Together with the twelve *juan* of prose and poetry, this edition also
evidently included an *Yijia yan bieji* 一家言別集 with a preface (*bianyan* 弁言) by
Li Yu dated a day after his birthday in 1678. His preface makes it clear that he
was planning to incorporate this section in his collected works. It is a thoroughgoing revision and adaptation, in four *juan*, of his *Discussions of the Past*, which he
refers to in the preface as *Liweng lun gu* 笠翁論古. Assuming, as I believe, that we
have the original *Liweng lun gu* essentially intact as reprinted in the 1730 *Liweng
yijia yan quanji*, we can easily see the scope of the revisions Li Yu made in 1678. It
is a selection, as he emphasizes; many items are omitted. But there are also some
additions—there are at least two items not in the 1730 edition. A number of
friends' comments have been omitted, and several new comments have been
added. My impression is that the newer comments tend to stress Li Yu's humor
rather than claim for him a historian's acumen. For example, there is an added
note by Wang Maolin 汪懋麟 on the item about Dongfang Shuo 東方朔 (*juan* 2):
"Liweng's talent is to excel in humor, and yet he is of upright and serious
character. He naturally belongs in the category of Dongfang—a fact on which he
surely prides himself." More important are the changes Li Yu made in format.
The subtitle is given as *Shi duan* 史斷 (Historical Judgments), not *Lun gu* (Discussions of the Past). Similarly, the word *lun* has been omitted before the titles of the
items. The historical anecdotes that are the occasion for Li Yu's remarks are
abridged and sometimes omitted, and his comments are altered, somewhat cut
down, and notably less ebullient. Even the introductory "Liweng says" is often
omitted.

3. *The combined edition.* Between Li Yu's death in 1680 and the publication by the Jieziyuan of his collected works in 1730, there appeared several editions combining his first and second collections, and sometimes adding others of
his works, perhaps as they went out of print. These constitute the "combined edition," although the word "edition" may be a misnomer since they all used the
original blocks of the first and second editions, both of which were by the
Yishengtang. I have seen four copies of the combined edition, in the possession
of Wu Xiaoling 吳曉鈴, in the Ma Lian 馬廉 Collection of Beijing University
Library (two editions, one a fragment), in the Library of Congress, and in the
possession of Itoh Sohei 伊藤漱平.

Wu Xiaoling's copy has no general title. Its title-page has the title *Liweng yi-*

jia yan chuji 笠翁一家言初集, together with a publisher's blurb by the owner of the Yishengtang. The word *chuji* is found only on the title-page. This copy carries the Bao preface, but lacks Li Changxiang's preface as well as Li Yu's "Yijia yan shiyi." This work, in four and eight *juan*, is followed by *Liweng yijia yan erji* 笠翁一家言二集 in twelve *juan*, and by *Yijia yan bieji* in four. The title-page of the former bears the title *Yijia yan erji* and another blurb by the owner of the Yishengtang. The *Yijia yan erji* has Ding Peng's preface, and the *Yijia yan bieji*, Li Yu's. The complete copy in the Ma Lian Collection has a general title-page with the title *Liweng yijia yan quanji* 笠翁一家言全集, preceded by the words "With collective comments by the most famous writers in the world" 宇内諸名家合評. The publisher is given as the Yishengtang. Apart from this title-page, and the fact that it includes Li Yu's "Yijia yan shiyi," the contents and format of this edition are exactly the same as in Wu Xiaoling's. The Library of Congress copy has the same contents, except that it lacks a title-page, the Bao preface, Li Yu's preface to the *Yijia yan bieji*, and a few other items. The copy in the possession of Itoh Sohei is generally the same as those in the Ma Lian Collection and in the Library of Congress, except for its addition of two other works by Li Yu: *Naige ci* 耐歌詞 in four *juan*, and *Ci yun* 詞韻, also in four *juan*. Both works appeared in 1678 or 1679, and were evidently out of print by the time of this printing. The incomplete copy in the Ma Lian Collection appears identical to the complete one. It contains *juan* 4 of the prose and all eight *juan* of the poetry of the first collection, plus *juan* 1–6 of the second collection.

The integrated edition. The editors of the Jieziyuan 芥子園 edition published in 1730 integrated the contents of the first and second editions by genre (perhaps using a combined edition), keeping the original order of the items the same in most cases. Although theirs is in general a reliable edition, it has many minor textual differences, most of which prove to be copying errors on their part. They compressed the prose and poetry into eight *juan*: three of prose, one of couplets, three of *shi* poetry, and one of *ci* lyrics. They appear to have added nothing, and to have omitted only two poems and three letters, all from the second collection. More serious is the omission of some of the upper-margin comments and the misplacement of others.

The editors did not reprint the *Yijia yan bieji*, Li Yu's drastic revision and abridgment of his *Liweng lun gu*, but instead, if my assumption is correct, chose to reprint the original *Liweng lun gu* itself, in *juan* 9 and 10, under the title of *Liweng bieji*. In *juan* 8, they did not reprint the *ci* section of the first collection, but instead incorporated the whole of Li Yu's *Naige ci*. This change is understandable; the *Naige ci* contains the *ci* of the first collection, often with new comments, plus more recent *ci*. A third significant change was to add the whole of the *Xianqing ouji* 閒情偶寄, compressing the sixteen *juan* of the original edition into six, and altering the title to *Liweng ouji* 笠翁偶集, probably for the sake of symmetry. The Jieziyuan edition as a whole was entitled *Liweng yijia yan quanji*. It was re-engraved at least once in the Qing dynasty with the same pagination, but still purporting to be by the Jieziyuan. The Harvard-Yenching Library at Harvard University has copies of both editions.

Bibliography

Abrams, M. H. *The Mirror and the Lamp: Romantic Theory and the Critical Tradition*. Oxford: Oxford University Press, 1953.

Aoki Masaru 青木正兒. *Shina kinsei gikyokushi* 支那近世戲曲史, Tokyo, 1930. Wang Gulu 王古魯, trans. and ed., *Zhongguo jinshi xiqushi* 中國近世戲曲史. Revised edition, 2 vols. Beijing: Zuojia, 1958.

Barnhart, Richard. "The 'Wild and Heterodox' School of Ming Painting," in Susan Bush and Christian Murck, eds., *Theories of the Arts in China*.

Birch, Cyril. *Anthology of Chinese Literature*. New York: Grove Press, 1965.

—— trans. *The Peony Pavilion*. Bloomington: Indiana University Press, 1980.

Bush, Susan, and Christian Murck, eds. *Theories of the Arts in China*. Princeton: Princeton University Press, 1983.

Cahill, James. *The Compelling Image: Nature and Style in Seventeenth-Century Chinese Painting*. Cambridge, Mass.: Harvard University Press, 1982.

Chai Shaibing 柴紹炳. *Chai Xingxuan xiansheng wenchao* 柴省軒先生文鈔. Early Qing edition. (Shanghai Library.)

—— *Yiwang shanren wenchao* 翼望山人文鈔. Qing edition. (Nanjing Library, Gujibu.)

Chaves, Jonathan. "Self in the Kung-an School," in Robert E. Hegel and Richard C. Hessney, eds., *Expressions of Self in Chinese Literature*. New York: Columbia University Press, 1985.

Chen Duo 陳多. *Li Liweng quhua* 李笠翁曲話. Changsha: Hunan renmin, 1980.

—— "Xingge xiju he 'Naikan ci'" 性格喜劇和「耐看詞」, in *Zhongguo gudian beiju xiju lunji* 中國古典悲劇喜劇論集 Shanghai wenyi, 1983.

Chen Jiru 陳繼儒. *Xiaochuang youji* 小窗幽記. Shanghai: Zhongyang shudian, 1935.

Chen Shaotang 陳少棠. *Wan Ming xiaopin lunxi* 晚明小品論析. Taipei: Yuanliu chubanshe, 1982.

Chi pozi zhuan 癡婆子傳. Meiji-period Kyoto edition. (Harvard-Yenching Library.)

Dai Bufan 戴不凡. "Li Liweng shilüe" 李笠翁事略, *Juben*, 1957.3:95–97. Reprinted in *Dai Bufan xiqu yanjiu lunwenji* 戴不凡戲曲研究論文集. Hangzhou: Zhejiang renmin, 1982.

de Bary, Wm. Theodore, ed. *Self and Society in Ming Thought*. New York: Columbia University Press, 1970.

—— "Individualism and Humanism in Late Ming Thought," in de Bary, ed., *Self and Society in Ming Thought.*

Deng Zhicheng 鄧之誠. *Qingshi jishi chubian* 清詩紀事初編, 2 vols. Shanghai guji, 1984.

Ding Peng 丁澎. *Fu li ci* 扶荔詞. Manuscript. (Institute of Literature, Chinese Academy of Social Sciences.)

—— *Fulitang wenjixuan* 扶荔堂文集選. Early Qing edition. (Beijing Library.)

Ding Yaokang 丁耀亢. *Jianggan cao* 江干草. In Ding Yaokang, *Ding Yehao xiansheng shicigao* 丁野鶴先生詩詞稿. Early Qing edition. (Beijing Library.)

—— *Xu Jin Ping Mei* 續金瓶梅. 64 chaps. Qing edition.

Doctrine of the Mean. In James Legge, trans., *The Confucian Classics*, vol. 1. Oxford: Clarendon Press, 1893.

Dong Han 董含. *Chunxiang zhuibi* 蓴鄉贅筆. In (1868) *Shuo ling* 說鈴.

Dong Qian 董遷. "Gong Zhilu nianpu" 龔芝麓年譜, *Zhonghe yuekan* 中和月刊 3.1–3 (January–March, 1942):35–51, 64–74, 79–88.

Du Chuang 杜濬. *Meihu yinji* 湄湖吟集. Qing edition.

Du Guangting 杜光庭. "Qiuran ke zhuan" 虬髯客傳. In *Taiping guangji*, 193.

Du Jun 杜濬. *Bianyatang ji* 變雅堂集. In *Huanggang erchushi ji.* 黃岡二處士集. 1935 edition.

—— *Bianyatang wenji bu fen juan* 變雅堂文集不分卷. Qing edition. (Chinese Academy of Sciences, Beijing.)

—— *Bianyatang jiwai shi* 變雅堂集外詩. Manuscript. (Chinese Academy of Sciences, Beijing.)

—— *Bianyatang yiji* 變雅堂遺集. 1894 edition.

—— *Du Chacun shichao* 杜茶村詩鈔. (Shanghai Library.)

Du Shuying 杜書瀛. *Lun Li Yu de xiju meixue* 論李漁的戲劇美學. Beijing: Zhongguo shehui kexue, 1982.

Elliott, Robert G. *The Literary Persona.* Chicago: Chicago University Press, 1982.

Elman, Benjamin A. *From Philosophy to Philology: Intellectual and Social Aspects of Change in Late Imperial China.* Cambridge, Mass.: Council on East Asian Studies, Harvard University, 1984.

Fang Wen 方文. *Tushanji* 嵞山集. Early Qing edition. (Beijing Library.) Facsimile edition, 3 vols., Shanghai guji, 1979.

Fu Xihua 傅惜華 ed. *Zhongguo gudian wenxue banhua xuanji* 中國古典文學版畫選集. Shanghai meishu, 1979.

Gao Lian 高濂. *Yuzanji* 玉簪記. In *Liushizhong qu.*

—— *Zunsheng bajian* 遵生八牋. Ming edition. (Beijing Library.)

Gao Ming 高明. *Pipaji* 琵琶記. In *Liushizhong qu.*

Goffman, Erving. *The Presentation of Self in Everyday Life.* London: Allen and Unwin, 1959.

Gong Dingzi 龔鼎孳. *Dingshan tang quanji* 定山堂全集. 1883 rpt.

Goodrich, L. C. "Chuang T'ing-lung," in Arthur W. Hummel, ed., *Eminent Chinese of the Ch'ing Period.*

—— and Chaoying Fang, eds. *Dictionary of Ming Biography: 1368–1644.* New

York: Columbia University Press, 1976.

Guben xiqu congkan 古本戲曲叢刊. Shanghai and Beijing. First series, 1954; second series, 1955; third series, 1957; fourth series, 1958.

Gu Dunrou 顧敦鍒. "Li Liweng cixue" 李笠翁詞學. In Gu Dunrou, *Wenyuan chanyou*.

—— "Li Liweng pengbei kao" 李笠翁朋輩考. In Gu Dunrou, *Wenyuan chanyou*.

—— "Li Liweng nianpu" 李笠翁年譜. Manuscript. (Beijing University Library.)

—— *Wenyuan chanyou* 文苑閑幽. Taizhong, Donghai daxue, 1969.

Gu Jingxing 顧景星. *Baimaotang ji* 白茅堂集. Qing edition.

Gu Yanwu 顧炎武. *Rizhi lu* 日知錄. 2 vols. Shanghai, Commercial Press, 1933.

—— *Gu Tinglin shiwenji* 顧亭林詩文集. Beijing, Zhonghua, 1983 rpt.

Guan Hanqing 關漢卿. *Zhao Pan'er fengyue jiu fengchen* 趙盼兒風月救風塵. In *Guan Hanqing xiquji* 關漢卿戲曲集, ed. Wu Xiaoling 吳曉鈴 et al. Beijing: Zhongguo xiju chubanshe, 1958.

Guan Zi 管子. *Guan Zi jiaozheng* 管子校正, ed. Dai Wang 戴望. Shanghai: Commercial Press, 1935 rpt.

Guo Shaoyu 郭紹虞. *Zhongguo wenxue pipingshi* 中國文學批評史. Revised edition, 2 vols. Shanghai: Commercial Press, 1947.

Guo shi liezhuan 國史列傳 (*Man Han dachen liezhuan* 滿漢大臣列傳). Dongfang xuehui 東方學會, n.d.

Han Yu 韓愈. *Han Changli wenji jiaozhu* 韓昌黎文集校注. Beijing, Zhonghua, 1972.

Hanan, Patrick. *The Chinese Vernacular Story*. Cambridge, Mass.: Harvard University Press, 1981.

Hegel, Robert E. *The Novel in Seventeenth-Century China*. New York; Columbia University Press, 1981.

Henry, Eric P. *Chinese Amusement: The Lively Plays of Li Yü*. Hamden, Conn.: Archon Books, 1980.

Hsia, C. T. "Time and the Human Condition in the Plays of T'ang Hsien-tsu." In Wm. Theodore de Bary, ed., *Self and Society in Ming Thought*.

Hsiao, K. C. "Li Chih." In L. Carrington Goodrich and Chaoying Fang, eds., *Dictionary of Ming Biography*.

Hu Jie 胡介. *Lütang shiwenji* 旅堂詩文集. (Chinese Academy of Sciences, Beijing.)

Huang Lizhen 黃麗貞. *Li Yu yanjiu* 李漁研究. Taipei: Chun wenxue, 1974.

Huang Tianji 黃天驥. "Lun Li Yu de sixiang he chuangzuo" 論李漁的思想和創作, *Wenxue pinglun*, 1983.1:107–118.

Huang Xun 黃訓. *Du shu yi de* 讀書一得. Ming edition. (Palace Museum, Taiwan.)

Huang Zhouxing 黃周星. "Zhi qu zhiyu" 製曲枝語. Attached to Huang's *Ren tian le* 人天樂. *Guben xiqu congkan*, third series.

Hummel, Arthur W., ed. *Eminent Chinese of the Ch'ing Period*. Washington, D. C., Government Printing Office, 1943–1944.

Itoh Sohei 伊藤漱平. "Ri Gyo no shōsetsu *Museigeki* no hampon ni tsuite" 李漁の小説「無聲戲の版本について, *Chū tetsubun gakkaihō* 中哲文學會報 9 (June 1984):126–133.

—— "Ri Gyo no shōsetsu no hampon to sono ryūden—*Museigeki* wo chūshin to shite" 李漁の小説の版本とその流傳—「無聲戲」を中心として, *Nihon Chūgokugaku kaihō* 日本中國學會報 36 (1984): 191–206.

Jiang Feng 江峰. "Li Yu jiashi ji qita" 李漁家世及其他, *Xiwen*, 1982.3:63–64.

Jiang Xingyu 蔣星煜. *Yi xi dai yao* 以戲代藥. Guangzhou. Guangdong renmin, 1980.

Jingchaiji 荊釵記. In *Liushizhong qu*.

Jing shi tongyan 警世通言, comp. Feng Menglong 馮夢龍. Facsimile edition of first (1624) edition. Taipei: Shijie shuju, 1958.

Kong Xianyi 孔憲易. "Guanyu Li Yu de *Wusheng xi* canben" 關於李漁的「無聲戲」殘本, *Wen shi* (Zhonghua shuju) 9 (June 1980):245–248.

Lau, D. C., trans. *The Analects*. London: Penguin Books, 1979.

—— trans. *Mencius*. London: Penguin Books, 1970.

Li Chaowei 李朝威. "Liu Yi zhuan" 柳毅傳. In *Taiping guangji, juan* 419.

Li Haogu 李好古. *Zhang sheng zhu hai* 張生煮海. In *Guben xiqu congkan*, fourth series.

Li Yu 李漁. *Bimuyu* 比目魚. In *Liweng shizhongqu*.

—— *Chidu chuzheng* 尺牘初徵. Early Qing edition. (Chinese Academy of Sciences, Library of Congress.)

—— *Fengzheng wu* 風箏誤. In *Liweng shizhongqu*. Also an early Qing edition in Beijing University Library.

—— *Huang qiu feng* 凰求鳳. In *Liweng shizhongqu*.

—— *Jeou-P'ou-T'ouan*, trans. Pierre Klossowski. Paris: Société des Editions Jean-Jacques Pauvert, 1962.

—— "Kui ci guanjian" 窺詞管見. Attached to *Naige ci. Liweng yijia yan quanji, juan* 8.

—— *Li Liweng chidu* 李笠翁尺牘, ed. Xu Jiayou 許嘉猷. Manuscript. (Shanghai Library.)

—— *Li Liweng chuanqi shizhong* 李笠翁傳奇十種. Yishengtang 翼聖堂 edition. (Wu Xiaoling.) Also a Shidetang 世德堂 edition (National Taiwan University). Facsimile edition of latter in *Li Yu quanji*. Alternative title: *Liweng shizhongqu*.

—— *Li Liweng xiaoshuo shiwuzhong* 李笠翁小説十五種, ed. Yu Wencao 于文藻. Hangzhou: Zhejiang renmin, 1983.

—— *Li Liweng xijuxuan* 李笠翁喜劇選, ed. Huang Tianji 黃天驥 and Ouyang Guang 歐陽光. Changsha: Yuelu, 1984.

—— *Liancheng bi* 連城璧. Early Qing edition. (Saeki Municipal Library, Japan.)

—— *Lianxiang ban* 憐香伴. In *Liweng shizhongqu*.

—— *Liweng ciyun* 笠翁詞韻. Qing edition. (Kuraishi Collection, Tōyō bunka kenkyūjo.) Also included in a Qing edition of Li Yu's *Naige ci* (Wu Xiaoling). Also included in *Liweng yijia yan quanji* (Itoh Sohei).

—— *Liweng lungu* 笠翁論古. Qing edition, under the title of *Liweng zengding lungu* 笠翁增定論古, formerly in Fu Xihua's possession. Abridged and revised as the *Bieji* 別集 of *Liweng yijia yan erji*, which survives in the combined edition (see below). Original version incorporated in the (1730) *Liweng yijia yan quanji*.

—— ed. *Liweng piyue Sanguo zhi* 笠翁批閱三國志. Early Qing edition. (Institute of Literature, Chinese Academy of Social Sciences, and Bibliothèque Nationale.)

—— *Liweng shiyun* 笠翁詩韻. Qing edition. (Kuraishi Collection, Tōyō bunka kenkyūjo, and University of California, Berkeley.)

—— *Liweng shizhongqu*. See under *Li Liweng chuanqi shizhong*.

—— *Liweng yijia yan* 笠翁一家言 (First collection). Early Qing edition. (Chinese Academy of Sciences, Beijing.)

—— *Liweng yijia yan quanji* 笠翁一家言全集 (Combined edition). Versions of this early Qing edition, with slightly differing contents, are in the possession of Wu Xiaoling, the Library of Congress, the Ma Lian Collection in Beijing University Library (two copies), and Itoh Sohei.

—— *Liweng yijia yan quanji* 笠翁一家言全集 (the integrated edition of 1730 by the Jieziyuan 芥子園). There are two separate Jieziyuan editions, with identical pagination; one is held by the Literature Department of Kyoto University and also by the Harvard-Yenching Library, and the second is held by the Harvard-Yenching and other libraries. The Kyoto University edition is reproduced in *Li Yu quanji*.

—— *Li Yu quanji* 李漁全集, ed. Helmut Martin. 15 vols. Taipei: Chengwen chubanshe, 1970.

—— *Naige ci* 耐歌詞. Qing edition. (Wu Xiaoling.) Also a Qing edition incorporating the *Liweng ciyun*. (Wu Xiaoling.) Reprinted in *juan* 8 of the (1730) *Liweng yijia yan quanji*.

—— *Naihe tian* 奈何天. In *Liweng shizhongqu*. Also an edition in the Ma Lian Collection, Beijing University Library.

—— *Qiao tuanyuan* 巧團圓. In *Liweng shizhongqu*.

—— *Rou putuan* 肉蒲團. Qing edition, with the alternative title of *Juehou chan* 覺後禪. (Harvard-Yenching Library.) The preface is dated *guiyou* 癸酉, there are 13 illustrations before the text proper, and the format is 21 characters in 12 columns. Also the Meiji-period Japanese edition. Also a late Qing, small-format, lithographic edition, entitled *Yesou qiyu zhongqing lu* 野叟奇語鍾情錄, 1894 preface.

—— *Shen luanjiao* 慎鸞交. In *Liweng shizhongqu*.

—— *Shenzhong lou* 蜃中樓. In *Liweng shizhongqu*.

—— *Shi'er lou* 十二樓. (Alternative, perhaps primary, title: *Jueshi mingyan* 覺世名言.) Early Qing edition by the Xiaoxianju 消閒居. (Ma Lian Collection, Beijing University Library.) Also a Qing edition (Academia Sinica, Taiwan.) The latter is reproduced in *Li Yu quanji*. Also a modern edition by Shanghai guji, 1986.

—— *Siliu chuzheng* 四六初徵. Yishengtang edition. Title-page has the title *Xin siliu chuzheng* 新四六初徵. (Harvard-Yenching Library.)

—— *Wusheng xi* 無聲戲 (First collection). Early Qing edition. (Sonkeikaku.) Facsimile edition in *Li Yu quanji*.

—— *Wusheng xi heji* 無聲戲合集. Early Qing edition, fragmentary. (Ma Lian Collection, Beijing University Library.)

—— *Xianqing ouji* 閒情偶寄. Early Qing edition by the Yishengtang 翼聖堂. (Harvard-Yenching Library.) Also a second edition, entitled *Liweng ouji* 笠翁偶集, incorporated in the (1730) *Liweng yijia yan quanji*. Also a modern edition of the latter, ed. Shan Jinheng 單錦珩, under the title of *Xianqing ouji* 閒情偶寄. Hangzhou: Zhejiang guji, 1985.

—— *Yijia yan bieji* 一家言別集. See above under *Liweng lungu.*

—— *Yizhong yuan* 意中緣. In *Liweng shizhongqu*. Also an early Qing edition with a preface by Fan Xiang dated 1659. (Beijing Library.)

—— *Yu saotou* 玉搔頭. In *Liweng shizhongqu.*

—— *Zizhi xinshu* 資治新書 (First collection). Early Qing edition by Wenjintang 文錦堂. (Chinese Academy of Sciences.) Also a second impression of the above by the same house, entitled *Xinzeng Zizhi xinshu* 新增資治新書全集, which is also in the Academy of Sciences.

—— *Zizhi xinshu*. Combined edition of the first and second collections. Mid-Qing edition by the Yingdetang 英德堂. (Gujibu, Nanjing Library.)

—— *Zizhi xinshu erji* 資治新書二集 (Second collection). Early Qing edition by the Jingyetang 敬業堂. (Harvard-Yenching Library.) Also a Qing edition by the Jieziyuan and a reprint, entitled *Xinzeng Zizhi xinshu erji* 新增資治新書二集, by the Youyutang 友于堂. (Chinese Academy of Sciences, Beijing.)

Li Yu (attribution). *Changxing ji* 悵性集. Qing edition. (Wu Xiaoling.)

—— *Gujin chidu daquan* 古今尺牘大全. Edition with preface dated 1688. (Beijing University Library.)

—— *Gujin liansou* 古今聯藪. Qing edition. (Beijing University Library.)

—— *Gujin shilüe* 古今史略. Qing edition. (Naikaku Bunko.)

—— *Yiqing ji* 怡情集. Qing edition. (Wu Xiaoling.)

Liang Yunzhi 梁允植. *Tengwu shiji* 藤塢詩集. Early Qing edition. (Chinese Academy of Sciences, Beijing.)

Lin Yutang. *The Importance of Understanding*. Cleveland: World Publishing Co., 1960.

Ling Mengchu 凌濛初. *Erke Pai'an jingqi* 二刻拍案驚奇, ed. Tien-yi Li. Taipei: Zhengzhong, 1960.

—— *Pai'an jingqi* 拍案驚奇, ed. Tien-yi Li. Hong Kong: Youlian, 1966.

Linqing 麟慶. *Hongxue yinyuan tuji* 鴻雪因緣圖記. Yangzhou, 1847.

Liu, James J. Y. *Chinese Theories of Literature*. Chicago: University of Chicago Press, 1975.

Liu Tingji 劉廷璣. *Zaiyuan zazhi* 在園雜志. In *Liaohai congshu* 遼海叢書.

Liushizhong qu 六十種書. Compiled by Mao Jin 毛晉. 12 vols. Beijing: Zhonghua, 1958.

Lu Cai 陸采. *Mingzhuji* 明珠記. In *Liushizhong qu.*

—— *Nan Xixiang* 南西廂. In *Liushizhong qu.*

Lu Qi 陸圻. *Weifengtang wenji* 威鳳堂文集. Early Qing edition. (Chinese Academy of Sciences, Beijing.)

Lü Tiancheng 呂天成. *Xiuta yeshi* 繡榻野史. Late Ming edition.

Lung, Conrad W., trans. "The Strong Kid of the Ch'in-huai Region." In Y. W.

Ma and Joseph S. M. Lau, eds., *Traditional Chinese Stories: Themes and Variations.*

Lynn, Richard John. "Alternate Routes to Self-Realization in Ming Theories of Poetry." In Susan Bush and Christian Murck, *Theories of the Arts in China.*

Ma, Y. W., and Joseph S. M. Lau, eds. *Traditional Chinese Stories: Themes and Variations.* New York: Columbia University Press, 1978.

Mao, Nathan K., and Liu Ts'un-yan. *Li Yü.* Boston: Twayne, 1977.

Mao Xianshu 毛先舒. *Kuang lin* 匡林. In his *Mao Zhihuang shi'erzhong shu.*

—— *Mao Zhihuang shi'erzhong shu* 毛穉黃十二種書. Qing edition. (Naikaku Bunko.)

—— *Sigutang ji* 四古堂集. In his *Mao Zhihuang shi'erzhong shu.*

—— *Sigutang shisizhong shu.* 四古堂十四種書. Manuscript. (Naikaku Bunko.)

—— *Sun shu* 渡書. In his *Mao Zhihuang shi'erzhong shu.*

—— *Xiao kuang wenchao* 小匡文鈔. In his *Sigutang shisizhong shu.*

Mao Xiang 冒襄. *Yingmei'an yiyu* 影梅庵憶語. In *Rugao Mao shi congshu* 如皋冒氏叢書.

Martin, Helmut. *Li Li-weng über das Theater.* Taipei: Meiya, 1966.

Matsuda, Shizue. "The Beauty and the Scholar in Li Yü's Short Stories." *Studies in Short Fiction* 10.3 (Summer 1973):271–280.

—— "Li Yü: His Life and Moral Philosophy as Reflected in His Fiction." Ph.D. diss., Columbia University, 1977.

Otsuka Hidetaka 大塚秀高. "*Jūni shō to Ri Gyo*" 十二笑と李漁. In *Itoh Sohei kyōju taikan kinen Chūgokugaku ronshū* 伊藤漱平教授退官記念中國學論集. Tokyo, Kyūko shoin, 1986.

Owen, Stephen. *Reminiscences: The Experience of the Past in Classical Chinese Literature.* Cambridge, Mass.: Harvard University Press, 1986.

Peterson, Willard J. *Bitter Gourd: Fang I-chih and the Impetus for Intellectual Change.* New Haven: Yale University Press, 1979.

Poetry Classic. See Shi jing.

Pollard, David E. *A Chinese Look at Literature.* Berkeley and Los Angeles: University of California Press, 1973.

Qian Qianyi 錢謙益. *Muzhai waiji* 牧齋外集. Manuscript. (Beijing Library.)

Qianjia shixuan 千家詩選. Compiled by Xie Fangde 謝枋得. Ming edition by the Wenhuaxuan 文華軒, Jianyang. (Harvard-Yenching Library.)

Qingdai jinhui shumu 清代禁燬書目. Compiled by Yao Jinyuan 姚覲元. Shanghai: Commercial Press, 1957.

Qingdai zhiguan nianbiao 清代職官年表. Compiled by Qian Shifu 錢實甫. Beijing: Zhonghua, 1980.

Qingshi gao 清史稿. Compiled by Zhao Erxun 趙爾巽. Beijing: Zhonghua, 1976–1977 rpt.

Quhai zongmu tiyao 曲海總目提要. Beijing: Renmin, 1959.

Ruan Dacheng 阮大鋮. *Yanzi jian* 燕子箋. In *Guben xiqu congkan,* second series.

Ruyi Jun zhuan 如意君傳. Meiji-period Kyoto edition. (Harvard-Yenching Library.)

Shan Jinheng 單錦珩. "Li Yu nianbiao" 李漁年表, *Zhejiang Shifan xueyuan xuebao* (Social Sciences number) 1982.4:36–46.

Shang Zhongxian 尚仲賢. *Liu Yi chuan shu* 柳毅傳書. In *Guben xiqu congkan*, fourth series.

Shen Qian 沈謙. *Dongjiang jichao* 東江集鈔. Early Qing edition. (Chinese Academy of Sciences, Beijing.)

Shen Shouzheng 沈守正. *Xuetangji* 雪堂集. Late Ming edition. (National Central Library, Taiwan.)

Shen Zijin 沈自晉. *Chongding Nanjiugong cipu* 重定南九宮詞譜. Facsimile edition of 1655 edition. Shanghai: Commercial Press, 1936.

Shengyu xiangjie 聖諭像解, ed. Liang Yannian 梁延年. 1681 edition.

Shi jing 詩經. *Mao shi yinde* 毛詩引得 edition. Harvard-Yenching Institute, Beijing, 1935.

Siku quanshu zongmu 四庫全書總目. Beijing: Zhonghua, 1965 rpt.

Siliu xinshu guangji 四六新書廣集. Compiled by Huang Shi 黃始. Early Qing edition. (Naikaku Bunko.)

Song Maocheng 宋懋澄. *Jiuyueji* 九籥集, ed. Wang Liqi 王利器. Beijing: Zhongguo shehui kexue, 1984.

Spence, Jonathan D., and John E. Wills, Jr., eds. *From Ming to Ch'ing: Conquest, Region, and Continuity in Seventeenth-Century China.* New Haven: Yale University Press, 1979.

Struve, Lynn A. "Ambivalence and Action: Some Frustrated Scholars of the K'ang-hsi Period." In Jonathan D. Spence and John E. Wills, Jr., *From Ming to Ch'ing.*

Sun Kaidi 孫楷第. *Riben Dongjing suo jian Zhongguo xiaoshuo shumu* 日本東京所見中國小説書目. Revised edition. Beijing: Renmin, 1958.

—— "Li Liweng yu *Shi'er lou*" 李笠翁與十二樓. Revised edition in Sun Kaidi, *Cangzhou houji* 滄州後集. Beijing: Zhonghua, 1985. Originally published in *Tushuguanxue jikan* 9.3–4 (1935): 379–441.

—— *Zhongguo tongsu xiaoshuo shumu* 中國通俗小説書目. Revised edition. Beijing: Renmin, 1982.

Sun Zhi 孫治. *Sun Yutai ji* 孫宇台集. Early Qing edition. (Naikaku Bunko.)

Taiping guangji 太平廣記. Compiled by Li Fang 李昉 et al. 5 vols. Beijing: Renmin, 1959.

Taishang ganying pian 太上感應篇. Compiled by Li Changling 李昌齡. In *Daozang*, vols. 834–839.

Tang Xianzu 湯顯祖. *Mudan ting* 牡丹亭. In *Tang Xianzu xiquji* 湯顯祖戲曲集, ed. Xu Shuofang 徐朔方. Shanghai: Shanghai guji, 1978.

Tanner, Tony. *Adultery and the Novel: Contract and Transgression.* Baltimore: Johns Hopkins University Press, 1979.

Tian Rucheng 田汝成. *Tian Shuhe wenji* 田叔禾文集. Ming edition.

Tong Shinan 佟世南, comp. *Dongbaitang cixuan chuji* 東白堂詞選初集. Early Qing edition. (Beijing Library.)

Tu Long 屠隆 (attribution). *Kaopan yushi* 考槃餘事. *Congshu jicheng* edition.

Van Gulik, Robert H. *Sexual Life in Ancient China.* Leiden: Brill, 1961.

Van Hecken, J. L., and W. A. Grotaers. "The Half Acre Garden, Pan-mou Yüan." *Monumenta Serica* 18 (1959): 360–387.

Wakeman, Frederic, Jr. *The Great Enterprise.* 2 vols. Berkeley and Los Angeles: University of California Press, 1985.

Waley, Arthur, trans. *The Book of Songs.* New York: Grove Press, 1960 rpt.

Wang, Chi-chen. *Traditional Chinese Tales.* New York: Columbia University Press, 1944.

Wang Gai 王槩 et al. *Jieziyuan huazhuan* 芥子園畫傳. Beijing: Renmin meishu, 1960.

Wang Ji 汪楫. *Shanwen shi* 山聞詩. Early Qing edition. (Naikaku Bunko.)

Wang, John C. Y. *Chin Sheng-t'an.* New York: Twayne, 1972.

Wang Rigao 王日高. *Huaixuan shiji* 槐軒詩集. Early Qing edition. (Chinese Academy of Sciences, Beijing.)

Wang Ruqian 汪汝謙. *Chunxingtang shiji* 春星堂詩集. In *Congmu Wang shi yishu* 叢睦汪氏遺書. 1886 edition.

Wang Shilu 王士祿. *Shihu caotang ji* 十笏草堂集. Early Qing edition. (Naikaku Bunko.)

Wang Zhuo 王晫. *Jin Shishuo* 今世説. Shanghai: Gudian wenxue, 1957.

—— *Xiajutang shiwen quanji* 霞舉堂詩文全集. Early Qing edition. (Chinese Academy of Sciences, Beijing.)

Watson, Burton, trans. *Chuang Tzu.* New York: Columbia University Press, 1968.

Wu Bing 吳炳. *Lü mudan* 綠牡丹. In Wu Mei 吳梅, ed., *Shemotashi qucong* 奢摩他室曲叢. Shanghai, 1928.

Wu Weiye 吳偉業. *Wu Meicun shiji jianzhu* 吳梅村詩集箋注, ed. Cheng Maoheng 程穆衡 and Yang Xuehang 楊學沆. Facsimile edition of Qing manuscript, Shanghai guji, 1983.

Wu Xiaoling 吳曉鈴. "Chuanqi bazhong zuozhe kaobian"「傳奇八種」作者考辨. B. A. thesis, Beijing University, 1937.

Wu Zhao zhuan 武曌傳. Excerpted in Ye Rubi 葉如壁, ed., *Zazuan xingshui bian* 雜纂醒睡編. Ming edition. (Library of Congress.)

Xia Xieshi 夏寫時. "Li Yu shengping chutan" 李漁生平初探. *Xiqu yanjiu* 10 (September 1983):162–181.

Xiao Rong 肖榮 (Xiao Xinqiao 蕭欣橋). *Li Yu pingzhuan* 李漁評傳. Hangzhou: Zhejiang wenyi, 1985.

Xiling shizi shixuan 西陵十子詩選. Compiled by Chai Shaobing 柴紹炳 and Mao Xianshu 毛先舒. Early Qing edition. (Beijing Library.)

Xinxiang xianzhi 新鄉縣志. Compiled by Chang Jun 暢俊 et al. 1747 edition.

Xing shi hengyan 醒世恆言. Compiled by Feng Menglong 馮夢龍. Facsimile edition of first edition, 1627. 3 vols. Taipei: Shijie shuju, 1959.

Xu Shoukai 徐壽凱. *Li Liweng quhua zhushi* 李笠翁曲話注釋. Anhui renmin, 1981.

Xu Qiu 徐釚. *Benshi shi* 本事詩. Qing edition.

Yang Hsien-yi and Gladys Yang, trans. *Selected Plays of Kuan Han-ch'ing.* Shanghai: New Art and Literature Publishing House, 1958.

Youguiji 幽閨記. (Also known as *Baiyue ting* 拜月亭.) In *Liushizhong qu.*

You Tong 尤侗. *Xitang quanji* 西堂全集. Early Qing edition. (Harvard-Yenching Library.)

—— *Xitang zazu* 西堂雜俎. In his *Xitang quanji*.

Yu Huai 余懷. *Banqiao zaji* 板橋雜記. In *Zhaodai congshu* 昭代叢書.

—— *Weiwaixuan shiji* 味外軒詩輯. Compiled by Kang Jue 康爵. Qing edition. (Shanghai Library.)

—— *Yuqin zhai ci* 玉琴齋詞. Guoxue tushuguan, 1928.

Yuan Hongdao 袁宏道. *Yuan Hongdao ji jianjiao* 袁宏道集箋校, ed. Qian Bocheng 錢伯城. 2 vols. Shanghai: Shanghai guji, 1981.

Yuan Yizhi 袁益之 (Yuan Zhenyu 袁振宇). "Li Yu shengzunian kaobian" 李漁生卒年考辨. *Wenxue pinglun congkan* 13 (January 1982): 200–205.

Zhao Wenqing 趙聞慶. "Li Yu shengping shiji de xin faxian" 李漁生平事迹的新發現. *Xiwen*, 1981.4:49–52.

—— "Youguan Li Yu shengping shiji de jige wenti" 有關李漁生平事迹的幾個問題. *Zhejiang shifan xueyuan xuebao* (Social Sciences number), 1981.1:58–63.

Zhong Xing 鍾惺. *Shi huai* 史懷. Late Ming edition. (Chinese Academy of Sciences, Beijing.)

Zhou Lianggong 周亮工. *Chidu xinchao* 尺牘新鈔. Shanghai zazhi gongsi, 1935.

—— *Laigutang ji* 賴古堂集. Shanghai guji, 1979.

Zhu Jianxin 朱劍心, ed. *Wan Ming xiaopin wenxuan*. 晚明小品文選. Shanghai: Commercial Press, 1937.

Zhu Yan 朱琰. *Jinhua shilu* 金華詩錄. 1883 rpt. (Chinese Academy of Sciences, Beijing.)

Zhuang Yifu 莊一拂. *Gudian xiqu cunmu huikao* 古典戲曲存目彙考. 3 vols. Shanghai guji, 1982.

Glossary

A Ji 阿寄

"A Qian Shen Yinbo sishi chudu shi ban yu ke Tiaochuan shiri chu zhi" 阿倩沈因伯四十初度時伴予客苕川是日初至

"Ao gongqing qi'er zhang yi" 傲公卿乞兒仗義

"Ao ju nan hao" 拗句難好

ba po ruan 罷頗軟

Ban Zhao 班昭

"Banghou jian tongshi xiadizhe" 榜後柬同時下第者

"Banmu ying yuan" 半畝營園

bao 報

Bao Xuan 郎瑄

benqian 本錢

"Benxing kuhao zhi yao" 本性酷好之藥

bian 緶

"Bian diao" 變調

"Bian jiu cheng xin" 變舊成新

biankan 編刊

bianyan 弁言

"Bie" 縶

bieji 別集

biji 筆記

Bimuyu 比目魚

"Binbai" 賓白

Bodao 伯道 (style of Deng You 鄧攸)

"Budeng gao fu" 不登高賦

buquan 不全

busi yingxiong 不死英雄

caizi jiaren 才子佳人

"Cang hou na wu" 藏垢納污

Cang Jie 倉頡

Cao 曹

"Cao ben" 草本

Cao Jiao 曹交

Cao Xi 曹璽

Cao Zhi 曹植

Chai Shaobing 柴紹炳

chantou 纏頭

Chen Aiyong 陳靉永

Chen Baifeng 陳百峯

Chen Jiru 陳繼儒

Chen Qitai 陳啓泰

Chen Tuan 陳摶

Cheng Hao 程顥

"Cheng Suo Yu'an xiangguo ershou" 呈索愚菴相國二首

chengti 承題

Chi pozi zhuan 癡婆子傳

Chidu chuzheng 尺牘初徵

Chidu xingao 尺牘新稿

Chidu xinpian 尺牘新篇

"Chongchang" 冲場

chou 丑

"Chou langjun pa jiao pian de yan" 醜郎君怕嬌偏得艷

"Chuang zhang" 牀帳

chuanqi 傳奇

"Chugui" 櫥櫃

ci 詞

"Ci bie fan jian" 詞別繁減

"Ci yun he Wu Xiuchan shijun guofang ershou" 次韻和吳修蟾使君過訪

過訪二首

"Ci yun he Xu Donglai zeng bie" 次韻和徐東來贈別

"Cuiyalou" 萃雅樓

"Da Gu Chifang" 答顧赤方

"Da shan" 大山

"Da Jiang Cisheng wen shanju jinzhuang" 答姜次生問山居近狀

"Da Li Yi shu" 答李翊書

dan 旦

daoxue 道學

Daxue 大學

"Dazongbo Gong Zhilu xiansheng wange" 大宗伯龔芝麓先生輓歌

"Deng zhu" 燈燭

"Dian ran" 點染

Ding Peng 丁澎

dizhu 地主

Dong Qichang 董其昌

Dongfang Shuo 東方朔

"Dongji xing le zhi fa" 冬季行樂之法

Dongmen Sheng 東門生

Du Chuang 杜濬

Du Fu 杜甫

Du Jun 杜濬

Du Liniang 杜麗娘

"Du Tianzhu, Xiong Xunshu, Xiong Yuanxian, Li Renshu . . ." 堵天柱，熊荀叔，熊元獻，李仁熟 . . .

Dunmutang 敦睦堂

"Duqi shou you fu zhi gua, nuofu huan busi zhi hun" 妬妻守有夫之寡，懦夫還不死之魂

"Erchen zhuan" 二臣傳

"Ersun qi haigu tongpu ben sang" 兒孫棄骸骨僮僕奔喪

fan an 翻案

Fan Chengmo 范承謨

Fan Qi 樊圻

Fan Wencheng 范文程

Fan Xiang 范驤

fang 方

"Fang Li Lihong" 訪李笠鴻

Fang Wen 方文

"Fangshe" 房舍

fanli 凡例

fengliu 風流

"Fengxianlou" 奉先樓

Fengzheng wu 風箏誤

"Fori cheng shang ji" 佛日稱觴記

"Fu Cao Gu'an taishi" 復曹顧菴太史

"Fu Chen Duanbo sikong" 復陳端伯司空

"Fu Chen Xueshan shaozai" 復陳學山少宰

"Fu ju fu" 福橘賦

"Fu Ke Yanchu zhangke" 復柯岸初掌科

"Fu Shen Zemin taiqinweng" 復沈澤民太親翁

"Fu Tang Junzong" 復唐君宗

"Fu Wang Zuoju" 復王左車

Fu Xihua 傅惜華

fu xing 拂性

"Furen xiewa bian" 婦人鞋襪辨

"Fuyunlou" 拂雲樓

Gao Zi 告子

"Geju" 格局

"Gewu" 歌舞

Gong Dingzi 龔鼎孳

gu 股

"Gu feng" 谷風

Gu Jingxing 顧景星

Gu Kaizhi 顧愷之

"Gu Liangfen dianji, yi ren zeng suguo jian yi, dai jian fuxie" 顧梁汾典籍，以人贈蔬果見貽，代束賦謝

Gu Yanwu 顧炎武

"Guafu she ji zhui xinlang, zhongmei qi xin duo caizi" 寡婦設計贅新郎，眾美齊心奪才子

Guan Hanqing 關漢卿

"Guangling gui zhi jiaci danri" 廣陵歸值家慈誕日

"Guanjie" 盥櫛

"Gudong" 骨董

"Gui huobian" 貴活變

"Gui xianqian" 貴顯淺

"Guimao yuanri" 癸卯元日

"Guiren xing le zhi fa" 貴人行樂之法

Glossary

"Guizhenglou" 歸正樓
"*Gujin xiao shi* xu" 古今笑史序
Guo Chuanfang 郭傳芳
"Guo Ziling diaotai" 過子陵釣臺
guowen 過文
"Gushi" 穀食
guwen 古文
Han shu 漢書
Han Xin 韓信
Handan 邯鄲
Hatano Tarō 波多野太郎
"Heguilou" 鶴歸樓
"He You Hui'an guan jiaji yan ju ci yuanyun" 和尤悔菴觀家姬演劇次原韻
"He zhuyou cheng shang xi ci lai yun" 和諸友稱觴悉次來韻
hehuan 合歡
"Heyinglou" 合影樓
Hongfu 紅拂
hongyan boming 紅顏薄命
"Hou duanchang shi shishou you xu" 後斷腸詩十首有序
houting hua 後庭花
Hu Jie 胡介
"Huai A Qian Shen Yinbo ji wu nü Shuzhao" 懷阿倩沈因伯暨吾女淑昭
huajing 化境
Huang qiu feng 凰求鳳
Huang Yuanjie 黃媛介
Huangheshan Nong 黃鶴山農
"Hui sha bian" 回煞辯
"Huqiu maihuashi" 虎丘賣花市
Hushang Liweng 湖上笠翁
ji (descriptive account) 記
ji (articulation) 機
"Ji da Chen Xueshan shaozai" 寄答陳學山少宰
"Ji Fujian jingnan xunhaidao Chen Dalai xiansheng wen" 祭福建靖難巡海道陳大來先生文
"Ji Fujian jingnan zongdu Fan Jingong xiansheng wen" 祭福建靖難總督范覲公先生文
"Ji Ji Bozi" 寄紀伯紫

"Ji leng re" 劑冷熱
"Ji pai'ou" 忌排偶
ji qing 寄情
"Ji su'e" 忌俗惡
Ji Yingzhong 紀映鍾
Ji Yuan 紀元
Jia Dao 賈島
Jia Hanfu 賈漢復
"Ji'an" 几案
"Jian Cong Muxu" 束叢木虛
"Jian touxu" 減頭緒
jiang 將
Jiang Zhengxue 姜正學
"Jianjian" 箋簡
jianxin 尖新
"Jiao bai" 教白
"Jie fengci" 戒諷刺
"Jie fufan" 戒浮泛
"Jie huangtang" 戒荒唐
"Jie longdong shengshu zhi yu" 節隆冬盛暑之慾
"Jie piaoqie chenyan" 戒剽竊陳言
"Jie wangluo jiuji" 戒網羅舊集
"Jie youhuan shang qing zhi yu" 節憂患傷情之慾
"Jie zhili buzou" 戒支離補奏
"Jiegou" 結構
Jieziyuan 芥子園
Jin Ping Mei 金瓶梅
Jin Shengtan 金聖歎
jing (outer world) 景
jing (role) 淨
Jingchaiji 荊釵記
"Jinqian" 金錢
"*Jinyouyuan shiji* xu" 今又園詩集序
Jiu fengchen 救風塵
"Jiuju" 酒具
"Jixie Jia Jiaohou dazhongcheng" 寄謝賈膠侯大中丞
"Jixie Liu Yaowei dazhongcheng" 寄謝劉耀薇大中丞
jueju 絕句
Jue shi baiguan 覺世稗官
Jue shi mingyan 覺世名言
kaozheng 考證

Ke Song 柯聳
"Kehun" 科諢
"Keshou ciyun" 恪守詞韻
Kunqu 崑曲
Kunlun nu 崑崙奴
"Lan" 蘭
Lanqi 蘭谿
Lao Can youji 老殘遊記
laoshi 老實
Li Bai 李白
Li Changxiang 李長祥
Li Liufang 李流芳
"Li Liweng chuanqi xiti" 李笠翁傳奇戲題
"Li Liweng chuanqi xu" 李笠翁傳奇序
"Li Liweng Fuboxuan" 李笠翁浮白軒
"Li Liweng zhaitou tong Wang Zuoju yu su" 李笠翁齋頭同王左車雨宿
"Li Shenyu kunjun shoulian" 李申玉閫君壽聯
"Li shi wuzhong zongxu" 李氏五種揔序
"Li yan dang jin shuo" 立言當謹説
Li Yu 李漁
Li Zhi 李贄
"Li zhunao" 立主腦
Li Zi 李子
Li Zicheng 李自成
"Lianbian" 聯匾
Liancheng bi 連城璧
Lianxiang ban 憐香伴
"Liao bing" 療病
Lin Tiansu 林天素
Ling Mengchu 凌濛初
"Ling Shizhong xiaocao xiaoyin" 凌士重小草小引
"Linzun qupu" 凜遵曲譜
Liu Biao 劉表
"Liu Dongshan" 劉東山
Liu Dou 劉斗
Liu E 劉鶚
Liu Qianqian 劉倩倩
"Liu Yi zhuan" 柳毅傳
Liu Zhengzong 劉正宗

"Liuzhi zi shou sishou" 六袠自壽四首
Liweng 笠翁
Liweng chuanqi shizhong 笠翁傳奇十種
Liweng yijia yan 笠翁一家言
Liweng yijia yan erji 笠翁一家言二集
Liweng zengding lun gu 笠翁增定論古
Longmen Lishi zongpu 龍門李氏宗譜
lou 樓
"Lu ping" 鑪瓶
Lu Qi 陸圻
lun 論
"Lun Cao Cao zi chen gongfa ji rang huan sanxian" 論曹操自陳功伐及讓還三縣
"Lun Cheng Ying li gu er si" 論程嬰立孤而死
"Lun Dongfang Shuo jian na Dong Yan zhi jiu xuanshi" 論東方朔諫內董偃置酒宣室
"Lun er Shu bu yi cai lei zisun" 論二疏不以財累子孫
"Lun er Shu qing lao" 論二疏請老
Lun gu 論古
"Lun Han Xin ci piaomu guan shaonian" 論韓信賜漂母官少年
"Lun Han zhao Liu Xiu dian ling wujing suo zou qilüe jiuliu zhi yi" 論漢詔劉秀典領五經所奏七略九流之議
"Lun Jin Wengong shang zongwangzhe er buji Jie Zitui" 論晉文公賞從亡者而不及介子推
"Lun Lin Xiangru qu yu Lian Po" 論藺相如屈于廉頗
"Lun Tang bing san bian Tang wen san bian" 論唐兵三變唐文三變
"Lun Tang Taizong yi gong shi jian wu yu zhi dao" 論唐太宗以弓矢建屋喻治道
"Lun Tang Taizong Zhou Qin xiuduan zhi yi" 論唐太宗周秦修短之議
"Lun Wei Jiang gui Jin Hou yi an le si zhong" 論魏絳規晉侯以安樂思終
"Lun Wei Zi xian bao jiqi gui Zhou"

論微子先抱祭器歸周
"Lun Xie Fei He Dian He Yin shu you" 論謝朓何點何胤執優
"Lun Yang Xiong Tao Qian chu chu" 論揚雄陶潛出處
"Lun Yao rang tianxia Xu You Tang rang tianxia yu Bian Sui Wu Guang" 論堯讓天下許由湯讓天下于卞隨務光
"Lun Yin Hao ni Guan Ge" 論殷浩擬管葛
"Lun Yuan Shizu zhi dai Wen Tianxiang" 論元世祖之待文天祥
"Lun Zhao Pu zhi jian Taizu" 論趙普之諫太祖
"Lü kuang" 旅況
Lü Tiancheng 呂天成
"Mai shan quan" 賣山券
Mao Xianshu 毛先舒
"Mei nanzi bi huo fan sheng yi" 美男子避惑反生疑
Meisheng 眉生
meitai 媚態
meixiang 梅香
Meng Haojan 孟浩然
Meng Jiao 孟郊
"Mi zhenxian" 密針線
miaofa 妙法
"Ming zhuzi shuo" 名諸子説
Mingci xuansheng 名詞選勝
"*Mingci xuansheng xu*" 名詞選勝序
"Minzhong shi xian lizhi" 閩中食鮮荔枝
mu 畝
mudan 牡丹
Mudan ting 牡丹亭
"Muyu" 沐浴
na hua 那畫
"Na ji" 納姬
nahua 那話
"Nai bing jie" 耐病解
Naige ci 耐歌詞
Naihe tian 奈何天
"Nan gui daoshang sheng er zi he ershou" 南歸道上生兒自賀二首

"Nan Meng mu jiao he san qian" 男孟母教合三遷
"Nei ye" 內業
Neiwai bazhong 內外八種
"Neizi yu ceshi bing buyi nan . . ." 內子與側室並不宜男 . . .
"Ni gou Yishan bieye wei sui" 擬搆伊山別業未遂
Ni Zan 倪瓚
Nuoru shanfang shuo you 娜如山房説尤
"Nü Chen Ping ji sheng qichu" 女陳平計生七出
Nü shi 女史
"Nüzi shou zhen lai yibang, pengchai xiang nüe zhi qiyuan" 女子守貞來異謗，朋儕相謔致奇冤
"Ou xia jian canshu fen qi keyi bu du zhe" 偶暇撿殘書焚其可以不讀者
"Ou xing" 偶興
paiyou 俳優
Pan An 潘安
Pan Gu 盤古
pinglun 評論
"Pinjian xing le zhi fa" 貧賤行樂之法
piruan 罷軟
poti 破題
qi 奇
"Qi guizheng fengsu" 期規正風俗
"Qi jingti renxin" 期警惕人心
Qian Qianyi 錢謙益
"Qiangbi" 牆壁
Qiangu qiwen 千古奇聞
Qianhou bazhong 前後八種
qiao 巧
Qiao Fusheng 喬復生
"Qiao Fusheng Wang Zailai erji hezhuan" 喬復生王再來二姬合傳
Qiao tuanyuan 巧團圓
"Qi'er xing haoshi, huangdi zuo meiren" 乞兒行好事，皇帝做媒人
"Qin you po zhuang gui hou jin chang jibu yi san wu yigan er fu ci" 秦游頗壯歸後僅償積逋一散無遺感而賦此
qing 情

"Qing fugui nüdan quan zhen" 輕富貴
　女旦全貞
Qingchi fanzheng daoren 情癡反正道
　人
qingke 清客
"Qingmingri Wang Ranming
　fengweng zhao yin hushang" 清明日
　汪然明封翁招飲湖上
qingtan 清談
qingzhong 情種
"Qinhuai jian'er zhuan" 秦淮健兒傳
"Qiqiong ge" 奇窮歌
"Qiu Changru" 丘長孺
Qiu sheng lu 求生錄
"Qiu sheng lu xu" 求生錄序
qu 趣
"Qu jing zai jie" 取景在借
"Qubu shici" 曲部誓詞
que 缺
re 熱
"Ren su ji qiong gui su piao yuan" 人
　宿妓窮鬼訴嫖冤
"Renwu chuxi" 壬午除夕
"Renyin ju disan zi fu ju disi zi" 壬寅
　舉第三子復舉第四子
Rou putuan 肉蒲團
Ruan Dacheng 阮大鋮
Rugao 如皋
Ruyi Jun zhuan 如意君傳
Sai Kunlun 賽崑崙
sang 嗓
Sanguo yanyi 三國演義
"Sanyulou" 三與樓
"Sasao" 灑掃
sha 煞
"Shan shi" 山石
"Shang dumen guren shu jiuzhuang
　shu" 上都門故人述舊狀書
Shang shu 尚書
shaoyao 芍藥
Shen luanjiao 慎鸞交
Shen Shouzheng 沈守正
Shen Xinyou 沈心友
"Shen yu chuyan" 慎獄芻言
sheng 生

"Sheng wu kengchiang" 聲務鏗鏘
shengrong 聲容
"Shengwolou" 生我樓
shenyun 神韻
Shenzhong lou 蜃中樓
shi 詩
Shi jing 詩經
Shidetang 世德堂
Shi'er lou 十二樓
"Shijinlou" 十卺樓
shilun 史論
Shiyinyuan 市隱園
shiyong meiguan 適用美觀
"Shiyun xu" 詩韻序
"Shou qu" 授曲
"Shoushi" 首飾
"Shou shi qi fang ba" 壽世奇方跋
"Shouzu" 手足
shu 數
"Shufang bi" 書房壁
"Shui" 睡
"Shuixian" 水仙
Shuixiang jijiu 睡鄉祭酒
si zhi si zhi guishen tong zhi 思之思之鬼
　神通之
Siliu chuzheng 四六初徵
Sima Xiangru 司馬相如
Siping 四平
Sishu 四書
"Sizhu" 絲竹
"Sizitie ci Wulin zhuqinyou zhi zhao"
　四字帖辭武林諸親友之招
Song Wan 宋琬
Song Yu 宋玉
Songgotu 索額圖
"Suchang le wei zhi yao" 素常樂為之
　藥
"Suishi ji jing jiu shi xing le zhi fa" 隨
　時即景就事行樂之法
Sun Zhi 孫治
"Suo chang wei duan" 縮長為短
"Sushi" 蔬食
"Taidu" 態度
Taishang ganying pian 太上感應篇
Taizong 太宗

Glossary

"Tan" 談
"Tan Chuyu xili chuan qing, Liu Maogu quzhong si jie" 譚楚玉戲裡傳情，劉藐姑曲終死節
"Tang" 湯
Tang Yin 唐寅
Tao Qian 陶潛
"Ti Suo xiangguo yuanting erlian" 題索相國園亭二聯
tian 天
"Tian ci yulun" 填詞餘論
Tian Rucheng 田汝成
Tiaolingji 齠齡集
"Ting bi" 廳壁
"Ting liao" 庭燎
ting wo dao lai 聽我道來
Tong 佟
"Tong Shaocun Xingzhai ji Lihong Fuboxuan ting qu ershou" 同邵村省齋集笠鴻浮白軒聽曲二首
"Tujing" 途徑
"Tuo kejiu" 脫窠臼
tuo xing 託興
waibian 外編
Wang Duanshu 王端淑
Wang Gai 王槩
Wang Ji 汪楫
Wang Ruqian 汪汝謙
Wang Shi 王著
Wang Shilu 王士祿
Wang Shizhen 王士禎
Wang Siren 王思任
Wang Wan 汪琬
Wang Zailai 王再來
"Wang Zhongzhao Sun Yutai Zhang Shijiu Li Liweng . . ." 王仲昭孫宇台章式九李笠翁 . . .
Wang Zuoju 王左車
Wei Yijie 魏裔介
Wei Yingwu 韋應物
Wei Zheng 魏徵
weiyang 未央
Weiyang Sheng 未央生
"Wen gui jiejing" 文貴潔淨
Wen Tianxiang 文天祥
Wen Tong 文同
"Wenguolou" 聞過樓
wenren 文人
"Wenren mofang zhi bing" 文人摹倣之病
"Wenyi" 文藝
wu 武
Wu Bing 吳炳
Wu Hong 吳宏
Wu Weiye 吳偉業
Wu Xiaoling 吳曉鈴
Wu Zetian 武則天
Wudi 武帝
wusheng shi 無聲詩
Wusheng shi shi 無聲詩史
Wusheng xi 無聲戲
Wusheng xi erji 無聲戲二集
Wusheng xi heji 無聲戲合集
Wusheng xi hexuan 無聲戲合選
Wuzong 武宗
"Xi ji" 習技
"Xiaji xing le zhi fa" 夏季行樂之法
Xiali Village 夏李村(下李村)
"Xian nei yin" 賢內吟
"Xiangcaoting chuanqi xu" 香草亭傳奇序
"Xiang long qie si" 箱籠篋笥
"Xiang xing moyi" 祥刑末議
xianqiao 纖巧
Xianqing ouji 閒情偶寄
Xiao Zhen 蕭震
xiaopin 小品
"Xiao shan" 小山
"Xiao shousha" 小收煞
"Xiao ya" 小雅
"Xiayilou" 夏宜樓
"Xie" 蟹
Xie Daoyun 謝道韞
"Xiewa" 鞋襪
Xiling 西冷
Ximen Qing 西門慶
xin 新
"Xin yu" 新浴
xing 性
"Xing le" 行樂

xingling 性靈
Xishi 西施
"Xiti Jinling zha jiuju" 戲題金陵閘舊居
Xiuta yeshi 繡榻野史
Xixiangji 西廂記
"Xu Chen Zhengfu *Huixinji*" 敍陳正甫會心集
Xu Du 許都
"Xu ke 'Wutong shi'" 續刻梧桐詩
Xu Xicai 許檄彩
"Xuan ju" 選劇
"Xuan zi" 選姿
"Xun mei" 尋梅
"Xuntao" 薰陶
yadan 雅淡
Yan Shifan 嚴世蕃
Yang Yunyou 楊雲友
yangmei 楊梅
"Ye meng xianci ze yu huangfei juye, xing shu zi cheng" 夜夢先慈責予荒廢舉業，醒書自懲
"Ye xing" 野性
"Yi qi huan qie guishen qi" 移妻換妾鬼神奇
"Yi qu jianxin" 意取尖新
"Yi quan wen" 瘞犬文
"Yi yuan shibian" 伊園十便
yijia yan 一家言
"Yijia yan shiyi" 一家言釋義
yilun 議論
"Yin lü" 音律
ying 穎
ying zhai 營債
yintou 引頭
"Yiren zhiji xing, zeng Tong Bimei shijun" 一人知己行，贈佟碧枚使君
Yishan 伊山
"Yishan" 衣衫
Yishengtang 翼聖堂
"Yisheng wei jian zhi yao" 一生未見之藥
"Yiwu" 椅杌
"Yixin zhongai zhi yao" 一心鍾愛之藥
Yiyang 弋陽
yiyang 頤養

"Yizhong qing" 一種情
Yizhong yuan 意中緣
"You fu pianzha" 又附片札
"You sui" 憂歲
You Tong 尤侗
"You yu Yanchu zhangke" 又與岸初掌科
"Yu Chen Duanbo shilang" 與陳端伯侍郎
"Yu Chen Xueshan shaozai" 與陳學山少宰
"Yu Du Yuhuang" 與杜于皇
"Yu Fang Shaocun shiyu" 與方紹村侍御
"Yu Gong Zhilu dazongbo" 與龔芝麓大宗伯
"Yu Han Ziju" 與韓子蘧
Yu Huai 余懷
"Yu Ji Bozi" 與紀伯紫
"Yu Li Renshu" 與李仁熟
"Yu Liu shijun" 與劉使君
Yu Lou 虞鏤
"Yu mougong" 與某公
"Yu qiu xiaosi" 語求肖似
"Yu ren qi qu pingyu shu" 與人乞去評語書
"Yu ren shu shi" 與人書十
Yu saotou 玉搔頭
"Yu Sun Yutai" 與孫宇台
Yu Wei 虞巍
"Yu Wei Danzu zhizhi" 與衛澹尼直指
"Yu Wei Zhen'an xiangguo" 與魏貞菴相國
"Yu Wu Meicun taishi" 與吳梅村太史
"Yu xi funü chu you you xiao qi shi ji zhe shi yi jie chao" 予攜婦女出游有笑其失計者詩以解嘲
"Yu Xu Dianfa" 與徐電發
"Yu Xu Donglai" 與徐東來
"Yu Zhao Jieshan" 與趙介山
"Yu Zhao Shengbo wenxue" 與趙聲伯文學
Yuan Hongdao 袁宏道
Yuan Yuling 袁于令
"Yuanxiao wu yue ci Wang Ranming

fengweng yun" 元宵無月次汪然明封
翁韻
"Yue you jiabao zhi si" 粵游家報之四
"Yuehu da Li Yu wushou" 月湖答李漁
五首
yun 韻
zaowu 造物
"Ze zi" 責子
"Zeng Bao Yeshan" 贈郋冶山
"Zeng niexian Guo Shengzhou
xiansheng" 贈臬憲郭生洲先生
"Zeng Sun Zi Yutai" 贈孫子宇台
"Zeng Suo Yu'an xiangguo" 贈索愚菴
相國
"Zeng Wulin Li Liweng" 贈武林李笠翁
Zha Jizuo 查繼佐
Zhang Dai 張岱
Zhang Jinyan 張縉彥
Zhang Zhou 張洲
Zhao Pan'er 趙盼兒
Zhao Shiji 趙時揖
Zheng Chenggong 鄭成功
zhengda guangming 正大光明
Zhengde 正德

"Zhi fu" 治服
"Zhi ti yi jian" 制體宜堅
"Zhi Xuanzi Zhao Jianzi zhi lihou" 智
宣子趙簡子之立後
"Zhi you zuo chuanqi shu" 止友作傳
奇書
"Zhidu" 制度
zhiji 知己
zhiwei 脂韋
"Zhiyi fu" 支頤賦
"Zhong ji qu" 重機趣
Zhongyong 中庸
Zhou Lianggong 周亮工
"Zhu" 豬
"Zhu Jingzi zhuan" 朱靜子傳
"Zhu mao wen" 逐貓文
"Zhu shu zhi nan" 著書之難
Zhu Xi 朱熹
zhunao 主腦
Zizhi tongjian gangmu 資治通鑑綱目
Zizhi xinshu 資治新書
Zizhi xinshu erji 資治新書二集
zuo 作

Index

Index

Jing (role), 144, 154, 155, 156
Jing (scene), 57
Jinhua, 10, 15
Jiu fengchen, 151

Kangxi Emperor, 74
Kaopan yushi, 243n22
Ke Song, 1, 4, 5
Kunqu, 61

Lesbianism, 15
Li Bo, 147
Li Changxiang, 37, 40, 41
Li Liufang, 214n21
Li Yu: journeys, 1, 2, 3, 6–7, 8, 18; in
   Beijing, 1, 3–4, 6; concubines, 1, 3,
   6, 7–8, 11, 15, 16, 19, 29, 38, 43,
   67, 200–203; in Nanjing, 1, 3, 8, 12,
   13, 14, 66, 69, 198; poverty, 1, 6, 8,
   9; size of family, 1, 8; gardens, 1, 29,
   56, 72, 76; in Hanyang, 2, 3, 6, 7, 8;
   decorative notepaper, 3, 5, 13, 14,
   73; in Shaanxi, 6, 7; in Guangzhou,
   6, 8; Mustard Seed Garden, 7, 8; in
   Hangzhou, 8, 10, 12, 13, 15, 17, 69,
   198; in Suzhou, 8, 12; family background, 9–10; and examinations, 9,
   10; as secretary, 10; in Lanqi, 11;
   means of livelihood, 11; at Mt. Yi,
   11, 12; indebtedness, 13, 40; wife,
   15; pseudonyms, 20, 22, 23; biographical sources, 209–210
      WRITING CAREER: patronage-seek-
         ing, 1, 2, 3–4, 5, 6–7, 11, 110;
         as professional writer, 2, 10, 12,
         14, 38, 75; literary friends, 6, 8,
         11, 38; books pirated, 12, 14,
         49; switch to classical genres, 13,
         24; bookshop in Nanjing, 13, 24;
         scandal of first play, 15–16; so-
         liciting commentaries on his
         work, 24, 196–197; revision, 47;
         process of composition, 52–58;
         sources of inspiration, 56
      ATTITUDES: to talk and laughter, 6,
         7, 35, 36–38, 40–41, 41–42,
         128, 158, 197–198, 199–200; to
         creativity and originality, 6, 14,
         26, 29, 36, 44–46, 48–49, 54,

   71, 76, 119–120, 157, 197; to
   thrift, 9, 28, 74; to aesthetic and
   instinctual pleasure, 9, 39, 59–
   67, 122–123, 203–207; to the
   Ming, 10; to the Manchus, 10,
   28; to comedy, 12, 42, 43, 50–
   51, 55, 75, 76–77, 97, 111,
   123, 125, 154–156; to the past,
   32, 34, 35, 46–47, 189; to his
   audience or readership, 41, 42–
   43, 75, 198–199, 200; to antiques, 47; to change, 47–48, 50;
   to tangible reality, 49–50; to
   construction (*jiegou*) in literature, 52, 54, 71, 78, 199; to
   health, 60–61, 203–207; to sexual love, 61, 62, 67, 128, 132,
   142–148, 149, 168; to high taste
   and low taste, 61–62, 74–75,
   187, 198–199; to self-interest,
   62–63, 76, 81, 150–154, 203–
   205; to food, 65–66; to flowers,
   66–67, 70; to patterning, 71; to
   naturalness, 72; to Confucian puritans and Confucianism, 78,
   118, 127, 128, 145, 187–188; to
   naturalism, 79, 230n28
      QUALITIES: outrageousness, 3, 6,
         25, 29, 37, 43, 76, 188, 189;
         role-playing, 6, 9, 35–36, 39;
         jesting, 7, 37–38, 41, 77; impul-
         siveness, 9; self-mockery, 9, 29,
         38, 78; stoicism, 11, 39, 168;
         fondness for inversion technique,
         18, 21, 26, 36, 50, 91–108; ri-
         baldry, 21, 38, 51, 68–69, 71,
         75, 103–104, 154, 162; analyti-
         cal ability, 25, 51, 68, 203; self-
         reference, 31–34, 35; personae,
         33, 35–44, 134, 197–198, 206;
         concern with the close-at-hand,
         34–35, 187, 195; discursiveness,
         34, 42, 76, 125, 128–134, 185,
         191; expressivism, 35; weakness
         of emotions, 35, 68–69, 123,
         148; inventiveness, 38, 45–57,
         145, 197–198; epicureanism, 39;
         ingenuity (*qiao*), 51, 55; eroti-
         cism, 67, 68, 201; personal ele-

268

Index

Li Yu (cont.)
246–247; "Fresh from the Bath,"
63; "In Search of Plum Blossom," 66; theory of lyric (Kui ci
guanjian), 225n121
STORIES: style, 42–43, 51–52, 74,
77, 91; characterization, 76;
comedy, 76–77; novel idea, 76,
192; narratorial comment, 77;
personal element, 77; prologues,
77, 80–81, 86, 90, 105, 189;
self-mockery, 78; and romantic
comedy, 78–101; reflexiveness,
89; inversion technique, 91–111
Silent Operas (Wusheng xi), 13, 17,
18, 19, 20, 21–22, 23, 25, 33,
76–78, 88–97, 102, 103–105,
106; editions, sequels, anthologies, 17–23; "Contemptuous of
Riches and Rank, an Actress
Preserves Her Honor," 88–91;
"An Ugly Husband Fears Marriage to a Pretty Wife but Gets a
Beautiful One," 92, 106; "A
Widow Hatches a Plot to Receive a Bridegroom, and Beautiful Women Unite to Seize a
Brilliant Poet," 96–97; "A Male
Mencius's Mother Educates His
Son and Moves House Three
Times," 97–98, 103; "A Son
and Grandson Abandon the
Corpse While a Servant Hastens
to the Funeral," 102; "The Fe-
male Chen Ping Saves Her Life
with Seven Schemes," 103–104;
"The Spirits Astonish by Switch-
ing Wife and Concubine," 104;
"A Beggar Scorns High Officials
and Upholds Justice," 105; "A
Chaste Girl Preserves Her Chastity but Incurs a Strange Slander,
While Friends' Jesting Produces a
Bizarre Injustice," 106; "A
Handsome Lad Raises Doubts by
Trying to Avoid Suspicion," 106
Twelve Structures (Shi'er lou), alt.
title, Famous Words to Awaken
the World (Jueshi mingyan), 17,
19, 23, 67, 76–78, 78–88, 98–
102, 102–103, 106–110, 125;
"The Summer Pavilion" ("Xiayi-
lou"), 78–81, 86, 123; "The
Cloudscraper" ("Fuyunlou"), 81–
86, 92, 107, 123; "The Pavilion
of Combined Reflections" ("He-
yinglou"), 86–88, 106–107; "The
House of Gathered Refinements"
("Cuiyalou"), 98–102; "The
House of My Birth" ("Sheng-
wolou"), 102–103; "Reformation
House" ("Guizhenglou"), 103,
125; "The Hall of the Homing
Crane" ("Heguilou"), 106–108;
"The Studio of the Three Teachers" ("Sanyulou"), 108–109;
"Corrigibility House" ("Wenguo-
lou"), 109–110
OTHER WORKS, 24–30; A First Collection of Letters (Chidu chuzheng),
24; A New Aid to Administration
(Zizhi xinshu), 25, 33; "Modest
Suggestions on the Proper Use of
Punishments," 25; "Humble Proposals for Due Care in Legal
Cases," 25; A New Aid to Admin-
istration, Second Collection (Zizhi
xinshu erji), 25–26; Preserving Life
(Qiu sheng lu), 26; A First Collec-
tion of Parallel Prose (Siliu chu-
zheng), 26; Discussions of the Past
(Lun gu), 26–28, 29, 33, 40,
46, 49, 185, 246–247; "A Com-
bined Biography," 43–44; rhap-
sodies, 44, 66; a classical tale,
221n87; works spuriously or
doubtfully attributed to Li Yu,
225n121
Li Zhi, 26, 34, 37, 45
Li Zhifang, 211n3
Li Zicheng, 21, 105
Liang Yunzhi, 227n27
Lin Tiansu, 16
Ling Mengchu, 49, 103, 231n30
Liu E, 106
Liu Qianqian, 17

270

Index